DRIVERLESS URBAN FUTURES

Since the industrial revolution, innovations in transportation technology have continued to re-shape the spatial organization and temporal occupation of the built environment. Today, autonomous vehicles (AVs, also referred to as self-driving cars) represent the next disruptive innovation in mobility, with particularly profound impacts for cities. At a moment of the fast-paced development of AVs by auto-making companies around the world, policymakers, planners, and designers need to anticipate and address the many questions concerning the impacts of this new technology on urbanism and society at large.

Conceived as a speculative atlas—a roadmap to unknown territories—this book presents a series of drawings and text that unpack the potential impacts of AVs on scales ranging from the metropolis to the street. The work is both grounded in a study of the history of urban transportation and current trajectories of technological innovation, and informed by an open-ended attitude of future envisioning and design. Through the drawings and essays, *Driverless Urban Futures* invites readers into a debate of how our future infrastructure could benefit all members of the public and levels of society.

AnnaLisa Meyboom is Associate Professor at the University of British Columbia in the School of Architecture and Landscape Architecture (SALA) as well as the Director of the Transportation Infrastructure and Public Space Lab (TIPSlab). Her research focus is the interrogation of future applications of technology in the design of our built environment. She emphasizes the need to integrate the highly technical, the beautiful, and the environmental simultaneously and seamlessly into built form. She holds a degree in engineering from University of Waterloo and a Masters in Architecture from the University of British Columbia. She designs and writes about future infrastructures and the use of advanced digital tools in the design and fabrication of architectural form.

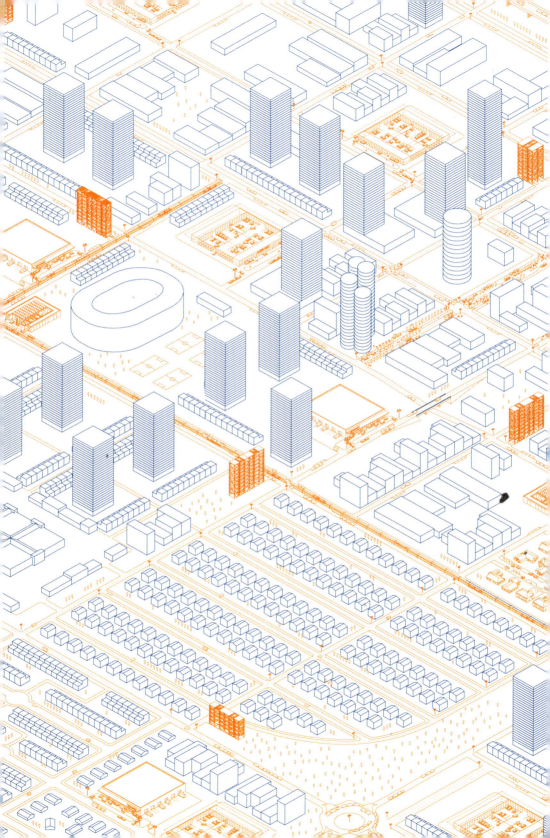

DRIVERLESS URBAN FUTURES

A Speculative Atlas for Autonomous Vehicles

AnnaLisa Meyboom

Drawings by Lőrinc Vass

Routledge
Taylor & Francis Group

NEW YORK AND LONDON

First published 2019
by Routledge
52 Vanderbilt Avenue, New York, NY 10017

and by Routledge
2 Park Square, Milton Park, Abingdon, Oxon, OX14 4RN

Routledge is an imprint of the Taylor & Francis Group, an informa business

© 2019 Taylor & Francis

The right of AnnaLisa Meyboom to be identified as author of this work has been asserted by her in accordance with sections 77 and 78 of the Copyright, Designs and Patents Act 1988.

All rights reserved. No part of this book may be reprinted or reproduced or utilised in any form or by any electronic, mechanical, or other means, now known or hereafter invented, including photocopying and recording, or in any information storage or retrieval system, without permission in writing from the publishers.

Trademark notice: Product or corporate names may be trademarks or registered trademarks, and are used only for identification and explanation without intent to infringe.

Artwork: Lőrinc Vass
Editor: Victoria Killington
Designer: Lőrinc Vass

British Library Cataloguing-in-Publication Data
A catalogue record for this book is available from the British Library

Library of Congress Cataloging-in-Publication Data
Names: Meyboom, AnnaLisa, author. | Vass, Lorinc, illustrator.
Title: Driverless urban futures : a speculative atlas for autonomous vehicles / AnnaLisa Meyboom ; drawings by Lorinc Vass.
Description: New York, NY : Routledge, 2019. | Includes bibliographical references.
Identifiers: LCCN 2018034595| ISBN 9780815354086 (hardback) | ISBN 9780815354109 (pbk.)
Subjects: LCSH: Autonomous vehicles--Forecasting. | Urban transportation--Forecasting. | Automobiles--Automatic control--Forecasting. | Technological forecasting.
Classification: LCC TL152.8 .M49 2019 | DDC 388.3/4--dc23
LC record available at https://lccn.loc.gov/2018034595

ISBN: 978-0-815-35408-6 (hbk)
ISBN: 978-0-815-35410-9 (pbk)
ISBN: 978-1-351-13403-3 (ebk)

Typeset in Lato
by Łukasz Dziedzic

Publisher's Note: This book has been prepared from camera-ready copy provided by the author.

Contents

Preface		vi
Acknowledgements		viii
Chapter 1	Envisioning Future Infrastructures	1
Chapter 2	Notes on Drawing	27
Chapter 3	Into the Future: Analytic Scenarios	37
Chapter 4	Historical Trajectory of Transportation Infrastructure	89
Chapter 5	Urban Scale Impacts	109
Chapter 6	Urban Theories and Autonomous Vehicles	159
Chapter 7	Street Scale Impacts	185
Chapter 8	Public Transportation	253
Chapter 9	Technology, the City and the Autonomous Vehicle	265
Chapter 10	Utopian Visions	277
Index		299

Preface

Since the Industrial Revolution, innovations in transportation technology have re-shaped the spatial organization and temporal occupation of the built environment. Today, autonomous vehicles (AVs) represent the next disruptive innovation in mobility, with particularly profound impacts for cities. At this moment, when automotive and technology companies around the world are engaged in the fast-paced development of AVs, policymakers, planners, and designers need to anticipate and address the many questions concerning the impacts of this new technology on urbanism and society at large. This is a particularly vexing problem when dealing with innovation and radical changes because of the unpredictability of the future. In researching the subject, however, it became clear that rather than passively waiting for the future to unfold, in this case it may be better for society to imagine and design the future for itself. In doing so, there is a better chance of influencing the introduction of this new technology to our society in ways that benefit everyone.

Architects have the ability to design a future and explain it to others through images. This is a powerful tool and one that is critically necessary when we are faced with the disruptive changes that AVs may bring. The purpose of this book is to bring this architectural design approach to the subject of autonomous vehicles and urban form.

Conceived as a speculative atlas—a roadmap to unknown territories—this book presents a series of drawings and text that unpack the potential impacts of AVs on scales ranging from the metropolis to the street. Speculative in nature, the work is both grounded in a study of the history of urban transportation and current trajectories of technological innovation, and informed by an open-ended approach to future envisioning and design. Through this approach, the work explores potential futures: some that we may aspire to and others that we may wish to avoid, although the intention here is to foster engagement with these futures rather than to be prescriptive or directive.

The speculative nature of the book is both its strength and its weakness. In being speculation, it lacks the authority of evidence-based research. Evidence-based research requires data to analyze; data is precisely what we do not have. The many social and technological factors which are involved in AV adoption are very complex and therefore difficult to model accurately, especially in light of the fact that there is limited relevant data to put in the model. And so conventional research is limited when faced with this type of problem. As an alternative, we have provided qualitative data in the form of informed speculation of multiple outcomes through both analytic discussion and drawings.

The intent of the drawings is to 'inhabit the future.' When we draw, we must envision: fill in the details of how things are configured and engage with the questions of why and how they became this way. In this way, an image of the future is drawn. The power of illustration is that sometimes the image becomes the blueprint of the future: as architects, we draw that which will then come into being. As architects of future infrastructures, we may be designing the future itself.

The analytic discussion fills in the details of the thinking behind the drawings, outlining the reasoning, the technology and the social assumptions that are the basis of the drawings. Through the drawings, discussions and the essays, we hope to draw readers into a debate of what our future infrastructure could be; through this debate, we are optimistic that deliberate infrastructural decisions will be made which will benefit all members of the public and levels of society.

Preface   vii

Acknowledgements

I would like to acknowledge the valuable inputs of those who have worked on this research with me. I would especially like to thank Lőrinc Vass, who contributed all the stunning illustrations and layout for the book as well as a significant amount of research work, and Sara Costa Maia, who contributed much research and specifically much of the excellent work on the future visioning methodology described in this book. I also thank the other students engaged in this research who have brought an immense amount of intellectual capital and hard work to the topic.

I would also like to thank my colleagues in the School of Architecture and Landscape Architecture, who are unfailingly supportive, particularly Sherry McKay, Sara Stevens, Adam Rysanek and Fionn Byrne, who dedicated their time to reviewing parts of the text, and also Ron Kellett, Mari Fujita and Leslie VanDuzer, who provided much appreciated advice and guidance at various points in the process.

Finally I would like to thank my editor, Victoria Killington, who was untiringly diligent and helpful throughout the process.

Funding for the original research for this book was provided by the Hampton Grants programme at the University of British Columbia.

One of the great privileges of working as a professor is that we engage with, and are challenged by, the bright minds around us on a daily basis. I hope that you, the reader, are in turn also enriched by the ideas put forward in these pages.

Chapter 1
Envisioning Future Infrastructures

Chapter 1
Envisioning Future Infrastructures

Introduction

A transportation revolution is imminent. By the time this book is published, there are likely to be self-driving cars operating taxi services. By the time you are reading this book, perhaps they are ubiquitous. It is the nature of research into this subject that by the time it is completed, technological advancement has outpaced the research. And while there is much talk about the impact of the autonomous vehicle (AV), there is very little true understanding of the revolution that this technology will bring—within society, on the design of the street, and on the urban realm. This book theorizes that in order to understand the impact of the technology, it is necessary to visualize the future with the technology well enough to understand it and, further, visualize it demonstrating multiple outcomes so that we can imagine the impacts of different decisions on the outcomes. By doing so, society at large will be able to make better informed decisions because they know the implications of those decisions, essentially collectively designing the future of the city.

The people who are actually at this point designing the future of the city are the leaders of the tech industry and the car companies. They may or may not have a thorough understanding of the future beyond their inventions but if there is an understanding, it has not been illustrated. The general discussion of the self-driving car is led by the heads of these organizations, thus providing a techno-utopian viewpoint and demonstrating only a limited understanding of the unforeseen impacts of these developments. The AV is presented as a great benefit to society without much evidence to back that up except for a predicted reduction in accident rates. Although these industry leaders present the technology as a social project, in fact the companies are developing this technology for profit and to keep up with the competition as others also race to develop and market their technical prowess. This is concerning: these companies are much more highly monetized than most governments and have some of the most talented people in the world working to deliver this technology as quickly as possible. The problem is not that the technology is being developed but the lack of critical discourse surrounding these developments. In and of itself, the technology cannot be defined as good or bad—but how it is used by society, and by whom it is used, are critical.[1]

The legislated relationship between the street and society helps in this regard, since there are well established societal norms regarding use of the street which have been codified through laws and regulations since the early 1900s. These developed over time as the space of the street became more contested—first by the introduction of cars and the desire to freely drive and park, and later on by the pedestrians and bicyclists who sought to take back the street from the car. As a result, the road is not a free market space but instead a highly controlled public space. In most cases the street is owned and under the jurisdiction of some level of government, and use of each part of the street is highly regulated by things such as speed limits, highway regulations, parking bylaws and bylaws regarding biking and walking, not to mention infrastructure control systems such as traffic lights and crosswalks.

It is clear that autonomous vehicles will have an impact on our society, our transportation choices and urban form. This raises many questions, such as what are the social and urban impacts of these changes? As noted by Hodge, who studies the relationship between equity and transportation, "urban transportation is important to defining which social groups, which factions of capital, which geographic areas in cities are to gain and which are to lose."[2] In the intense and expensive race to realize these technologies, what areas have not been thought through and should be? What will be the impact of these technologies on urban form, public transportation and decisions with regard to public infrastructure design? The answers to these questions will clarify what is at stake and what should be investigated thoroughly prior to the implementation of these technologies in order that they contribute as positively as possible to our society; the discussion within these pages is designed to advance this aim.

Conceived as a speculative atlas—a roadmap to unknown territories—this book presents a series of drawings and text that unpack the potential impacts of AVs on scales ranging from the metropolis to the street. The work is grounded both in a study of the history of urban transportation and current trajectories of technological innovation, and further informed by an open-ended attitude of future envisioning and design. The intent of the drawings is to allow readers to 'inhabit the future.' When we draw something in the future we must fill in the details of how things have changed or stayed the same, raising questions of why and how they became this way. The power of the drawing is that, sometimes, the image becomes the blueprint of the future. As architects, we draw that which will then come into being; as architects of future infrastructures, we may be designing the future itself. In the case of this book, multiple futures are depicted and this is intended to present a range of options for discussion so more informed choices can be made.

This book takes the reader through the development, assumptions and speculations about the future of urban space as influenced by the autonomous vehicle. The images run from street-scale specific infrastructures to urban-scale diagrams. Each image is designed to question how the future of technology will impact the space we live in and the ways in which we interact with that space and its other occupants, be they human or robot. Within the discussion of the images, technological assumptions will be outlined; for example, is the intelligence assumed to be within a controlling infrastructure or a vehicle itself? How is the infrastructural intelligence interacting with humans who are walking or biking and not in digital communication with the car or its network? What are the assumptions behind the technology in the drawing? What questions are raised for the city itself or for the ownership of the infrastructure? The intention of these images is to catalyze future thinking about the city and the transportation systems and networks that symbiotically exist to form and be formed by it.

Interspersed within the drawings are texts that elaborate and clarify specific aspects of how the topic has been thought about. Following this introduction is a glossary of vehicles, as well as a discussion of ownership models, and a brief consideration of the positioning of infrastructure with relation to the AVs themselves as well as a discussion about standards. This provides background context to orient a reader who may not be familiar with the technology under discussion. Secondly there is an exposition regarding drawing and its critical importance as it is conceived in this book.

The third chapter launches the reader into the future in two ways. Firstly, this chapter examines the future-visioning model that has been employed in this book. This model is based on a methodology used by companies who need to make decisions about the future for business purposes and the discussion elaborates on how this process was applied to the AV. Secondly, it depicts scenarios for different occupants of the future city and explains how, under a variety of different conditions, both the technology and the ways in which occupants use it are different

Beginning the discussion of urban scale impacts in Chapter 4 is an essay about the history of the car's influence on streets and urban form; technology, and its interplay with societal concerns from the different periods, is emphasized. This frames the drawings and discussion in the Urban Scale Impacts chapter.

The next section, including Chapters 6 and 7, opens with a discussion of street-scale impacts that reflects on disciplinary roles regarding design of the street and which cultural and social theories may be useful when designing the AV city. This examination extends the discussion in the previous essay to amplify the concerns within society at this time and how they may be incorporated into the critical design decisions that will need to be made in the next few decades.

It is clear as our discussion progresses that technology and the city is a topic which needs to be looked at more holistically and this is incorporated in the final chapters on future evolutions. While there has been much talk about Smart Cities as a topic, it becomes clear that the AV is really the catalyst for the implementation of future digital city infrastructure and, unlike many Smart Cities proposals, a clear way forward for this to benefit its inhabitants.

The book concludes with an essay about historical utopian images of future cities and transportation, the intent of which is to position the techno-utopian visions being put forward by large technology firms today in the context of previous utopian visions. It examines the societal outcomes and impacts of these earlier utopias with the wider intention of providing some thought-provoking reflections on our own future visions.

Explaining the New Paradigm

Vehicles

This book represents vehicles in a schematic way more related to function (see Figure 1.1). The AV is classified differently from current classification conventions, because the types of vehicles required in the future—and therefore their design and how we think about them—are likely to change. Categories will shift as Shared Autonomous Vehicles (SAVs) gain prevalence and become a type of public transit. As such, the vehicles are classified by function: Personal Mobility, Shared Mobility, Mass Mobility and Goods Transport (see Figures 1.2 and 1.3). Ownership models are likely to vary and as the distinction between public transit and ride-sharing blurs, it is increasingly unlikely that we will be able to distinguish between them (see Chapter 8 on Public Transportation).

Notes on General Design for AVs

There are several critical features to note with regard to AV design. The first is that there is no necessity for people to sit facing forward or in a driver position. This is relatively well understood; a driver is not required and therefore a passenger is free to sit in any direction and the cars can facilitate that. The second is that there is no longer a necessity for a front or back of a vehicle since cars can travel in either direction—this follows from the first point. Regulations regarding lights on vehicles are one of the main factors which may result in the traditional front/back design being retained, but from an operational perspective, driverless cars should be able to reverse direction without difficulty. However, these are radical changes in automobile design and it is not likely that vehicle design will undergo extreme change in the short term. This is because there are two diverging forces at work: on the one hand, tradition and familiarity; on the other, technological necessity and efficiency. Society is by now very familiar with this design tug-of-war as it was famously illustrated at Apple. From 2007 to 2013, Apple's graphic interface used skeumorphism—a design approach that references that which we already know, such as the calendar image with leather like book edges or a folder on a computer that looks like a paper folder. This design approach was promoted by Scott Forstall and Steve Jobs,[3,4] who understood that people would be able to adapt to something new more quickly when it offered something that gave a visual indication of its function in a familiar framework. This approach was extremely successful and Apple enjoyed massive popularity due in large part to its user-friendly interfaces. In 2013, however, under the new design direction of Jony

Ives, skeumorphic references were removed from Apple interfaces in favour of cleaner, more logical interfaces which do not reference the 'paper era.' Interfaces which do not relate to a previous era have a significant functional advantage over skeumorphic models: because they can work on their own internal logics, they provide optimum functionality of the technology. By contrast, interfaces which have to reference anachronistic characteristics, such as a page turning feature on an e-reader, make the technology less efficient for users to operate. Ives explained that people now understood the new paradigm of the digital interface and did not need the 'clues' that skeumorphic design had originally provided in order to help users adapt to the interface and the technology itself.

Much research has been done on product preferences and comfort with technology and it is consistently shown that consumers prefer both novelty *and* familiarity within new designs.[5] As such, new designs for AVs are likely to continue this trend of combining both innovative and traditional design in cars. There is an interesting caveat, however, relating to the AV; research indicates that prototypical objects, where no previous knowledge of the form exists, may then become the preferred industry standard.[6] This may be more relevant in the vehicle discussion when we look at new vehicles that are not used as passenger cars—vehicles such as

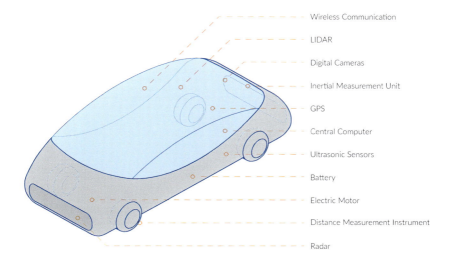

Figure 1.1. AV technology.

autonomous small delivery vehicles or delivery trucks. These are also not as likely to be influenced by consumer trends since companies buy them for more functional reasons.

Clearly one of the potential major design changes in an AV is the removal of the requirement to have a driver seat facing forward. In the case of goods vehicles, there is no requirement to have a seat for a person at all. However, what is perhaps more significant, is the idea of removing layers and layers of structure which provides safety from impact. It is estimated that using AV technology rather than sheer physical bulk to increase safety will allow a reduction of 35 to 50 per cent of the vehicle weight. Ultralight single-occupant AVs could even be developed that are only 250 pounds.[7] Once accident rates drop significantly and vehicle speeds are controlled autonomously, there is little reason to have extensive amounts of structure to protect the inhabitants of the vehicles. The AVs then become automated platforms, potentially battery platforms, with seats and a light covering over them.

Personal Mobility

In this book, various sizes of personal mobility vehicles are shown: these are classified into AV pods and AVs. AV pods are ultra-light commute-type

Explaining the New Paradigm

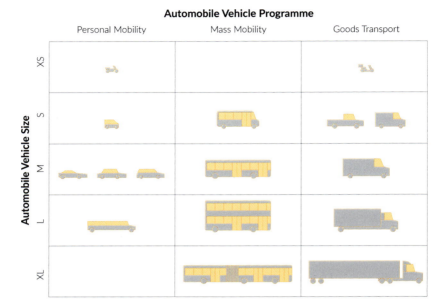

Figure 1.2. Current automobile classifications.

vehicles that provide basic sheltered transportation for either one or two occupants. AVs are larger vehicles for two to four people and similar to a family car in that they would also be able to accommodate luggage and/or shopping. These vehicles would be marketed to and owned by individuals.

Shared Mobility Vehicles

The shared mobility vehicles shown are two-, four- and six-seat vehicles. These are proposed to be more focused on function than image and make up the smaller end of the shared mobility market.

Mass Mobility Vehicles

Vehicles intended for mass mobility are shown as eight person shuttles, 12 person shuttles, and more standard size autonomous buses; any public transit vehicle could, of course, be autonomous. The only anticipated difference in vehicle design in these cases is the lack of a driver. In fact, the current shuttles being produced by Easymile and Navya and autonomous buses by Mercedes are

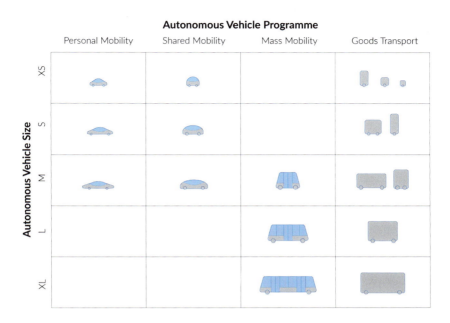

Figure 1.3. Potential AV classifications.

remarkably unremarkable in terms of the language of the vehicle—they are clearly visually identifiable as public transit vehicles since they look like small buses, having the familiar rectangular form, doors and buttons for operation. If more vehicles can be deployed because of reduced operating costs, smaller public transit vehicles may result, reducing greenhouse gas (GHG) emissions and providing better transit responsiveness.

Goods Transportation

As with other types of AVs, goods vehicles will no longer require a driver and therefore will have no need for a driver's cab in the vehicle. The major issue posed by delivery with AVs is the last 100m problem—i.e. how does the package get from the AV to the residence or business? There are multiple industry experiments happening in this area, from small autonomous sidewalks using delivery boxes[8] to larger trucks where people can unlock their packages from a locker with a code.[9] Boston Dynamics has even developed a humanoid robot capable of climbing stairs and carrying packages up to 45 kg.[10] The goods vehicles shown in this book are of various

Explaining the New Paradigm   9

scales from small to extra large. A variety of shapes and proportions are shown. Although the illustrations are of plain box-type vehicles, it is anticipated that advertisements, potentially digital, will feature on the exterior surfaces.

Freight Delivery

There is also extensive effort being made by various companies including Scania,[11] Volvo, Daimler, Uber and Waymo[12] in the area of self-driving and auto-platooning long-haul freight vehicles. Technologies in this sector are anticipated to have benefits such as saving fuel by having vehicles platoon, decreasing shipping costs through a reduction in driver costs, and improved safety by reducing crashes. While not the main focus of this book, the impact of these technologies on the shipping industry is expected to be huge and to be introduced relatively quickly since highway driving is much easier to automate than city driving.

Ownership Models

It is anticipated that AVs will fundamentally change our concepts of planning, owning, using, and paying for mobility. As American automobile designer Michael Robinson states, "People won't buy cars—they will use cars."[13] Future mobility will likely take the form of Shared Autonomous Vehicle (SAV) networks of some description. The concept of the SAV is basically car sharing but with a

driverless vehicle: you hail a car, the car comes and takes you where you want to go, and then it moves on to service another customer. This model is closest to an autonomous taxi system. While people are generally assuming these schemes will be like current car sharing services, there are other, more sophisticated versions, as discussed below. The greatest benefits of SAVs are safety, cost and convenience: for example, in a SAV scenario the cost per trip-mile could be reduced by 80% when compared to personally owned vehicles.[14] Individual car ownership is both possible and probable; however, it is likely to be a more expensive and unnecessary mode, even when image and lifestyle issues are factored in.

Moving to a mobility-on-demand model is expected to happen relatively quickly with major automakers seeing a revenue generation opportunity in SAVs even in light of the potentially reduced number of vehicles. A study by Stanford University and McKinsey Group suggests that SAVs could increase automotive company revenues by almost 30% and lead to a market penetration of 10% by 2025 and 33% by 2050.[15] This is a relatively conservative timeline estimate compared to others;[16] however, it explains the large automakers' interest in the SAV ecology.[17] Other studies have anticipated that a single SAV could replace between 9 and 13 cars.[18]

Ride sharing with more than one person per vehicle is critical in the AV discussion because Vehicle Miles Travelled (VMT) are anticipated to rise since more people will have access to less expensive and more convenient transportation options. Putting more people in one vehicle is the key to avoid increasing congestion. Economic incentives are the most likely to succeed at making people receptive to this version of the SAV service. Research on networks and dynamic ride sharing has shown that ride sharing with more than one occupant in the vehicle can service trips better at peak hours than solo occupancy trips, which may also help motivate people when demand is high.[19] Both the models discussed below incorporate the potential for carpooling.

On-Demand Taxi Services

Car-share and ride-share programmes are anticipated to be the first step in terms of consumers accepting autonomous vehicles.[20] Current car-share and ride-share programmes that operate as short-term vehicle rentals are quickly expanding, with the number of users worldwide increasing by 32% a year and expected to reach 26 million by 2020.[21] There are currently two main models of car sharing in use. One model features cars positioned within the city which individuals can 'sign out' a for a specified period of time: by the minute, hour or day. They either return them to where they got them or leave them at their destination in designated zones. In this model they are sharing the car with others but not at the same time. The second model is the ride-share model where people drive their own cars but they share them with others. This can be on longer trips between cities where everyone shares gas prices, for example, or can be mediated by now more common app services like Uber, Lyft, and Grab (sometimes called ride hailing services). These two major models are anticipated to merge into one type of service with SAVs: the SAVs will drive themselves to your door rather than you having to travel to the car, making the short-term car rental model obsolete, and the ride-share model will no longer require a driver. Almost all car share services now use web- and app-based electronic dispatch of vehicles using smartphones or tablets. This growth is expected to accelerate with the introduction of AVs as they are anticipated to be introduced as shared mobility, and will therefore increase the car-sharing market drastically.

The future prevalence of relatively inexpensive, on-demand SAVs could make car ownership no longer cost effective for the vast majority of people. SAVs will allow for real-time 24/7 access, charge per use, and eliminate the need to park and maintain the vehicle. The convenience of being able to call an autonomous vehicle when it is needed (and easily release it for others to use when it is not) is likely to make autonomous car-sharing a much more convenient and cost-efficient mode of transportation for many.

Some potential reasons why this model may not be successful include the vehicle being unable to act as a status symbol and/or lifestyle image contributor for the user, in addition to the inconvenience of not having a personal vehicle in which to store your belongings and keep them on hand. However, this second factor is only an inconvenience to those who are accustomed to having their own car so this may not be a factor once the social shift to car-sharing occurs. During times of congestion, the wait for vehicles to arrive may be longer than usual. Also the vehicle may be used for advertising geared towards its user, and some may find the mobile advertisements displayed on SAVs in and of themselves off-putting.

Subscription Model SAV Services

Car companies will undoubtedly see any consumer dissatisfaction (such as the points mentioned above) as an opportunity; as such, SAV networks as envisioned in this book also include a more sophisticated model of a car share scheme where you subscribe to a particular service rather than calling an open service such as an autonomous Uber or Lyft. Through this type of subscription model, you

could select to always be driven in a car of a specific quality—addressing the image and lifestyle aspects of car ownership but in a shared model— and the service would prioritise your requests over those of subscribers at a lower subscription tier. Students doing research for the Transportation Infrastructure and Public Space Lab (TIPSlab) at UBC have speculated that subscription services for SAVs could be set up like a mobile phone company, with different levels of service and car models for different subscription rates. This model would still not address the issue of storing personal belongings but it would address convenience, image and lifestyle issues so that the trade-off becomes attractive. For example, a company providing SAV services could have three tiers available to meet the needs of various customer profiles:

- Tier One: $125/month – AV guaranteed within 10 minutes, have to share with others, advertisements, plus goods delivery within 8 hours – 500 miles per month limit (overages apply).
- Tier Two: $300/month – AV guaranteed within 5 minutes, sometimes have to share depending upon demand, limited advertisements, plus goods delivery within 4 hours – 1,000 miles/month limit (overages apply).
- Tier Three: $1,000/month – AV is ready when the person opens their door, no sharing with

others and no advertisements, plus goods delivery within 1 hour – Unlimited distance per month.

A range of price points allows users to select the level most appropriate for their needs and budget—a subscription on-demand model is still significantly less costly than an ownership model. Furthermore, tiers one and two are not just car-share: they are *ride* share—key for reducing congestion. In this model we could also consider SAVs that only deliver goods, serving as an autonomous courier service; this allows for the possibility of smaller SAVs that only deliver groceries, documents, etc.

Individually Dedicated AVs

Individually owned AVs in the future are still likely but are anticipated to be quite expensive compared to the shared models. These may be desirable for people who are very wealthy, who own businesses where the AV doubles as their mobile office, or for people who live in more remote areas that are not serviced by SAV networks. Households outside the SAV networks could find transportation costs very high relative to current car ownership costs.

It may also be that when customers become more used to shared mobility services that they still wish to have a car solely dedicated to their household—in this case it would be more like a lease, with the AV company

keeping the software and hardware updated and the car cleaned and maintained. In this model the car could be dispatched to a parkade or other location overnight for charging and maintenance.

Infrastructure

One of the major issues concerning the future of road-based transportation is the development and balance between so called 'vehicle intelligence' and 'infrastructure intelligence.'[22] While the former concerns the sensory and responsive capabilities of autonomous vehicles, the latter includes various changes to the supporting infrastructure, including road networks, traffic control and management systems, the ability for infrastructure to communicate with vehicles, and very importantly, for vehicles to communicate with other vehicles. There are many ways intelligence can be coordinated between systems.[23] Vehicle ad hoc networks (VANETs) are one of the most useful infrastructural types currently discussed. These are roadside infrastructure units that enable vehicle-to-vehicle (V2V) or vehicle-to-infrastructure (V2I) communication. These units relay information to vehicles originating either from the infrastructure or other vehicles. VANETs are open-ended in what they can support, including applications related to aspects such as local mapping, surrounding vehicles, traffic, and/or pedestrians;

Explaining the New Paradigm   13

additionally, they can provide information which can include everything from traffic safety to infotainment. VANETs are a core element of next generation intelligent transportation systems (ITS).[24] In this book, we have represented these as road-side beacons called Compass Poles with Wi-Fi information transmitted from them (see Chapter 7). In reality, these could be very unobtrusive and unnoticeable in the roadside environment. They are shown in this book as being multi-functional elements that also contain sensors, lighting and communications information.

There is tremendous potential to use infrastructure intelligence to increase efficiency, sustainability, reliability and safety of roadways as well as to decrease computing requirements for onboard computers in AVs.[25] For example, if infrastructure can direct right of way at intersections, more vehicles can move through more efficiently as each vehicle doesn't have to individually assess what other vehicles are doing. In addition, infrastructure can pass information about traffic congestion, accidents and intended actions of other cars to people and other vehicles: imagine a lighting system in curbs which would indicate to pedestrians whether a car will be going straight or making a right-hand turn. In terms of environmental benefits, the infrastructure could direct cars to optimize flow and reduce idling times at traffic lights or optimize the current

traffic to reduce congestion at any one place. Research on this type of infrastructure has been carried out by University of Michigan Transportation Research Institute (UMTRI), ITS-Davis and many others.[26]

However, a comprehensive infrastructural system will rely on government investment in advanced technological systems and their maintenance. Compatibility between infrastructural systems will need to be considered on a city level as well as across state, province and country borders. Whether governments have the resources and ability (and inclination) to direct such systems is a significant question. As a result of this uncertainty, all AV technology developers are currently developing their technology independently of infrastructure technology. They are not waiting for governments to develop any infrastructure but instead rely on their own mapping, sometimes even live mapping, and computation to identify speed limits and road restrictions. Even with a lack of infrastructure, vehicles can still communicate to each other through vehicle-to-vehicle (V2V) protocols, passing on information about traffic conditions and potentially even using agent-based rules to organize platooning and optimize traffic flow.[27]

Here, several scenarios are presented which rely on infrastructure to coordinate traffic—specifically at intersections and interchanges. It is possible that the beacons shown as the infrastructure communications tools may be only local facilitators of vehicle-to-vehicle information with the ability to resolve traffic problems on an intersection-only basis, thereby avoiding the need for significant investment in a large-scale system and the potential security issues. With a smaller scale infrastructure investment of this type, it is more likely that these beacons would become ubiquitous. (See also discussion in Chapter 9.)

Standards

The importance of the role of standards in transportation cannot be overstated, whether it be the design of the vehicle or the infrastructure. Standards have many benefits including guarantees of safety of course (e.g. crash barriers), ease and efficiency of construction (e.g. road curbs, subway stops), cost efficiency in fabrication (road signs), recognizability for the general public (e.g. subway entrances, road signs), understanding of function (e.g. rest stops, traffic lights), and interoperability of systems across countries (universal symbols, sign standards). However, in spite of these benefits, in design of the city and street there is a tension between standards and specificity that is constantly playing out: a push and pull between standardization and design for site and context specificity. This is an interesting design problem

on many levels and will continue to have a large impact on urban form. In the case of AVs, the standards will not only encompass road standards for future infrastructure development but, probably more importantly, standards of digital coding: the instructions on how an AV should interpret the environment and respond. These may become implicit standards—adopted because everyone uses Delphi or Mobileye technology, for example—or they may become explicit standards in that they are stated as standards by agencies and written down. These two sets of standards, for the infrastructure and for the vehicle, will both have an impact on the form of the city.

At this critical point, where we are about to embark on creating regulations and standards for AVs, it is worth looking at some of the impacts and problems that can result from standards. When there is an inconsistency of standards (plugs, for example), inefficiencies are created and sometimes (as in software) there is an impediment to functionality as well as efficiency across the systems. The debate about standards primarily rests on two aspects: the suitability of the standards for the elements to which they are being applied, and any unintentional influence they may have—with unintentional being the operative word.

Keller Easterling is one of the most interesting and critical voices in terms

Standards   15

of discussing standards. She explains,

> If law is the currency of governments, standards are the currency of international organizations and multinational enterprises. ISO (International Organization for Standardization) is an extra-state parliament of this global standard-making activity. A private nongovernmental organization, convening both private companies and national representatives, ISO oversees global technical standards for everything from credit card thickness to dashboard pictograms, computer protocols and the pitch of screw threads. [...] Standards create a "soft law" of global exchange.[28]

Easterling is concerned that not only do we not realize the implications of the standards, but that these standards are created by extra-state entities or entities that are beyond government reach and thus have no accountability. They are beyond the reach of the public and even the government.

As Easterling points out, many of the standards which govern our built environment today and the way we go about our business lives are developed by private non-governmental organizations and/or corporations. Our assumptions about our environment are generally that standards are put in place by some level of government, and in a democratic society we elect that government. By this logic we would expect to have some control over the standards set and that they are in the best interest of our relative societies, within the limits and imperfections of our democratic processes. Easterling makes a good argument that this assumption is likely flawed and our world is a reflection of standards outside of our control. This is worth thinking about in the context of the new transportation technology of the AV.

The development of AVs and their technologies so far are not conforming to any standards, simply because no agencies have published any for them.[29,30] This lack of development of standards is partly at the behest of the companies involved since there is intense competition in the field and each company wants complete freedom to innovate. Currently each company decides on their own standards: these standards are likely set in order to interface with other control systems, either of their own company or outside hardware or software,[31] and, most importantly, for reasons of limiting and controlling their own liability and preventing negative press coverage of any negative incidents involving their cars.

There are many discussions of standards that one could embark on, but one of the most interesting scenarios in terms of AVs is perhaps the 'disposition' of the cars. Consider this description of the dispositions of two different makes of AV:

16   Chapter 1 Envisioning Future Infrastructures

Riding in Hyundai's self-driving Ioniq, for example, is like taking a Sunday drive with your grand-mother. The car is extremely ad-ept at staying squarely in its lane without ping-ponging back and forth, but it is also cautious in the extreme, stopping nine feet short of crosswalks and stubbornly refusing to go forward if a pedes-trian looks poised to step off the sidewalk. It is behavior that can ignite road rage in nearby human drivers.

By comparison, Delphi's test car, which uses an Intel computing platform installed in an Audi Q5, is more aggressive. It can easily merge into highway traffic and negotiate complex intersections. However, it treats pedestrians with less deference, taking right-hand corners more quickly — even though pedestrians may be contemplating entering the crosswalk.[32]

How can we set standards for a car's disposition? Should we even bother? The details of the car's disposition are contained within the code: how close does the pedestrian need to be to the curb before the car stops moving and allows the pedestrian to have the right of way? If the car is already moving and knows the trajectory of the person and car will not intersect, should the car go forward? Does the car need to predict the trajectory of the pedestrian at all or just react the second the person's foot crosses the curb? If we can be assured that the pedestrian will not be hit if they decide to step off the curb, should

we worry about the 'manners' of an aggressive car on the road?

And then there are the questions of what type of standards should be set. Would you standardize the distance the pedestrian is from the curb at the point that their trajectory is headed towards the intersection? Or should it be the trajectory of the car and the pedestrian intersection? Should it be the behaviour of the car as the pedestrian's foot steps over the curb? And who is going to inspect the code of the AV to ensure conformance?

To date this issue has been dealt with only by a driving test—the AV is required to undergo a driving test similar to that which a person has to pass. If the car has multiple dispositions (or settings regarding aggressiveness), would each dispo-sition have to be tested? Perhaps people will, in the end, be able to choose which disposition they would like for their car. Perhaps they will even choose their AV depending on the model's disposition. And perhaps that disposition will affect street standards—either requiring or not requiring different crosswalk and in-tersection configuration. At this point it is hard to tell.

Moving back to the standards of the streets, about which we know considerably more having had many decades to develop and study them, Easterling writes:

Standards   17

Picture the places where we live: the parking places, sky-scrapers, turning radii, garages, street lights, driveways, airport lounges, highway exits, big boxes, strip malls, shopping malls, small boxes, free zones, casinos, retail outlets, fast food restaurants, hotels, cash machines, tract housing, container ports, industrial parks, call centres, golf courses, suburbs, office buildings, business parks, resorts. In the retinal afterglow is a soupy matrix of details and repeatable formulas that generate most of the space in the world—what we might call infrastructure space.[33]

Much of the infrastructure space she mentions is the space and paraphernalia of the vehicle. In *Streets and the Shaping of Towns and Cities*, Michael Southworth claims "street standards may appear benign but are powerful in the way they shape the environments we live in."[34] He points out that the public will rail against planners, developers and designers for urban sprawl but much of this 'sprawl' is a direct result of street standards which require huge lanes and rights of way. The standard right of way width for a residential neighbourhood as specified by the Institute of Transportation Engineers has remained at 15.2m–18.3m for the last 30 years.[35] Multiply that requirement by many streets and there is a resulting huge sea of asphalt as well as large amounts of land to be maintained. Southworth further highlights that worldwide at least one third of all urban developed land is dedicated

to parking lots, roads and other motor vehicle infrastructure. In this case both the suitability of the standards and the outsize influence they have point to the need to revisit standards as well as to understand the influence of the decisions on urban form when multiplied by exponential factors.

But there are also standards that are created without any company or government writing them. The car in the suburb, for example, is not regulated by any standards. However, the technological innovation of the car "hacked the suburban software,"[36] requiring a garage for every house. This has given rise to the societal norm of the addition of a garage and driveway to every household in suburbia and has had an immense impact on the form of the city. The question now is what will the AV do to the 'standard' configuration of the new city fabric? This is more thoroughly discussed in the chapters that follow.

Safety and Deployment of Autonomous Technologies

The deployment of self-driving technologies in the public realm is a risk which is currently being heavily debated — and rightly so. The challenge with self-driving technology is that, unlike many other technologies, it cannot be fully tested within controlled conditions. Centres such as Mcity at University of Michigan and Castle Air Force Base in California try to recreate conditions such as trees over roadways, grates in the street, railway crossings, overhead electrical interference, graffitied stop signs and many others which may be problematic for an AV's intelligence. However, there are an incalculable number of unforeseen conditions which AVs may encounter on a street; these unpredictable events can only be tested on real roads where, inevitably, unforeseen and therefore un-programmed situations will occur. The solution to date has been to allow the cars to drive 'supervised' on the road for thousands of kilometres, with a supervising engineer behind the wheel to take over should the car not be able to assess the situation. This seems a reasonable approach, but the question remains: what level of risk is acceptable before allowing the vehicles unsupervised on the streets?

A simple answer would be to say that AVs would need to demonstrate that they are at least as safe or safer than human drivers on a balance of probability. However, although road accident rates for human drivers are high, there are still relatively few if considered per number of kilometres driven. Currently, Americans drive over 5 trillion kilometres per year.[37] In 2013 there were 2.3 million reported injuries, corresponding to a rate of 48 injuries per 100 million kilometres driven.[38] There were also 32,719 fatalities, corresponding to a rate of 0.7 per 100 million kilometres driven.[39]

Looking to statistics for AVs, the most extensive testing and documentation comes from Google (now Waymo). Google's cars drove over 2 million kilometres between 2009 and 2015 and were involved in 11 crashes, 9 of which involved no injury[40] and only two crashes which have been reported as resulting in injuries. Furthermore, these cars are all supervised so any serious circumstances may have been dealt with by the human who was supervising and thus the data is not truly representative of regular driving conditions. A detailed analysis has been done on these statistics[41] but clearly even this extensive testing programme gives us little information on what would happen with an extensively deployed fully autonomous fleet. As Kalra and Paddock point out:

> Autonomous vehicles would have to be driven hundreds of millions of miles and sometimes hundreds of billions of miles to demonstrate their reliability in terms of fatalities and injuries. Under even aggressive testing assumptions, existing fleets would take tens and sometimes hundreds of years to drive these miles—an impossible proposition if the aim is to demonstrate their performance prior to releasing them on the roads for consumer use.[42]

More precisely, their detailed analysis demonstrates that, using a fleet of 100 autonomous vehicles driving 24 hours a day, it would take 400 years or 14 billion kilometres of driving to demonstrate with 95% confidence

Safety   19

their failure rate to within 20% of the true rate of fatalities with human drivers.[43]

Further complicating the discussion, but generally not mentioned, is that other companies have different software and would also need to test their cars for these same billions of kilometres in order to prove their reliability. Testing a Google car is not the same as testing a self-driving BMW. Some of the sensors used may be the same but the software for each AV developer is proprietary to those companies.[44] As such, our method of testing reliability is currently unworkable and will remain unresolved in terms of certifying safety to a similar level with current statistically acceptable methods.

Since testing our way to a solution to safety is unlikely, then, to be fruitful, AV companies will have to prove through other methods that the cars are equivalently safe. It may be that innovative methods of doing so may evolve; however, the validity of these methods may not be accepted by all. Overall this leaves us with a knotty problem and no easy answer. Within a democratic society, decisions which are unclear and cannot be statistically determined are typically appraised in the court of public opinion. The public express their views, through various means, to the politicians who create laws and regulations to direct society. This brings us to another messy discussion in light of the alleged influencing of public opinion by social media efforts. However, this discussion is far from new — it is only the media through which it is working and the global reach of the media that is different. The 'Motordom' lobby from the 1920s changed the court of public opinion from anti-car to pro-car through an extensive, far-reaching and very cleverly executed media and influence campaign.[45,46] The movement developed from the banding together of automotive interest groups who joined with chambers of commerce and local safety councils to "fight accidents and congestion on the terms of Safety First and efficiency."[47] As Norton explains, "Motordom socially reconstructed city streets as motor thoroughfares — places where cars pre-eminently belong [...] Motordom's struggle and relative success reveal much about how social groups succeed or fail at remaking the world to suit their needs."[48]

It could be argued that the AV companies are not doing enough to sway this court of public opinion, since news reports of any crashes are proliferating significantly, especially following the preventable first death of a pedestrian hit by an AV.[49] There are, however, AV lobbies such as the 'Self-Driving Coalition for Safer Streets' whose mandate is "to work with lawmakers, regulators, and the public to realize the safety and societal benefits of self-driving vehicles"[50] as well as the recently created 'Automated Vehicle Coalition'[51] which emphasizes the benefits of AVs in regard to safety, job creation, sustainability and economic efficiency. These coalitions hark back to the creation of Motordom; whether or not they can be as successful in swaying public opinion is still an open question but they have the business savvy, the technological resources and the skill with social media as well as a deep pool of extremely talented engineers to draw on — all the criteria which made the Motordom lobby so successful in its day.

Notes

1 Melvin Kranzberg, "Technology and History: 'Kranzberg's Laws,'" *Technology and Culture* 27, no. 3 (1986): 544–60.

2 David C. Hodge, "Geography and the Political Economy of Urban Transportation," *Urban Geography* 11, no. 1 (1990): 97.

3 Zac Hall, "Scott Forstall Finally Weighs in on the Flat versus Skeuomorphic Design Debate," *9to5Mac* (blog), June 21, 2017, https://9to5mac.com/2017/06/21/scott-forstall-design-debate/.

4 Buster Hein, "Jony Ive Explains Why He Decided to Gut Skeuomorphism from IOS 7," *Cult of Mac* (blog), September 19, 2013, https://www.cultofmac.com/246312/jony-ive-explains-why-he-decided-to-gut-skeuomorphism-out-of-ios/.

5 Paul Hekkert, Dirk Snelders, and Piet CW Wieringen, "'Most Advanced, yet Acceptable': Typicality and Novelty as Joint Predictors of Aesthetic Preference in Industrial Design," *British Journal of Psychology* 94, no. 1 (2003): 111–124.

6 TW Allan Whitfield and Philip E Slatter, "The Effects of Categorization and Prototypicality on Aesthetic Choice in a Furniture Selection Task," *British Journal of Psychology* 70, no. 1 (1979): 65–75.

7 James M Anderson et al., *Autonomous Vehicle Technology: A Guide for Policymakers* (Rand Corporation, 2014), https://www.rand.org/pubs/research_briefs/RB9755.html.

8 "About," Starship Technologies, accessed October 18, 2017, https://www.starship.xyz/.

9 Myllymaki, Jussi. "Autonomous delivery platform." U.S. Patent 9,256,852, issued February 9, 2016.

10 "Handle" Handle | Boston Dynamics, accessed October 18, 2017. https://www.bostondynamics.com/handle.

11 James Vincent, "Self-Driving Truck Convoy Completes Its First Major Journey across Europe," *The Verge*, April 7, 2016, https://www.theverge.com/2016/4/7/11383392/self-driving-truck-platooning-europe.

12 Jack Stewart, "Of Course Google's Waymo Is Building Self-Driving Trucks," *Wired*, accessed October 18, 2017, https://www.wired.com/2017/06/course-googles-waymo-building-self-driving-trucks/.

13 Ken Pyle and Managing Editor, "Autonomous Vehicle View—10/17/14—Blurred Lines," *The Viodi View*, October 18, 2014, http://viodi.com/2014/10/17/autonomous-vehicle-view-101714-blurred-lines/.

14 Chunka Mai, "Fasten Your Seatbelts: Google's Driverless Car Is Worth Trillions," accessed October 18, 2017, https://www.forbes.com/sites/chunkamui/2013/01/22/fasten-your-seatbelts-googles-driverless-car-is-worth-trillions/#61a8ade879dd.

15 P Gao, HW Kaas, and D Mohr, "Automotive Revolution-Perspective towards 2030" (McKinsey & Company, January 2016), 20.

16 Biz Carson, "Lyft President: Car Ownership Will 'All-But End' in Cities by 2025," *Business Insider*, September 18, 2016.

17 US Energy Information Administration, "Study of the Potential Energy Consumption Impacts of Connected and Automated Vehicles," Department of Energy Washington, USA, 65.

18 Daniel Fagnant and Kara Kockelman, "The Travel and Environmental Implications of Shared Autonomous Vehicles, Using Agent-Based Model Scenarios," *Transportation Research Part C: Emerging Technologies* 40 (March 2014), 1–13.

19 Daniel Fagnant and Kara Kockelman, "Dynamic ride-sharing and optimal fleet sizing for a system of shared autonomous vehicles," *Transportation Research Board 94th Annual Meeting*, no. 15-1962, 2015.

20 Joseph Okpaku, VP Operations for Lyft and Adam Gromis, lead on sustainability and environmental impact, commenting at AUVSI July 13, 2017. http://www.auvsi.org/industry-news/ride-sharing-first-step-automated-vehicles-speakers-say

21 Ludovic Privat, "Carsharing: 26M Users Worldwide in 2020," *GPS Business News*, accessed December 16, 2017,

https://www.gpsbusinessnews.com/Carsharing-26M-Users-Worldwide-in-2020_a5752.html.

22 Sadayuki Tsugawa, "Issues and Recent trends in Vehicle Safety Communication Systems," *IATSS Research* 29, no. 1 (2005): 7–15.

23 Sadayuki Tsugawa, Shin Kato, Takeshi Matsui, Hiroshi Naganawa, and H. Fujii, "An Architecture for Cooperative Driving of Automated Vehicles," in *Intelligent Transportation Systems, 2000. Proceedings. 2000 IEEE*, 422–427.

24 Liu, Jianqi, Jiafu Wan, Qinruo Wang, Pan Deng, Keliang Zhou, and Yupeng Qiao, "A Survey on Position-based Routing for Vehicular ad hoc Networks." *Telecommunication Systems* 62, no. 1 (2016): 15–30.

25 Heiko G. Seif, and Xiaolong Hu, "Autonomous Driving in the iCity—HD Maps as a Key Challenge of the Automotive Industry," *Engineering* 2, no. 2 (2016): 159-162.

26 Transportation Research Institute at University of Michigan & Institute of Transportation Studies, University of California at Davis.

27 Tsugawa et al., "An Architecture for Cooperative Driving of Automated Vehicles."

28 Keller Easterling, *Extrastatecraft: The Power of Infrastructure Space* (London: Verso, 2014), 18.

29 "Given the nascent nature of technologies for AVs and CVs, no federal safety standards exist specifically for these vehicles in Canada," as stated in Jed Chong, "Automated and Connected Vehicles: Status of the Technology and Key Issues for Canadian Governments" Background Paper 2016-98-E for the Library of Parliament, Current Publications, accessed October 21, 2017, under 4.1 Regulation.

30 The US has published 'guidance' standards but not specific standards for AVs: "Federal Automated Vehicles Policy—September 2016," US Department of Transportation.

September 19, 2016. https://www.transportation.gov/AV/federal-automated-vehicles-policy-september-2016.

31 John R. Quain, "Self-Driving Cars Might Need Standards, but Whose?," *The New York Times*, February 23, 2017, https://www.nytimes.com/2017/02/23/automobiles/wheels/self-driving-cars-standards.html.

32 Ibid.

33 Easterling, *Extrastatescraft*, 11.

34 Michael Southworth and Eran Ben-Joseph, *Streets and the Shaping of Towns and Cities* (New York: McGraw Hill, 1997), 3.

35 Ibid, 4–5.

36 Easterling, *Extrastatecraft*, 21.

37 Federal Highway Transportation Adminstration, "Press Release: 3.2 Trillion Miles Driven On U.S. Roads In 2016," February 21, 2017, https://www.fhwa.dot.gov/pressroom/fhwa1704.cfm.

38 Nidhi Kalra and Susan M. Paddock, "Driving to Safety: How Many Miles of Driving Would It Take to Demonstrate Autonomous Vehicle Reliability?," *Transportation Research Part A: Policy and Practice* 94 (December 1, 2016): 2, https://doi.org/10.1016/j.tra.2016.09.010.

39 Ibid, 2.

40 Myra Blanco et al., "Automated Vehicle Crash Rate Comparison Using Naturalistic Data" (Virginia Tech Transportation Institute, 2016).

41 Ibid.

42 Kalra and Paddock, "Driving to Safety," 1.

43 Ibid.

44 As evidenced by the lawsuit launched by Waymo against Uber Arrian Marschall, "Uber and Waymo Abruptly Settle For $245 Million," *Wired*, February 9, 2018, https://www.wired.com/story/uber-waymo-lawsuit-settlement/.

45 Peter D. Norton, *Fighting Traffic* (Cambridge, Massachusetts: The MIT Press, 2008).

46 Also see Chapter 4.

47 Norton, *Fighting Traffic*, 173.

48 Ibid, 255.

49 The Associated Press, "Police Release Video of Fatal Crash by Uber Self-Driving SUV," CBCnews, *CBC/Radio Canada*, March 22, 2018, http://www.cbc.ca/news/world/uber-self-driving-accident-video-1.4587439.

50 "Self-Driving Coalition for Safer Streets," April 7, 2018, http://www.selfdrivingcoalition.org/.

51 "The Automated Vehicle Coalition," AVC, accessed April 7, 2018, http://www.avcoalition.net/.

Chapter 2
Notes on Drawing

Chapter 2
Notes on Drawing

Lőrinc Vass

(Im)possible Futures[1]

Drawing is a process of creation, a making-visible of possible alternatives from which material or virtual realities may be constructed. Insofar as the world comprises the 'real' and the 'possible,' drawing can serve as a powerful tool not only to *represent* things that are real, but also to *actualize* possible futures. Its projective apparatus may be used to produce eminently realizable schemes, or be tuned to conjure seemingly unbuildable constructions. Ever since the Renaissance, drawing has enjoyed an intrinsic role in architectural practice: architects and other spatial designers draw lines and pictures, and in doing so, they also draw together ideas and conclusions. At times, this takes the form of exact blueprints that directly result in physical manifestations; at other times, the form of exploratory representations that set in motion indirect but potentially substantial consequences.

This dynamic is particularly clear in past urban visions that speculated on the role of the automobile, which have exerted a substantial influence on urbanism largely by way of iconic drawings. As a marvel of engineering and industrial mass-production, automotive technology captured the imagination of architects through the 20th century, and became a key protagonist in the urban utopias produced on both sides of the Atlantic. Many of Le Corbusier's perspectival renderings for *Ville Contemporaine* (1922) and other urban-scale projects feature vast swaths of highways in the foreground—images that became reality in the post-war decades with the proliferation of functionalist urban planning. Similarly, Frank Lloyd Wright's drawings for *Broadacre City* (1932–1959) depict personally-owned automobiles travelling on a network of superhighways that connect a dispersed, continental-scale urbanity. Naive in its lack of anticipation of the scale of impending population growth and concurrent explosion of traffic, the scheme is often (and somewhat unfairly) seen as a precursor to postwar suburban sprawl.[2]

Fast-forward to the present. Whereas automobiles have long fallen out of favour amongst architects and planners alike, the urban imagination has lately been populated by their presumed successors, driverless cars. When introduced in the near future, such vehicles are anticipated to be the first independent robots widely encountered by the public. Capable of sensing and navigating their surroundings, they are the embodiments of a digitally networked future urban ecology, characterized by a paradigm shift in the relationship between vehicles, users, infrastructure, material flows, and the built environment at large.

As traditional auto-manufacturers race against up-and-coming tech companies to produce their own driverless car, a multitude of arguments that support or criticize the technology are exchanged in public discourse: the media, think-tank reports, and policy documents. Rarely, however, have the unique disciplinary tools of architecture and design (particularly, the special representational and discursive agencies of drawing) been called into action in these debates—a contribution the drawings in this book seek to make. The following briefly explores some of the dilemmas and opportunities underlying the drawing of possible and probable futures: first, the contested and constructed nature of the future, and the related questions concerning the social role of architecture; second, the frequently technological bias of future envisioning, and the simultaneous embeddedness of drawing

in technology; and third, socially engaged drawing as a form of design practice, and the particular aesthetic considerations of such speculative work.

Drawing Context: Disparate Visions

Late-modern society, as the sociologist Anthony Giddens contends, is the most future-oriented there has ever been,[3] with notions of social and technological progress, environmental collapse, and irreversible change permeating the social imagination. Consequently, it is of the utmost importance to view the future not only as an indeterminate yet objective succession of the present, but as a heterogeneous and constantly negotiated discursive field. As outlined by the editors of *Contested Futures: A Sociology of Prospective Techno-Science*, the future:

> comes to be defined as a contested object of social and material action: if actors are to secure successfully for themselves a specific kind of future then they must engage in a range of rhetorical, organisational and material activities through which the future might be able to be 'colonised.'[4] ... Like all discourses, 'the future' is constituted through an unstable field of language, practice and materiality in which various disciplines, capacities and actors compete for the right to represent near and far term developments.[5]

Concerned with creating new spatial conditions and social configurations, architecture and allied spatial design disciplines have always been fundamentally projective endeavours, ever leaning towards possible successions and alternatives to the present, even while building on or borrowing from the past. Architectural drawings of the future, then, need to be situated within the discursive field of contested futures, as devices that simultaneously open particular possibilities while foreclosing others. And in a broader sense, a discursive view of the future, whether it takes a material or virtual form, also evokes the debates concerning architecture's relationship with, and influence on, its political, economic, and social contexts. As the architectural theorists Isabelle Doucet and Kenny Cupers articulate:

> Architecture is, by its very nature, 'in the world,' in both spatial and temporal terms: buildings are concrete and tangible elements of our everyday life-world. Yet, also architectural designs, urban plans, utopian schemes or paper architecture are 'in the world': they might not define the way things work, but they do change the way we think about how they work, or should work. It is this peculiar, myriad being-in-the-world-ness of architecture that raises fundamental questions about how architecture enacts, how it performs, and consequently, how it might 'act otherwise' or lead to other possible

futures. This possibility underlies all questions regarding architecture's ability to be critical.[6]

In other words, if the critical–projective debate of the past two decades has eroded criticality as the assumed source of architecture's agency (as it has been extensively argued elsewhere[7]), it has also brought to the forefront the very notion of agency—the ability to act, or in other words, the ability to *make a difference*. Within the context of architectural practice, Doucet and Cuper define agency in relation to three key questions: the 'what'—the source of agency; the 'how'—the means, modes and vehicles of agency; and the 'why'—the effect or intention of agency.[8] In other words: who (or what) is contributing towards visions of the (im)possible? By what means and methods are images of the future drawn? And to what end are prospective scenarios created? These questions are examined in the following, in relation to technology as both the problematic source and unavoidable means of agency, and in regard to socially engaged drawing practice as the goal of agency.

Drawing Technology: Post-Digital Fictions

The problem concerning technology pervades future envisioning in two distinct ways. Firstly, visions of the future produced since the advent of modernity have typically been dominated by advances in technology.[9] A problematic consequence of this fact is that agency is often attributed to a particular technology, at the expense of other human and non-human actors in complex socio-technical systems. The future then, is seen:

> as unfolding or developing naturally along identifiable lines as its 'self-evident' benefits are taken up by users. This view is typically found in commentaries on the 'future impact' of a list of new technologies. Here, the key question is not whether a certain option will be pursued, but rather when it will come in being.[10]

The way in which such uncritical and celebratory views of technology continue to permeate architecture is aptly expressed by the architect Keller Easterling:

> Architects still long to be modern like the old days. Having put faith in every successive new technology, believing in the obsolescence of the old and the superiority of the "new," architecture easily flocks toward ubiquitous computing, smart cities, and the "internet of things." Architects have embraced Kevin Kelly's twentieth-century digital enthusiasm about cars as "chips with wheels," airplanes as "chips with wings, farms as chips with soil, houses as chips with inhabitants." OSARC (open source architecture) proposes a universal digital platform for the design and production of space in which, they argue, many of the

modernists' dreams can finally be realized. A new technology like Google Car will solve transportation problems. With something like Airbnb, we see tools to make architecture dance to immaterial instructions. New technologies will finally deliver the dematerialization of space into information. The whole world is Turing complete.[11]

Such deterministic views of new technologies as uncomplicated solutions to complex issues are especially problematic due to the extreme difficulty in predicting the future impacts of technology, whereas inventions can (and often do) create their own necessity.[12] For example, the MP3 format was created to allow for efficient data storage; in the long run, it made online streaming possible. Likewise, mobile phones allowed for making calls from anywhere; ultimately, they became personal gateways to the internet.[13] Thus, while inventors imagine and foresee certain uses for their creations, the unforeseen uses of new technologies—within a complex matrix of competing interests and interactions—are an even more potent field for speculation, especially by those who are expert at inventively recombining technological means and representing this through drawing: designers of the built environment.

Secondly, whereas the role of agency in future envisioning is too often surrendered to technology in place

Drawing Technology: Post-Digital Fictions   31

of human actors or social matrices, it has likewise become commonplace to evaluate the status of architectural drawing in relation to the so-called post-digital technological paradigm. If the post-digital can be defined as an *imminent* condition in which the digital is suffusing into everyday urban life through innovations such as driverless cars, 'smart' household appliances, or artificial intelligence and machine learning, a similar state of affairs has *already* transformed the practice of architecture over the past two decades. Computer-aided design (CAD), building information modelling (BIM) and graphic visualization software packages have instrumentalized architectural production since the 1990s, and have been seen by many as grave threats to drawing's status as an expressive tool that is simultaneously critical and creative—a role it has enjoyed since the modern movement from the early 20th century.[14] Some, then, characterize the current, post-digital paradigm of drawing as a divergence between a technical exactitude "that equates drawing to blueprints of realizable artifacts and narrows the space of creativity" and an artistic extravagance that "remov[es] it from the material and tangible world."[15]

While on the one hand it is worth acknowledging the intrinsic value of engagements with digital visualization and simulation technologies in broadening the conceptual boundaries of architecture, it is also necessary to point out a problem with the above assessment of the post-digital. As the media theorist Florian Cramer argues, the post-digital condition is best understood as the *stabilized* state of affairs following the intense upheaval of technological innovation, in which 'new' and 'old' media and technology coexist in various hybrid forms, and choices between them are made according to their suitability to each task.[16] Likewise, the architect Sam Jacob describes the occurrence of precisely this phenomenon amongst many avant-garde practitioners of architectural drawing today: "Instead of striving for pseudo-photo-realism, this new cult of the drawing explores and exploits its artificiality, making us as viewers aware that we are looking at space as a fictional form of representation."[17] Rather than surrendering the discursive and representational agencies of future envisioning to technology, instead it becomes both subject and method: drawings *of* technology and drawing *as* technology can be deployed towards other, socially focused agendas.

Drawing Practice: Speculative Matters

As an alternative to evaluating drawing solely by its role *within* architecture—where it is at risk of being seen as an intermediary between thought and action, with 'action' understood as 'building'—it is worthwhile to consider *drawing as action*, a possible means of *practising* architecture, the product of which is not necessarily built realizations. As the architect John Bass articulates:

> Precise and focused drawings are among the skills closest to the core of an architect's education and practice. The discipline of drawing does not, however, need to be subordinate to the ultimate objective of building. Drawing can be an end in itself, or more accurately, be produced in the service of alternative ends.[18]

Drawings of possible alternatives to the status quo of spatial and social arrangements, then, can be *sources* of agency, by acting as visual repositories of speculation, critique, and invention. Simultaneously, socially disposed drawings can also be *vehicles* of agency in a given situation, by serving as catalysts of imagination, facilitators of communication, and instigators of debate.

Conceived with these objectives in mind as a speculative atlas, *Driverless Urban Futures* visualizes the possible spatial, and consequentially, social, impacts of driverless vehicles on the city of the near-future. The drawings in the book comprise three open-ended 'roadmaps': illustrations of narrative scenarios, diagrams of urban-scale spatial structures and temporal patterns, and vignettes of street-scale assemblies and interactions. In contrast to both the glossy renderings of car-manufacturers and the overly technical graphs of transportation researchers, these spatial diagrams and perspective collages seek to be simultaneously exacting and experimental. They are purposefully characterized by a graphic flatness and a display of their artificiality, drawn with a simple and slightly cartoonish hand, so as to make them legible and engaging for broad audiences. Likewise, while the specific elements of the drawings are rendered with care and precision, they are left purposefully abstract so as to suggest a *possible*, as opposed to a *certain*, future. The comparative pairings and scenarios, along with the graphic annotations and accompanying texts, also intend to offer multiple entry points and readings. Engendering a plurality of interpretations—or even, of productive misreadings—can then become a means for drawing closer to the unpredictable consequences and unforeseen uses characteristic of new technologies.

In addition, even though the drawings are predominantly speculations on probable changes to the form and function of elements of the built environment as a result of driverless vehicle technology, also implicit within this assembly of line-work is a drawing together of many other matters of concern: from public space, infrastructure and energy consumption to spatial practices, well-being and social interaction. These various social, economic and cultural

Drawing Practice: Speculative Matters   33

phenomena, which by necessity will shape the realization of driverless vehicles, are addressed to a greater degree in the accompanying texts.

Just as important as the explosion of technology in architecture—in particular, of the tools related to drawing—has been the expansion of architectural practice itself. While a rigorous training in techniques and methods of drawing that are simultaneously exact and exploratory remains essential to architecture and its allied disciplines, these fields are also increasingly positioned within an expanded territory. Spatial designers can, and should, act as spatial facilitators, analysts, advocates, and collaborators—not to undermine but to preserve and extend the relevance and efficacy of their field. Drawing can act as a form of critical projection, taking advantage of contemporary technologies in responsive yet imaginative, focused yet open-ended, ways in order to make visible and expose to debate the possible—but not inevitable—futures of the city. Ultimately, the agency of the drawings in the book is seen to reside in the spaces between these contested futures, contingent technologies, and collective (mis)readings.

Notes

I would like to thank Roy Cloutier, Nicole Sylvia, and Zherui Wang for their valuable comments and suggestions.

1   Parts of this essay were presented at the 106th ACSA Annual Meeting "The Ethical Imperative," March 15–17, 2018, Denver, Colorado, and published in the conference proceedings (forthcoming).

2   Katherine Don, "Frank Lloyd Wright's Utopian Dystopia," *Next City*, April 8, 2010, https://nextcity.org/daily/entry/frank-lloyd-wrights-utopian-dystopia.

3   Nik Brown, Brian Rappert, and Andrew Webster, eds., *Contested Futures: A Sociology of Prospective Techno-Science* (London: Routledge, 2016), 5.

4   Ibid, 3.

5   Ibid, 5.

6   Isabelle Doucet and Kenny Cupers, "Agency in Architecture: Reframing Criticality in Theory and Practice," *Footprint* no. 4 (Spring 2009): 1, http://dx.doi.org/10.7480/footprint.3.1.694.

7   Ibid, 6, endnote 1.

8   Ibid, 2–3.

9   Brown, Rappert, and Webster, *Contested Futures*, 4–6.

10 Ibid, 9.

11 Keller Easterling, "IIRS," *e-flux Journal* no. 64 (April 2015): 4, http://www.e-flux.com/journal/64/60837/iirs/.

12 Jesse Reiser and Nanako Umemoto, *Atlas of Novel Tectonics* (New York: Princeton Architectural Press, 2012), 188.

13 Tom Goodwin, "The Three Ages of the Digital," TechCrunch, June 23, 2016, https://techcrunch.com/2016/06/23/the-three-ages-of-digital/.

14 Frédéric Migayrou and Bob Sheil, eds., *Drawing Futures: Speculations in Contemporary Drawing for Art and Architecture* (London: UCL Press, 2016), 3.

15 ACSA, "Call for Papers, Drawing in the Post-Digital Era: From Exactitude to Extravagance," 2017, https://www.acsa-arch.org/programs-events/conferences/annual-meeting/106th-annual-meeting/call-for-papers.

16 Florian Cramer, "What is 'Post-digital'?" *APRJA Journal 3*, no. 1 (2014), http://www.aprja.net/what-is-post-digital/?pdf=1318.

17 Sam Jacob, "Architecture Enters the Age of Post-Digital Drawing," *Metropolis*, March 21, 2017, http://www.metropolismag.com/architecture/architecture-enters-age-post-digital-drawing/.

18 John Bass, "The end of drawing: narrative visualization and community-based collaboration," paper presented at ARCC 2009 Leadership in Architectural Research, San Antonio, TX, 15–18 April 2009, http://www.arcc-journal.org/index.php/repository/article/view/132/101.

Chapter 3
Into the Future: Analytic Scenarios

Chapter 3
Into the Future: Analytic Scenarios

Sara Costa Maia and AnnaLisa Meyboom

Introduction[1]

At the advent of this research into the impact of automated vehicles (AVs) on urban form itself, it was necessary to place ourselves, as researchers, in the future. As with other new technologies, such as the iPhone, it is not easy to understand the implications of a technology until it is already well-established. Being trained in architecture, we could formulate a future and inhabit this imagined design future (as per the exposition on drawing in Chapter 2); this could potentially give us a better perspective on the impacts of the technology, but the major problem becomes the inability to determine which futures are most likely. In the case of AVs, there are very large differences in potential outcomes depending on many factors; two of the strongest determining factors in the configuration of cities are arguably the modes and technologies that define urban transportation. There is clearly also a strong relationship between the interurban transportation system and the spatial form and organization of the city as discussed in the next chapter and borne out

in analytic studies.[2] To respond to this problem, the researchers at the Transportation Infrastructure and Public Space Lab (TIPSlab), a research group headed by the author, researched future-visioning methodologies. The outcome is described in this chapter.[3]

We then apply our findings to 'scenarios.' This is a methodology used by TIPSlab to bring government decision makers and the public at large into the future so that they can better understand the impact of the technology by understanding 'projective lived examples' regarding whatever transportation technology is in question. In the scenarios are characters who represent typical users of the technology. The characters are admittedly and intentionally undeveloped since the point of the exercise is to quickly bring the audience into an imagined future—at which point they can adapt the scene to how it might be applicable to them or others. It is worth acknowledging here the many serious and complex social implications of transportation technologies decisions, which are explored further in Chapter 8.

The scenarios outlined here are also examples of the different outcomes found from the future-visioning methodology, which further demonstrates how this methodology might be useful. Analytic methods applied to the scenarios resulting from the future-visioning methodologies would be the more classic way of applying this technique.

Future-Visioning Methodology

Understanding the full implications of introducing a new technology is no simple task. Since the beginning of the 20th century, when technology started to progress at an exponential rate, a multitude of researchers and enthusiasts have put efforts into envisioning the future scenarios enabled by new inventions. These speculations range from Villemard's far from accurate illustrations for the year 2000[4] to Nikola Tesla's impressive technology-specific predictions.[5]

One of the developments of the work of McLuhan[6] is the assumption that any technology in itself brings unforeseen consequences beyond its original purpose or content. Tenner, in *Why Things Bite Back: Technology and the Revenge of Unintended Consequences*, also identifies the unavoidable unknowns—consequences, potentialities and developments—which surround any new technology.[7] McLuhan uses the invention of

the printing press as an example, pointing out its far-reaching role in the emergence of modern national states in Europe.[8] Despite its primary goal of accelerating the production of books, the press also allowed for the standardization of education and the imposition of a national language, besides supporting the advent of the Industrial Revolution. McLuhan argues that these consequences were already present in the conception of the press, but would only reveal themselves slowly over time. Analogously, the consequences of AVs are also present in their conception and revealing these consequences is an interesting and important exercise.

In order to investigate the systemic urban impact of new transportation technologies, an innovative and comprehensive methodology is required. This chapter proposes one such methodology; it is based primarily on existing future-envisioning techniques for business decision making with some modifications for the adaptation to the more complex issue of the impact of AVs. This methodology was put forward not as a precise method for future prediction, but rather as a useful and robust tool that can be used by decision makers to make better informed assessments on maximizing benefits and mitigating problems of new transportation technologies with regard to their impact on the quality of urban environments.

In the fields of architecture and urban planning, technology has been embedded in 20th century visionary thinking about the city just as social issues were central to 19th century speculative design.[9] These visionary works, however, are of an arguably different nature than Villemard's or Tesla's. Architectural visionary thinking is unconcerned with predictive accuracy; it is more a social commentary and a way of proposing radical speculative futures in order to solve social problems. It is not solely concerned with what cities will be, but with what they *could* be, and how they reflect values and ideas in a very intentional way. It aspires towards an improved reality according to the authors' particular ideals, and then strives to influence the making of the world with such ideals (see Chapter 10 for a discussion of utopian visions and transportation technologies).

Apart from the aforementioned modes of envisioning the impact of technologies, it is also worth noting the abundance of literature that offers technical/scientific predictions for aspects of certain technologies, typically based on statistical models. For example, the journal *Technological Forecasting & Social Change* (published by Elsevier), presents several robust studies of this sort. These studies, however, are commonly focused on overly-specific aspects of technologies. They cannot illustrate comprehensive, speculative scenarios that allow for a broad understanding

of the impact of AVs and other transportation technologies on urban form and quality.

Looking into the Future: The Tools Available

At the time of this research, the only known attempt to build future scenarios of AV impact on urban environments using established methodologies is the work by Anthony Townsend.[10] Townsend uses the "alternative futures method," which posits that any story about the future can be grouped into one of four archetypes: Growth, Collapse, Constraint, and Transformation. He then presents his considerations for each scenario in regard to AVs, following each archetype's defining characteristics, and develops the story of each scenario around these.

While Townsend's paper is fascinating to read, we do not believe that this method is sufficiently robust to serve as a decision-making support for planners, politicians and the public. The method is static, not allowing for the weighting of different decisions on the outcome. It is also overly deterministic and focuses on a limited number of aspects. Instead of the "alternative futures method," we chose to base our proposal on what Townsend refers to as the "Shell approach," a traditional method widely adopted in large companies as a support for decision-making; the approach will be returned to later in this chapter.[11]

In *Learning from the Future*, Liam Fahey and Robert stress that the "Shell" method should not be considered as a hard prediction of the future, nor be used as an end in itself.[12] Rather, its objective is to explore possible developments, acknowledge uncertainties and understand the ways in which they might evolve. This information can then be used by people to manage the future strategically, which is why we adopt the term "scenario learning." The scenario learning methodology is fundamentally based on the identification of as many key factors and driving forces as possible that can have an influence on the development of future scenarios. Key factors that are thought to be high impact or of high uncertainty are then chosen to define which scenarios are to be explored, while the remaining factors are considered to be less critically influential.

The methodology proposed here has its foundations in this scenario learning approach. However, we specify a particular form of analyzing and selecting key factors which is most relevant to the context of transportation technologies and urban impact. We also develop a unique method for analyzing and developing each scenario based on architectural and urban design theories. The whole process is described in detail in the following section, preceded by an overview of our overall approach to the future scenario development problem.

Approach overview

Despite his claims of the existence of unforeseeable consequences for technologies, McLuhan suggests that when we look back in history for new technologies and their developments, it is possible to identify the seeds of these developments at the technology's very beginnings.[13] Critical theorists like McLuhan, Postman[14] and others share a determinism that is, above all, complex.[15] It accepts multiple variations and it happens in fields of constant negotiations. What exists is an ecology, a systemic environment where several conditionings are already at play. Each and every entity in such a system in connected to everything else, and every change propagates further. Because the system is overly complex, the number of variables are unmanageable, and unforeseen effects are bound to happen. Based on this understanding, the intention of the methodology proposed here is not to generate a precise portrait of a future that is still under construction. Instead, the objective is to provide support for informed intervention in such a system.

Each step of the methodology is described in the sub-sections below. After each description, we provide

CATEGORY	DRIVING FORCE	U	I
Demographic Patterns	Population growth	1	2
	Ageing population	1	1
	Continued immigration	1	1
	Decline in the share of active workforce	1	2
	Increase in one-person households & other configurations	1	2
Social &Lifestyle Factors	Automation-induced unemployment	2	2
	Automobile's image and desirability	3	3
	Conveniences of personal car ownership	1	3
	Attachment to driving	2	3
	Increase of flexible lifestyles	1	3
	Increase in work hours	2	2
	Increase in productivity	2	2
	Emergence of AV hacking and customization	3	2
	Attitudes towards new technology	2	2
	Emerging consumer demands	3	3
Natural Resources	Availability and accessibility of conventional vehicle fuels	1	2
	Availability and accessibility of alternative vehicle fuels	1	2
	Makeup of electricity production	1	1
	Availability of land	1	3
	Availability and accessibility of raw materials for AVs	1	3
Physical Environment & Urban Planning	Land use	2	3
	Urban movement patterns	2	3
	Type, size, age of urban fabric	1	3
	Scale of AV infrastructure implementation	1	3
	Existing transportation options and trends	2	3
	Connectivity between transportation modes	2	3
	Urban planning trends	3	3
	Relative importance of planning	2	3
	Consideration of AVs in planning	3	3
Political & Regulatory Forces	Pressure for climate change action	1	1
	Pressure to reduce accidents	2	2
	Political trend towards privatization and deregulation	3	2
	Government subsidizing power	2	2
	Resolutions on sustainability and energy efficiency	2	1

Table 3.1. Driving forces: uncertainty/impact scores.

CATEGORY	DRIVING FORCE	U	I
Political &Regulatory Forces (cont.)	Governmental agenda and development plans	2	2
	Subsidies for public/shared transportation	3	3
	Lobbying and Protectionism	2	3
	Regulations on AV use, driving standards and maintenance	3	2
	Regulations on personal and public safety	3	1
Technological Forces	Powering options for AVs	3	1
	Development of AI and possible limits of AV capability	3	2
	Digital user connectivity to transportation platforms	2	3
	Development of technologies for use inside AVs	3	1
	Development of other new transportation technologies	3	3
	Ubiquity of EV charging infrastructure	1	2
	Fast development of EV/AV battery technology	1	2
	Organization of AV software and hardware upgrades	3	1
	Development of vehicle only intelligence	2	3
	Development of infrastructure only intelligence	2	3
	Development of AV technological standards	1	3
	Integration of AVs into "Internet of Things"	2	3
	Speed and trajectory of AV uptake	3	3
Market Forces	Stability of macro economy	2	2
	Configuration of stakeholder interests	1	3
	Cost of energy	2	2
	Cost of key raw materials	2	2
	Cost of key technologies	2	2
	Cost of skilled labour	2	2
	Cost of AV maintenance	2	2
	Local cost of land	2	3
	Monetization strategies for AVs	3	2
	Car manufacturers' interest in maximizing sales	1	3
	Service providers' interest in offering continued services	1	3
	Real estate market trends	2	3
	AV financing schemes	2	2
	Insurance risks	1	2
	Cost of AV purchase	2	2
	Effectiveness of publicity strategies	2	1

Looking into the Future   43

a summary of the outcome for each step. These outcomes should be treated as examples of the product expected for each step, rather than definitive findings. Given the limitation of space, this chapter focuses on presenting the methodology in itself rather than expanding on and grounding the scenario results. This study was mainly concerned with AV impact in North American cities in the next 40 years.

Steps in Process

The steps described here explain the Shell methodology as well as what modifications were made to the process for this particular application. More details on the original methodology can be found in Fahey and Randall's *Learning from the Future: Competitive Foresight Scenarios.*[16]

Step 1: Identifying key factors and driving forces in the system

Based on the methods described for scenario learning,[17] the largest possible number of relevant factors and driving forces must be amassed through collective brainstorming sessions. For a comprehensive exploration, the Shell methodology suggests using the SEPT formula,[18] which considers five general categories: social, technological, economic, environmental and political forces. These five categories can then be broken down further into more relevant and specific categories. In this investigation, we found nearly 70 key

factors that we judged pertinent to the problem of AVs and urban form, across several categories. These factors are presented in Table 3.1.

Step 2: Classifying the key factors

The next step was to distinguish pre-determined elements from uncertainties. The point of this step is to indicate which factors have high uncertainty and high impact. Those with high impact and high uncertainty help bracket the possible outcomes. This is done as follows:

All the key factors and driving forces are studied individually and each is assigned a number from 1 to 3. 1 indicates low uncertainty, 2 indicates average uncertainty, and 3 indicates high uncertainty. If any factors are considered inevitable, these factors should be reflected implicitly or explicitly in each and all of the scenarios to be developed. In this investigation, for instance, we assigned low uncertainty to the fact that the average age of the North American population will increase in the next decades. High uncertainty was assigned to the fact that coming generations will be less attached to the ideal of owning a personal vehicle.

Next, every key factor was then classified with their impact, again with a number ranging from 1 to 3. 1 is assigned for aspects of low impact, 2 for aspects of some impact and 3 for aspects of high impact.

44   Chapter 3 Into the Future: Analytic Scenarios

These classifications are also part of the original scenario learning methodology.[19]

Table 3.1 presents a summary (descriptions and details omitted) of all key factors found, with the uncertainty (U) and impact (I) numbers assigned to each. These factors resulted from focus groups and an extensive literature review on AVs.

Step 3: Connecting the system

The next critical step is identifying which factors directly influence the outcomes of other factors. The purpose of this is to identify which factors are interdependent or interrelated. In order to facilitate this process, we connected all factors in a network of influences. This step is not a standard technique in the scenario learning methodology we have adopted as a foundation, but since the topic under discussion is highly complex and there are many interrelated factors, it became necessary. Similar approaches have been discussed in this field of study.[20]

Figure 3.1 presents the final network diagram. All of the key factors listed in Table 3.1 are present in the network, shown inside circles, and interconnected to the factors which they influence and by which they are influenced. They have been grouped into general categories which are indicated by the colours of the circles. The direction of the arrow connecting

the factors indicates the direction of influence. For clarity, the arrow has the same colour as the factor from which it issues. The thickness of the circle's border indicates the factor's level of impact, while the darkness of the grey shade of the fill colour indicates the degree of uncertainty.

Step 4: Defining the structure of the scenarios

Given the complex network presented in the previous step, it would be unfeasible to carefully consider every possibility generated by every single variation within the system. Consequently, the possible scenarios that could be constructed as a result of all factors' interactions are too numerous to be useful. This is why it is critical to identify the events that can be most impactful in the final outcomes, as well as to identify the factors whose certainty presents the greatest challenge.

Ideally, the Shell methodology proposes focussing only on two key factors for structuring the scenarios' main variances, namely those which are identified as being *very uncertain* and *very impactful* (i.e. the critical uncertainties). Because of their uncertainty, at least two opposite behaviours can be defined for each key factor. Finally, the combination of these variations would result in four scenarios, a reasonable number for in-depth exploration. All the remaining factors should then be considered

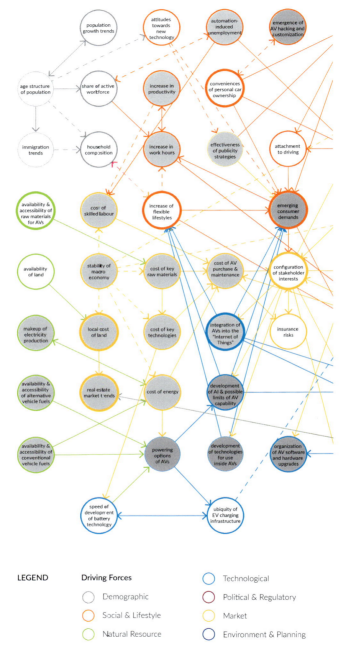

Figure 3.1. Network of influence factors.

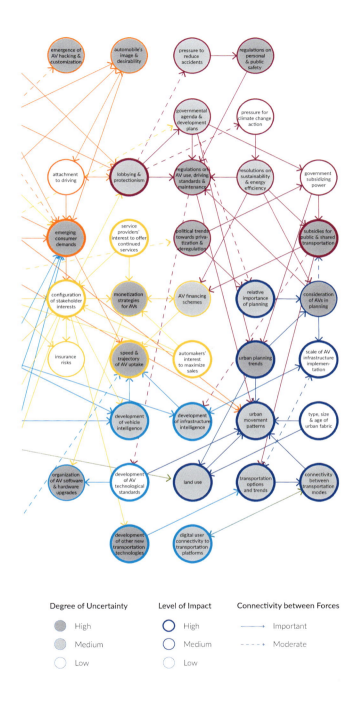

Looking into the Future   47

in relation to the structuring variances in each scenario. However, in the case of this study, there were too many factors of high uncertainty and high impact to be able to identify clearly the critical uncertainties. Further analysis of the factors was therefore undertaken and it was observed that there were common social drivers that underlaic them. When grouped according to these underlying common social drivers, a variation on the methodology was proposed which took these underlying drivers and made clusters of the factors influenced by them. It was the clusters of factors which were inter-related and had high uncertainty and high impact, rather than individual factors, which were then chosen to be the 'key factors' from the original Shell methodologies.

These *clusters* are recognizable by two aspects: firstly, by the number of connections between core factors; and secondly and most importantly, by the coherent behaviour within the group. By coherent behaviour, we refer to the tendency of a cluster of factors to vary together in a coherent direction, given they are very closely related. Two main clusters were selected as the structuring elements for the scenarios. Each structuring cluster was articulated as two plausible outcomes—these are the extreme outcomes of each cluster. The orthogonal combination of structuring clusters and their outcomes created four scenarios, as described in the

next paragraphs.

In the network created from these clusters, we observed that the factor named "emerging consumer demands" occupies a clearly central role. Its cluster, which we titled "Lifestyle and market forces" is simplified in Figure 3.2. The two opposite outcomes of the cluster were organized under the titles "conservative" and "progressive." As examples, some characterizing aspects of the "conservative" outcome are:

- Consumers want to keep the option of manual driving
- Consumers are heavily supportive of current ownership models
- Automaker companies control the market for automobiles
- Extended warranty bundles do not compete with insurance companies

Comparatively, some examples of a progressive outcome could include aspects such as:

- Consumers support a long-term ban on manual driving
- Consumers are open to different ownership models, such as car sharing
- A diverse landscape of software and hardware companies emerge and become main players in the automobile industry
- Insurance companies need to drastically adapt their business models to survive in the long term

The second most relevant cluster identified was named "Regulatory and urban environmental forces." This cluster comprises factors that planners and decision makers can directly act on, and that are of great interest to the developers of this study. The core factors of the second cluster are "urban planning trends," "considerations of AVs in planning" and "subsidies for transportation"; its diagram is simplified in Figure 3.3.

The two opposite outcomes of the cluster were organized under the titles "transit-oriented investment" and "AV investment." Some characteristic aspects of the first outcome are:

- Neglect of AVs in main planning strategies
- Direct support for compact urban growth
- Limited infrastructure intelligence
- Advance in public transportation and its intermodal technologies and structures

By comparison, an "AV investment" outcome could include aspects such as:

- Faster implementation of favourable legislation on AV traffic
- Indirect support for sprawling growth
- Infrastructure intelligence as a main public enterprise
- Incentivized AV technology development

Step 5: Defining the structure of scenarios

In the Shell methodology, the decision-making matrix is formulated next. To define the decision-making matrix, each of the factor groups becomes an axis. Each axis has two boxes—an extreme for one outcome and an extreme for the other. The orthogonal combination of the outcomes discussed thus far forms the basic structure of the scenarios to be developed. Figure 3.4 provides a brief description of the four scenarios and their fundamental contexts. The two factors which become the axes—'Regulatory and Urban Environmental Forces' and 'Lifestyle and Market Forces'—create four scenarios which can then be used to play out various futures for planning and governmental agencies. In the case of the 'Regulatory and Urban Environmental Forces,' the choices are between support for public transit or support for AVs. Support is defined as government policy at any level which provides financing, incentives, or disincentives to push adoption in either one of these directions. Because the AV operates within a highly regulated framework of publicly controlled roads and safety legislation, government policies and funding can have a large influence on outcomes.

On the other axis is 'Lifestyle and Market Forces' which is either a progressive and quick acceptance and uptake of technology by the

Looking into the Future   49

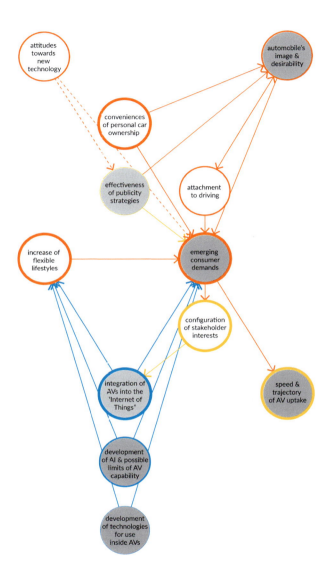

Figure 3.2. Lifestyle and market forces.

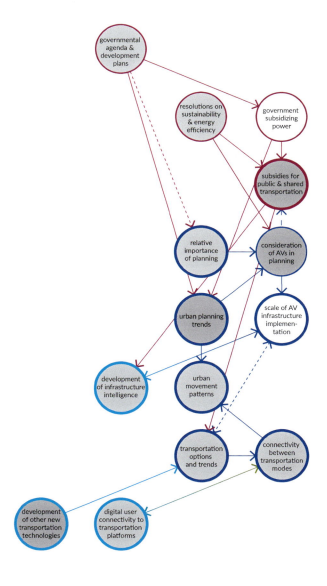

Figure 3.3. Regulatory and urban environmental forces.

Looking into the Future 51

Cluster B
Regulatory and Urban Environmental Forces

	Intervention for Public Transportation	Intervention for Autonomous Vehicles
Conservative Scenario	*AV uptake progresses very slowly and governments continue to focus on public transit to reduce congestion, pollution and accidents. Variety and connectivity of public transit is cushioned by users' conservative needs and expectations; this includes AV integration in public transit systems, which takes a relaively long time to be considered.*	*Level 4 AV uptake happens at relatively accelerated pace. A few models of familiar forms, functions and roles from main automakers become best-sellers. Commute-related habits are similar to today's. Car sharing services take the market share of taxis, with small relative growth.*
Progressive Scenario	*AV sharing services becomes highly attractive with the support of a robust public transit system and less people owning cars. In the long term, there's inclusion of AV fleets (buses and personal cars) in an intermodal transit system. Individual AVs, noteworthy, are only one of several transport modes.*	*Level 4 AV uptake happens at most accelerated pace, reaching full ban of manual driving in the long term. Different companies and vehicle models appear in the market, offering a diversity of services, features and even roles for personally owned AVs. A variety of ownership models exist. Vehicles that function as office space or sleeping space, among others, are common, and commute habits change.*

Cluster A
Lifestyle and Market Forces

Figure 3.4. Four scenarios and their fundamental contexts.

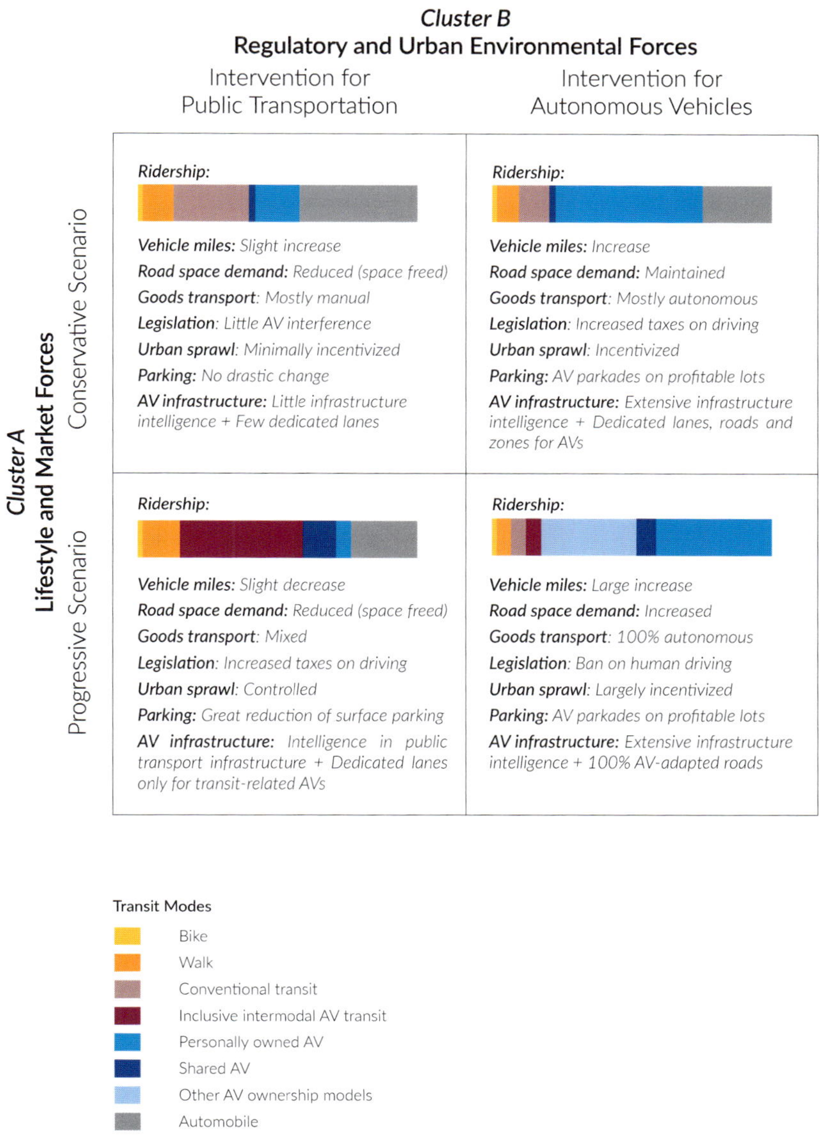

Cluster B
Regulatory and Urban Environmental Forces

Intervention for
Public Transportation

Intervention for
Autonomous Vehicles

Ridership:

Vehicle miles: *Slight increase*
Road space demand: *Reduced (space freed)*
Goods transport: *Mostly manual*
Legislation: *Little AV interference*
Urban sprawl: *Minimally incentivized*
Parking: *No drastic change*
AV infrastructure: *Little infrastructure intelligence + Few dedicated lanes*

Ridership:

Vehicle miles: *Increase*
Road space demand: *Maintained*
Goods transport: *Mostly autonomous*
Legislation: *Increased taxes on driving*
Urban sprawl: *Incentivized*
Parking: *AV parkades on profitable lots*
AV infrastructure: *Extensive infrastructure intelligence + Dedicated lanes, roads and zones for AVs*

Ridership:

Vehicle miles: *Slight decrease*
Road space demand: *Reduced (space freed)*
Goods transport: *Mixed*
Legislation: *Increased taxes on driving*
Urban sprawl: *Controlled*
Parking: *Great reduction of surface parking*
AV infrastructure: *Intelligence in public transport infrastructure + Dedicated lanes only for transit-related AVs*

Ridership:

Vehicle miles: *Large increase*
Road space demand: *Increased*
Goods transport: *100% autonomous*
Legislation: *Ban on human driving*
Urban sprawl: *Largely incentivized*
Parking: *AV parkades on profitable lots*
AV infrastructure: *Extensive infrastructure intelligence + 100% AV-adapted roads*

Cluster A
Lifestyle and Market Forces

Conservative Scenario

Progressive Scenario

Transit Modes

- Bike
- Walk
- Conventional transit
- Inclusive intermodal AV transit
- Personally owned AV
- Shared AV
- Other AV ownership models
- Automobile

Figure 3.5. Theoretical example of use of scenarios in transportation planning.

Looking into the Future   53

public (labelled 'progressive') or a slow and resistant adaptation to the technology by the public (labelled 'conservative'). This may vary highly even from district to district. This is the second highly influential and highly unpredictable group of factors.

Implementation: Running Scenarios

Figure 3.5 shows a theoretical example of what may be the outcome from running the four scenarios for a particular region. In this case we are demonstrating how an interested agency could predict the effects of AVs on transportation mode-share given the four scenarios. This type of analysis could be done for many of the aspects that agencies are concerned with; it has the added advantage of nicely framing outcomes that may be encountered in terms of different policy decisions that governments may be dealing with in the current political environment.

It is worth noting at this point that one of these key factors is the policies made by governmental agencies themselves. This is a critical observation, since in our experience, there is often a 'wait and see' attitude about new technologies; however, this analysis notes that the decisions made by regulatory agencies—incentives and rules—have a huge impact on the future outcome. What this means is that if the government takes a 'do nothing' approach, outcomes are more likely to be determined by the lobbying of large multinational organizations who intervene in their own interests resulting in the the pro-AV regions in the right-hand side of the matrix.

Typological Case Studies: AV User Group Narratives

As a tool to transport the reader to the futures that have now been framed by the future-visioning methodology, a series of future speculations for the autonomous vehicle (AV) future are described. The following ensemble of narratives attempts to illustrate the new ways in which sections of the region's demographic will use and live with the AV, aiming to depict the various changes in social habits and infrastructure attributed to a progressive-minded AV-oriented city. By this time the driver's licence has become a relic. Fully driver-less autonomous vehicles have redefined the way many sections of the typical North American city's population transport themselves and go about their daily activities and businesses.

Each group has two scenarios put forward—one which shows a progressive AV-centred policy environment and one showing a progressive public transit policy environment as per the scenarios from the methodology described earlier in this chapter. The user groups discussed are:

1.   The Suburban Family (suburb)
2.   The Urbanite (downtown)
3.   The Elderly (urbanized suburb)
4.   The Student (urban)
5.   The Commercial Trader (local urban centre/suburb)

SUBURBAN FAMILY

Scenario 1 (Pro AV)

Alan and Alex Astor are hard-working partners in a small-size tech start-up. Their investment in the company demands a great deal of time at the downtown office—a commute they make daily. The couple use an AV-share programme for which they pay a monthly fee. It's a medium-price service that many of their peers subscribe to with relatively short wait times and an image which is sporty but family-oriented. Alan and Alex use their smartphones to book a car in the mornings and again in the evenings to come back home.

The car service that Alan and Alex subscribe to is separate from the public transportation system. The on-demand AV service is more expensive than public transportation, but the public transit system has been eroded by private companies running transit services more efficiently. The service allows the two to determine their own commute time and have privacy during the journey, something Alan prefers so he can make private phone calls and start his work day en route to the office. When asked to describe the quality of the ride in the AVs, Alex relates the experience to that of the rapid transit trains in Japan—the AVs ability to maintain a consistent speed makes the trip quick and efficient. Because of automation, highway interchanges have been reduced to adaptations of the traffic circle, which allow AVs to enter the interchange at higher speeds while reducing the scale of infrastructure. During the day, Alan uses the company's on-demand car share service to drive him to meetings across town and back.

The family also currently own their own AV and depend on it for shuttling the children, running household errands and ease of access for weekend excursions out of the city. During the week, Alan and Alex depart in the car share service early to beat the morning rush, leaving Asher, 12, and Alice, 14, to take the personal AV to school. They have set their car to send an automated message when the car leaves the house and also once the children arrive at the school. Throughout the day, Alan and Alex can order household goods and groceries online and remotely direct the family AV to a "drive-through grocery market" where the order is loaded into the AV.

After classes at school end, the AV meets Asher and Alice at the school drop-off area. Alice has soccer practice nearby and is dropped off there, picking up her soccer bag from the AV, after which Asher is taken to piano lessons. During the children's activities, the AV waits at the nearest parking and charging station. The family reunites in the early evening at home and the AV retreats back into its compact garage for overnight charging.

Name: Alan (37) and Alex (42) Astor;
two children, Alice (14) and Asher (12)
Home location: Urbanizing suburb outside the
metropolitan core

Living configuration: Nuclear family
Occupations (adults): Business administrator;
creative development in a tech start-up
Interests: Outdoor and hiking enthusiasts

Scenario 2 (Pro Public Transit)

Alan and Alex Astor are hard-working partners in a small-size tech start-up. Their investment in the company demands a great deal of time at the downtown office—a commute they make daily. In 2040, the public transit system has expanded into an extensive network of automated regional trains, arterial streetcars, electric buses and community shuttles throughout the region, all of which are on-demand AVs controlled by the regional public transit service. In the suburban city where the Astor family resides, a community-dedicated transit system links into the regional commuting trains. The Astor family takes full advantage of this network by almost exclusively using transit, only subscribing to the more expensive car-share services occasionally. Both children are registered as minors in the transit system and have automated notifications sent out to their parents of their trip status and safe arrival each time they use transit.

Alan and Alex commute into work by meeting an on-demand last-mile shuttle a short distance from their home. Alex calls a shuttle with her smart phone for herself and Alan—timed to leave after the dedicated school shuttle—and the trip is automatically booked through to the shuttle stop near their office. Since the system adjusts in real time for passengers, they can always be assured of seats on both shuttles and the train involved in the trip. She then checks in Asher and Alice to the community school bus and the whole family walks to the end of their residential street.

By day's end, Alan had made one trip to a meeting across town, again using public transit. He knows one of the fixed-route shuttles runs every 2 minutes on this particular route downtown and he hails the next one at his stop. The AV shuttle maintains a quick speed, only speeding up and slowing down in relation to surrounding cars. Intersection lights are reduced to only those at pedestrian crosswalks—AVs navigate their surroundings with a system controlled via information beacons which guide and organize cross-traffic flow. This system is used and accessible by all.

The last school bell rings and Asher makes her way to the waiting AV pre-ordered by her mother with a car-share service. The service drives Asher to her piano lesson and then home again afterwards. In a few years she will take the community shuttle as well, but since she is younger her parents prefer her to use the AV service for her lessons. Alice walks to a nearby field for soccer practice. After practice she heads to the community shuttle stop nearest to the field and uses her phone to hail a shuttle home. Meanwhile, a notification goes out to Alex that the request has been made, and in a short while Alice arrives home.

Daily Commute

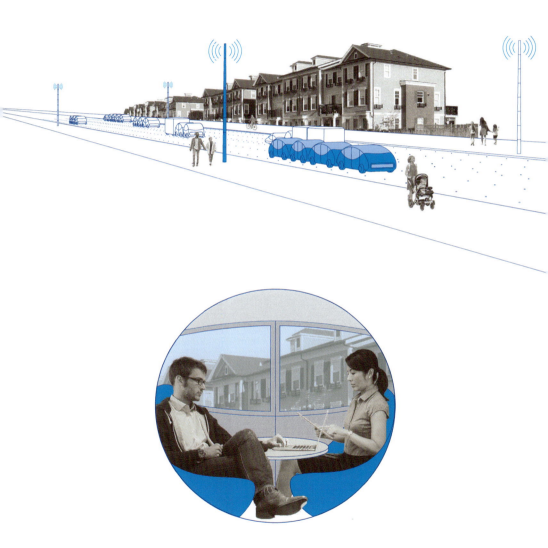

Daily commute to work with AV-share vehicle.

Daily commute to work with on-demand last-mile AV shuttles.

Typological Case Studies: Suburban Family

Kids in Transit

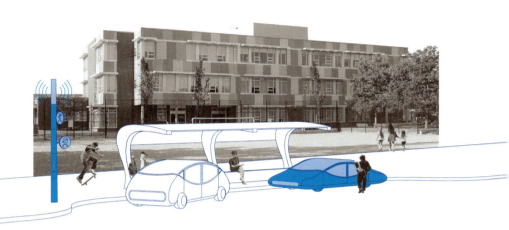

The children getting around using the family AV.

60   Chapter 3 Into the Future: Analytic Scenarios

The children getting around using a transit AV.

Typological Case Studies: Suburban Family   61

URBANITE

Scenario 1 (Pro AV)

Basia works, a lot. Her fast-pace job involves maintaining and sustaining relationships with a number of physicians and practices, keeping them informed about new drugs and treatment plans her company is researching and releasing. Her assigned district includes the downtown area and nearby neighbourhoods, which is convenient as she just moved into a new condo near downtown. Basia's company provides AVs to their sales representatives instead of an office space. Fully equipped with a desk, phone, computer, and all the promotional material she needs for meetings, the vehicle drives her to and from appointments throughout the day.

Following her early morning jog in a large park nearby, Basia gets ready for work and summons her AV out of the underground charging garage. Basia steps in and syncs the day's schedule from her phone to the car. First stop, company headquarters, where she attends the monthly face-to-face meeting with other sales representatives within the metropolitan area. After dropping off Basia at street level, her AV rolls into the underground parkade. Equipped with compact, stacked parking spaces and induction chargers, the garage is crowded with AVs, the ceilings high enough only to allow the vehicles to travel through the underground matrix.

At noon, Basia walks nearby to grab lunch and some snacks for a long afternoon of appointments across town, and summons her AV to pick her up at the marketplace where she is shopping. For the rest of the day, her vehicle drives her to various medical clinics as per her calendar. At each location, her AV enquires for available

parking within the building, or locates the nearest parking spots. Basia continues working in her AV while driving from place to place, and during a longer gap between appointments she parks at a "Mobile Office Dock," a co-working hub with basic amenities, designed for people working from their AVs.

By day's end, Basia instructs her AV to return to her apartment. As she completes her paperwork at the end of her workday, the AV parks and connects to the charger in its parking space. Basia's evening is free from her company vehicle, as she prefers instead to walk to a nearby restaurant for dinner with a friend. Once a week the car drives off at 1am for its automated software update, weekly cleaning and maintenance service.

Name: Basia Baker (28)
Home location: Downtown area
Living configuration: Single adult

Occupation: Pharmaceutical representative
Interests: Avid amateur food and fashion blogger

Scenario 2 (Pro Public Transit)

Beetling her way around the city, Basia knows the city's transit system like the back of her hand. Her position as a travelling pharmaceutical representative for the downtown core requires familiarity with the whereabouts of dozens of medical clinics. A city girl at heart, Basia relies solely on public transit to take her to the places she needs to go.

Basia starts her day early, requesting a transit AV to take her to the park for a run and stretch. She requires nothing other than the shoes on her feet and her watch, which serves as her transit pass, music player, and fitness monitor. As it is early in the morning, she is picked up by a six-person Flexishuttle, a transit shuttle that navigates the streets on a flexible route based on requests from customers. By the time she finishes her run, the streets are busy with people heading to work and summer tourists; many more transit AVs can be seen, some of them moving along in tightly spaced platoons, their numbers based on real-time traffic demand throughout the day.

Following a quick shuttle ride back to her apartment, Basia eats breakfast and gets ready for work. She checks her appointments, and instructs her smartphone to plan her route for the day. The transit navigation app, a staple for all portable devices, offers choices of routes based on convenience and expedience, and also easily takes care of payment. It is, of course, also possible to use transit without a smartphone, by making a request for a shuttle at a digital interface installed at designated transit stops. Basia's transit app is set with different settings for her

home and work account—she has asked it to search for less expensive routes for her personal trips but for work she prioritizes efficiency over cost. Since the refurbishing of the transit network with AVs and the reduction in the number of parking spaces, transit ridership has expanded while car ownership in the metropolitan core has markedly declined, improving the day-to-day experience of pedestrians and cyclists. Thanks to the reduction in the number and width of vehicle lanes, the sidewalks in most streets are wide, have ample greenery, and are busy with people. The only thing that has not changed is the amount of rain in the winter.

Today, the first meeting is at corporate headquarters and the transit software recommends walking to a nearby fixed route shuttle. The fixed route shuttles are less expensive than the Flexishuttles but still come every few minutes. If demand is high on the fixed routes, additional shuttles are deployed and the shuttles come even more often. Sometimes a Flexishuttle takes a longer time to arrive, especially during peak times and the transit app takes this into account live, giving Basia the best options for her preferences. Basia takes the fixed route shuttle, at this time travelling in a platoon of three ten-seat vehicles. After her first appointment at headquarters she grabs lunch at the nearby marketplace and from there takes the subway to her next appointment at a clinic across downtown. Throughout the day, she navigates the city on foot and via transit shuttles to her various appointments.

At the end of the day, Basia buys groceries at a nearby market and takes a last transit ride to meet a friend for dinner at a restaurant near home.

Urban Drop-off

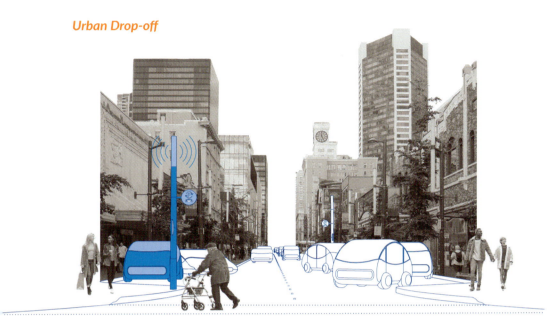

AV pick-up/drop-off station in an urban street.

AV transit stop in an urban street.

Typological Case Studies: Urbanite

Work on the Go

Working on the go in a personal AV.

66   Chapter 3 Into the Future: Analytic Scenarios

Travelling on a Flexi-shuttle.

Typological Case Studies: Urbanite

ELDERLY

Scenario 1 (Pro AV)

Craig does not like to see himself as a man in the later years of his life. Following a stroke a year ago, he moved into a nursing home, where he occupies most of his time reading, maintaining a regular exercise routine and cultivating a small garden. One of the things he particularly likes about this home is that they have a dedicated fleet of AVs which are specially designed for people with physical disabilities. This allows him to easily get around independently and when he wants to. This morning he is going to a doctor's appointment at the hospital and has already booked the AV through reception. When he is ready, he tells reception and the AV comes around to the front door of the nursing home and adjusts its settings to those customized for Craig. The vehicles have custom settings entered by the nursing home staff for each occupant depending on their requirements; for Craig, who can't hear well, the voice communication is louder and since he also has a walker, the car unfolds a ramp for entry and has a place to store the walker. The seat in the vehicle is custom-adjusted to his height, and even the temperature is set to his preference. Craig gets into the vehicle and sets off. The vehicle is tracked by the nursing home so that, in case of difficulties, Craig can always be found.

After being dropped off at the hospital, the AV moves to a dedicated waiting zone set up by the hospital. Parking the car here is free, since the hospital determined that having cars drive offsite was environmentally wasteful and so it no longer charges for this parking space. This has meant a considerable loss of revenue for the hospital but it makes up for some of it by having car-share services pay to store their cars overnight in the parkade.

When he is finished at his hospital appointment, Craig presses the button on his key to call the car. Craig, like many others in the care home, doesn't feel comfortable with operating apps on a smartphone, so he simply takes the key from the car and presses the button when he's ready; this calls the car to the key's location. Craig then returns back to the care home and has lunch.

Once a week, he is provided with a caregiver, Martha, for an afternoon to help with household chores and errands he is unable to do alone. This afternoon Martha is accompanying Craig on a short trip to the gardening centre, again using one of the home's AVs. After checking that one of the community-owned AVs is available, Martha summons the car to the front entrance. Martha instructs the AV to drive at a slower speed for better travel comfort, and the vehicle quietly departs.

The two are dropped off at the dedicated passenger island outside the garden centre and wander into the shop. As they walk around, Martha helps Craig load items into a cart. He buys gloves, soil, rhododendron bushes and a series of bulbs, all of which are loaded into their AV by staff while they pay. Summoning the car to the front, Craig and Martha drive back to the nursing home. Here, Martha helps to carry the new purchases to the back garden. After a bit of gardening help, Martha departs.

Name: Craig Connors (78)
Home location: Urbanized suburb
Living configuration: Single adult senior: widower, three adult children

Occupation: Retired family physician
Interests: Community gardening and reading

Scenario 2 (Pro Public Transit)

Remaining active is one of Craig's priorities. Following a stroke a year ago, he is able to continue low-impact activities such as gardening and walking within the safety of the nursing home where he lives, but requires help with some household errands that require lifting and carrying. Once a week a caregiver comes to help him with these. Having been an urbanite all his life, and being budget conscious, Craig prefers to use public transit for these trips rather than a more expensive AV service. Transit quality and experience has improved greatly with the adoption of AV technology and a sophisticated dispatch network. The transit system has Craig's personal requirements stored in its database so when he calls for transit the dispatch knows his requirements—in his case he has a walker, takes slightly longer to board and get seated than average, and needs instructions in English and a little bit louder than usual for his slight hearing problem.

Today, his caregiver Martha comes by after lunch. They plan to make a trip out to a nearby shopping centre for some gardening supplies and to restock some household groceries. Through her app, Martha makes a request for an upcoming vehicle to make a stop at the nursing home entrance. All AV shuttles are wheelchair accessible so the walker is not a problem, but in cases where the maximum number of walkers, wheelchairs and/or strollers are on a shuttle, the next available one will be dispatched to the nursing home. Again, this is arranged by the automated dispatch system. The system then informs Martha via her app when the shuttle will arrive.

Once the shuttle quietly arrives, the two get on and chat as the AV speeds them off a short distance to the nearby shopping centre. They dismount and cross at an intersection lit with LED patterns on the ground, which indicate the time for safe pedestrian walking. Once in the store, they walk the aisles making note of the items Craig needs. At the counter, the two place an order for delivery service for their purchases, which they request to arrive later in the afternoon. The store will take care of loading and dispatching the goods into a compact delivery vehicle for delivery later. In the meantime, Craig and Martha enjoy a drink in the nearby specialty coffee shop. After they are finished, Martha again calls for a transit shuttle and they navigate to the transit island in front of the mall, where an AV shuttle arrives shortly. They recognize their shuttle by the shuttle number, which matches that which they are given on the app. Later on, back at the nursing home, the delivery gets dropped off at reception, and Craig begins his planting.

Typological Case Studies: Elderly   69

Out to Town

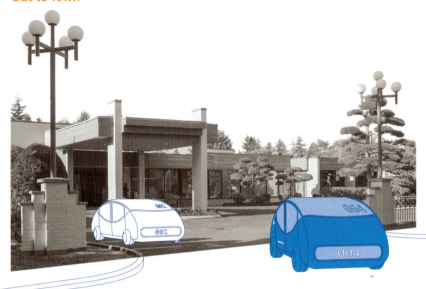

Departing from nursing home via accessible AV.

Departing from nursing home via accessible transit shuttle.

Typological Case Studies: Elderly

Accessible Around

AV drop-off zone at the hospital.

Transit AV stop at the hospital.

Typological Case Studies: Elderly 73

STUDENT

Scenario 1 (Pro AV)

A full-time student and part-time employee at an artisan café, Diana is a relatively recent arrival to the city. Originally from a smaller city, Diana made the move west just over three years ago.

Diana likes to start her weekdays very early, and bike to work or school after a quick breakfast. Thanks to a reduction in the width and number of vehicle lanes, most roads now feature dedicated bike lanes. Even the streets without bike lanes are safe for cyclists, and accidents are extremely rare.

After working the morning rush in the café, school classes fill Diana's time until the early afternoon, after which she usually works on her final exhibition project. She has been incorporating relatively large found objects into her installations, and the transportation of these materials requires some planning. Tomorrow, she is going on a weekend trip to the countryside with a friend to scavenge materials from an abandoned factory. She has a membership in a ride-share programme which allows her to reserve an AV for hours, or even days, at a time. Requesting the AV on her phone only takes minutes and a vacant AV is rerouted from the streets or released from the closest satellite charging and storage station. For her project Diana has requested a passenger AV pod along with a goods transport AV, which allow her to transport larger items back to the studio.

Working on her project until the early evening, Diana jumps on her bike again to meet with friends downtown for dinner and an art opening. With natural light
fading, the street pavement starts to light up. This "Smart Tarmac" is a system of inductive coils and embedded sensors that illuminates with the desired path of travelling vehicles. While riding on designated bike lanes, Diana's bike presence causes lights to illuminate on the road which help highlight her location. Additionally, her presence on the road transmits a signal to intersection and road beacons, which helps keep intersections working as efficiently as possible. At intersections, she has a choice to indicate her desired turn or direction on a "Compass Pole" (see drawing Chapter 7), or to stand in a specific zone so the sensors in the infrastructure identify which direction she wants to cross. After her evening out, Diana rides her bike home. She double-checks her AV reservation for the weekend and goes to bed early, excited for the trip the next morning.*

The next morning Diana's AV arrives. She hops in and selects her friend's house on her app, directing the AV to swing round there first to pick up two of her friends who will help her lift and carry. She then enters the location of the salvage on her app, an old abandoned fish cannery from which she has been granted permission to salvage. She also informs the transport vehicle to leave and to meet her at the site. After a few hours of exploring, photographing and salvaging, the group load the salvaged wood and old machinery into the transport vehicle and then get into the passenger AV. The car pulls out and the transport vehicle drops into a platoon formation behind it. After unloading it at her studio at school, Diana releases the transport AV and drives her friends home before returning home herself and releasing her rented AV.

Name: Diana Dalke (22)
Home location: Urban
Living configuration: Single adult

Occupation: Sculpture and fine arts student and part-time barista
Interests: Active in the arts and culture scene

Scenario 2 (Pro Public Transit)

It is an early start for Diana. Her apartment is a spacious bachelor suite that once was a double-car garage. Her landlord realized the opportunity for additional profit by renovating and renting out the space for living. Diana and the other tenants in the house rental do not own their own vehicles; they all rely on the transit system, with some bike riding, and very occasionally the more expensive AV car-sharing programmes when transit is not available. After a quick breakfast, she requests a neighbourhood last-mile transit shuttle on her phone. She notes the arrival time of 6 minutes, finishes packing her bag and walks to the front of the house to be picked up.

Changing to a fixed-route shuttle at a major intersection, she rides to the historic neighbourhood where she works at a café in the mornings. After her shift, she attends art classes at her university nearby, and spends the early afternoon working on her graduation project, for which she is investigating abandoned industrial buildings and collecting found objects from them for her studio work. Diana can manage her everyday errands and grocery shopping using the city's transit network, but for her weekend salvaging trips to remote abandoned industrial areas she has subscribed to one of the many AV car-share programmes. These, along with the new AV shuttle transit network, have significantly reduced individual vehicle ownership in the city. To save on costs, Diana often makes an initial reconnaissance trip using a one-person AV pod, and returns the next weekend with a larger transport AV and a friend to help.

Tonight, after an afternoon of work on a sculpture at her studio, Diana hops on a transit shuttle to meet with a friend downtown for dinner and an art gallery opening. Depending on the time of day and the volume of passengers, additional shuttles are quickly added to the circulating fleet, and, save for the late nights, buses are neither overcrowded nor empty. Thanks to automation, night bus service in the city has been greatly extended, allowing Diana to return home quickly after her evening out. At home, she double-checks her reservation for an AV the next day, and catches a few hours of sleep before the early start.

Wanting to minimize her usage of the AV rentals, Diana has decided to travel out to the abandoned fish cannery first and call the transport AV later in the day once they are ready to load up. She has also had her friends come to her place by transit. Once they arrive, she indicates they are ready to go; the AV arrives shortly at the curb and they head to the site. Since the cannery is an hour away from the city, the AV stays on site while they forage.

After a few hours of exploring, photographing and salvaging, they call the transport AV. The vehicle will take 45 minutes to arrive so they organize the load and take a break. Once the transport AV arrives they load it with the salvaged wood and old machinery and then hop into their AV. The car pulls out and the transport vehicle drops into a platoon formation behind it. On arriving back at school, Diana releases the regular AV and she and her friends unload the transport AV. She then releases that AV, and takes her friends out for burgers and beers to thank them.

Typological Case Studies: Student 75

Infrastructure Interactions

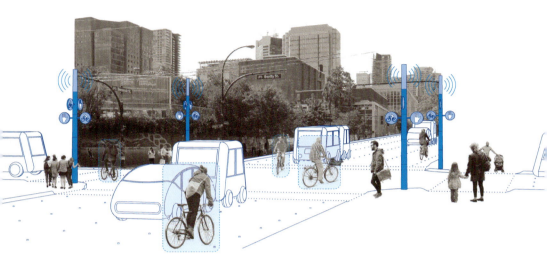

Cyclist-vehicle interaction in a four-way automated intersection.

76   Chapter 3 Into the Future: Analytic Scenarios

Pedestrian-vechicle interaction in a four-way automated intersection.

Typological Case Studies: Student 77

Scavenging Excursion

Using a passenger + cargo rental service.

Using a specially priced X-zone transit shuttle.

COMMERCIAL TRADER

Scenario 1 (Pro AV)

Evan's work at the micro-brewery involves an in-depth knowledge of local bars, restaurants and liquor stores in his locale, a gentrified area of the metropolis. His company, E-Brews, creates and delivers a variety of craft beers that focus on local sustainable production and distribution in and around his city, and occasionally, downtown Vancouver. Evan's specific role is to manage all the relationships with, and deliveries to, these businesses. Working from a shared industrial warehouse in the local town centre, Evan relies on the company's electric AVs to make deliveries and drop-offs. Living in a suburban home, Evan rides his personal AV to work, which is then stored at the company's compact stacked parking storage during the day.

At E-Brews, deliveries start early in the morning before busy traffic times and before the operating times of the stores and bars they stock. Evan requires vendors to place orders two days in advance; this is to ensure the production facility has enough time to produce and bottle the request. Working in small batches, the beer produced is always fresh and intended to be consumed within a few weeks. This morning, Evan dispatches four compact AVs filled with products to a dozen different locations. The majority of the AVs at E-Brews are unassuming pods, bearing only the company logo, with the whole interior space open for the loading and transportation of goods. A few larger ones are fitted with a pair of seats, in case Evan or other employees need to take a ride.

Each AV is loaded with the quantity and types of beer the buyers have ordered. Evan inputs the delivery location on each pod and watches the vehicles shuttle out of the production house. He can then monitor and track the deliveries from his office computer, making sure each arrives without a hitch. The AVs follow each other in a platoon until the internal GPS directs them to their respective locations. On arrival, the buyer retrieves their order using their personal passcode to unlock the pod's storage compartment. Once deliveries are made, buyers load empty kegs and bottles back into the AV to be returned to the E-Brew headquarters. By lunchtime, the fleet returns back to the warehouse to charge. Smaller deliveries are also made throughout the day using the AVs as required.

Name: Evan Eggles (34)
Home location: Local urban centre of an urbanized suburb
Living configuration: Single adult

Occupation: Distribution & Marketing Manager
Company description: Micro-brewery bar and distribution centee
Interests: Craft beer, live music

Scenario 2 (Pro Public Transit)

Evan works at a micro-brewery established three years ago in a suburban centre. A relatively young business, E-Brews has become well-known amongst local bars, restaurants and liquor stores in the area for its quality craft beer products and sustainable work ethic. Evan manages marketing and distribution, overseeing day-to-day deliveries to various businesses. Living in a suburban home, Evan takes transit to work. He rides an on-demand AV transit shuttle to the regional train system which he takes for a few stops to his workplace. He does not commute into the metropolitan core, just to the centre of the suburban city near which he lives.

Deliveries at E-Brews begin before the morning rush hour. Vendors have to place orders two days in advance, to ensure that there is enough fresh product available and bottled. Himself a beer connoisseur, Evan prides himself on the high quality of their brew. Today, Evan dispatches the AVs filled with bottle crates to a dozen different locations using seven delivery vehicles—five small and two large. Working from a shared industrial warehouse in the town centre, the company relies on a new AV transport share model to make its deliveries and drop-offs. Evan orders his required vehicles from this service and specifies the drop-off locations. The logo on the trucks is customized to whoever rents them by changing a digital sign on the sides of the box: this happens automatically when the vehicles are hired by E-Brews.

After Evan loads the delivery on to each vehicle, they shuttle off in a platoon, until their internal GPS directs them to their respective destinations. Evan tracks the deliveries on his smartphone from his office while processing the orders for the next two days. Several of the larger vehicles have smaller delivery pods within them which all dispatch from the larger vehicle to local bars in popular entertainment districts. This is convenient for the customers as the product waits outside the restaurant until someone is ready to retrieve it. Once the pods arrive, the crates are retrieved at each destination using a personal passcode to unlock the pod's storage compartment. The customer loads the empties back into the pod and the vehicles return to the warehouse. By lunchtime, the empty bottles returned in the shuttles have been unloaded, and the vehicles are released.

Shipment Trail

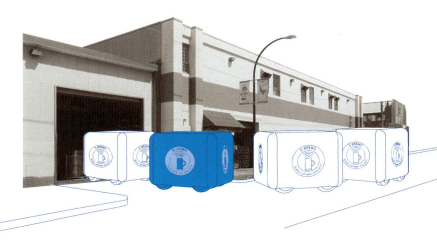

Tracking company delivery vehicles.

Delivery at a restaurant.

Typological Case Studies: Commercial Trader   83

Delivery Done

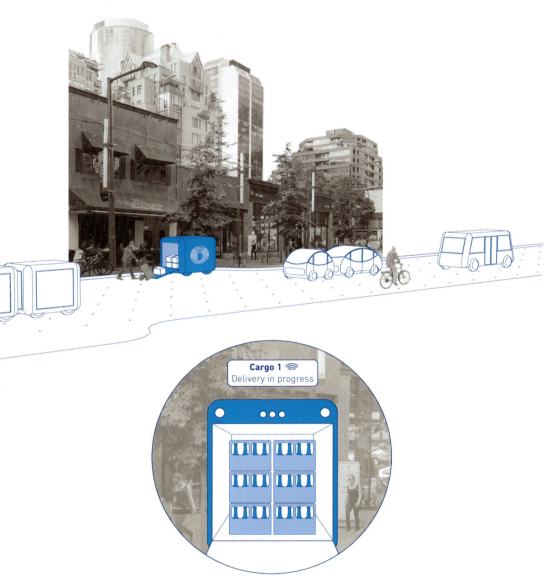

Using a third-party delivery rental service.

Door-to-door shipping with small delivery vehicles.

Typological Case Studies: Commercial Trader

Notes

1 Excerpts and diagrams have been published previously in the chapter "Understanding the Effects of Autonomous Vehicles on Urban Form," Sara Costa Maia and AnnaLisa Meyboom, in *Road Vehicle Automation 4* (Springer, 2018).

2 Peter O. Muller, "Transportation and Urban Form-Stages in the Spatial Evolution of the American Metropolis," in *The Geography of Urban Transportation*, eds. Susan Hanson, Genevieve Giuliano (New York: Guilford Press, 2004).

3 While we were researching future-visioning methodologies, we realized that our methodology may be of benefit to policy makers, engineers and others. We presented it at the Autonomous Vehicles conference in 2016 and also as a chapter in *Road Vehicle Automation 4*. This chapter is a summary of that information.

4 Bibliothèque nationale de France, "BnF—Utopie—Feuilleter," *Utopia: Visions of the Year 2000 from the Year 1910 by Villemard*, accessed December 10, 2017, http://expositions.bnf.fr/utopie/feuill/index.htm.

5 C. Dommermuth-Costa, *Nikola Tesla: A Spark of Genius* (Minneapolis: Lerner Publications, 1994).

6 C. A. Vassão, "Arquitetura Livre: Complexidade, Metadesign e Ciência Nômade" (Universidade de São Paulo, 2008).

7 Edward Tenner, *Why Things Bite Back: Technology and the Revenge of Unintended Consequences* (New York: Vintage Books, 1996).

8 Marshall McLuhan, *The Gutenberg Galaxy: The Making of Typographic Man* (Toronto: University of Toronto Press, 1962).

9 George R. Collins, "Visionary Drawings of Architecture and Planning: 20th Century through the 1960s," *Art Journal* 38, no. 4 (1979): 244–256.

10 Anthony Townsend, "Re-Programming Mobility: The Digital Transformation of Transportation in the United States," (New York: Rudin Center for Transportation Policy & Management, New York University, 2014).

11 Liam Fahey and Robert M. Randall, *Learning from the Future: Competitive Foresight Scenarios* (New York: Wiley, 1998).

12 Ibid.

13 McLuhan, *The Gutenberg Galaxy: The Making of Typographic Man*.

14 "Neil Postman," Wikipedia, January 15, 2018, https://en.wikipedia.org/w/index.php?title=Neil_Postman&oldid=820625423.

15 Vassão, "Arquitetura Livre."

16 Fahey and Randall, *Learning from the Future: Competitive Foresight Scenarios*.

17 Ibid.

18 Ibid.

19 Peter Schwartz and Jay Ogilvy, "Plotting Your Scenarios," in *Learning from the Future: Competitive Foresight Scenarios*, eds. Liam Fahey and Robert M. Randall (New York: Wiley, 1998).

20 Edward Ward and Audrey Schriefer, "Dynamic Scenarios: Systems Thinking Meets Scenario Planning. Plotting Your Scenarios," in *Learning from the Future: Competitive Foresight Scenarios*, eds. Liam Fahey and Robert M. Randall (New York: Wiley, 1998).

Chapter 4
Historical Trajectory of Transportation Infrastructure

Chapter 4

Historical Trajectory of Transportation Infrastructure: Impact on Urban Form and Spatial Configuration

Introduction

In order to try to understand the impact of AVs on urban form, it may be beneficial to look at past transportation technologies and their impact on the city, especially the influence of cars. The introduction of cars was a disruptive technology of its time, even more revolutionary than the introduction of AVs to our streets. As such, there is potentially much to learn from this last revolution in the streets. However, transportation technology is not the only factor in the shaping of streets; the social construction of the street is an equally powerful influence in how we view what a street is and should be.[1,2] Today we view the street as a thoroughfare for cars and we tend to project this thinking onto the past, but this view was not prevalent prior to the 1920s.[3] Before this period, the street was for people to walk in and children to play in. It was the social reconstruction of the street that produced the image we currently have of it and its resultant urban form, a fact that becomes increasingly obvious when looking back closely at this time period.[4] It is therefore also worthwhile examining the history of social attitudes to the street and how changes in attitude have corresponded with changes in transportation technology. Through examination of both the technology and the social attitudes towards that technology, we will get a better idea of how the social construction of the street and our hierarchical street network came about—and what we can anticipate with the next technological transportation revolution.

The impact of a transportation technology has effects on the city at two scales. The first is the impact on the cross-section of the street itself—its scale and how it is divided in terms of uses. The second effect is the impact of technology on the form and scale of the city. These two factors are interconnected since road typologies are used in specific locations in cities; as the smaller scale of the street is replicated, this replicated form becomes the form of the city. As such, these factors will be discussed here firstly at the scale of the street and then expanded to the urban form.[5]

Revolution in the Streets

While we think that the coming of AVs is happening unbelievably quickly and that technology today is rapidly advancing, it pales in comparison to the technological changes that occurred at the time of the invention of the automobile. In the early 1900s the automobile was a rare occurrence on the street with only 8000 existing on American roads, most of them fueled by steam. Gasoline was still just a waste product of the kerosene industry and not many dared experiment with it as a fuel.[6,7] However, between 1900 and 1929 some 1200 new models of cars were introduced. In 1916, after Henry Ford's revolutionary mass production of the automobile made the car available to the majority of Americans, the number of cars on the road increased to 2 million and then quadrupled to 8 million by 1920, even despite wartime constraints, and then again tripled to 23 million by the end of the 1920s.[8]

Thus, within the space of 20 years automobiles went from almost non-existent to a product available to every consumer and adopted at a ferocious pace. The rapid change of use in the streets and the speed of the car caused mayhem. In 1921, 1054 children were killed in accidents—most of them in city streets in the United States. In New York's safety week in 1922, 10,000 children walked in a procession in the streets to mourn these children. Over 200 mothers, called "white star mothers," were present who had lost their children in traffic accidents. Parades with open cars filled with children who were injured and maimed further reinforced the message. In Baltimore, 130 children were killed in traffic accidents in 1921. Similarly, in Pittsburgh, 286 children were killed. Thousands gathered in different cities to mourn their children and outrage and court cases ensued. In an article entitled "City Wide War is Declared on Death Drivers," a Philadelphia judge was quoted as warning, "It won't be long before children won't have any rights at all in the streets [...] Something drastic must be done to end this menace to pedestrians and to children in particular."[9]

Judges vilified the drivers and reinforced pedestrian rights. In Chicago in 1926, the city clarified that "nothing" in the law "prohibits a pedestrian from using any part of the roadway of any street or highways, at any time or at any place as he may desire."[10] And in the traffic court in New York in 1923, the judge stated "Nobody has any inherent right to run an automobile at all" and further that "the courts have held that the right to operate a motor vehicle is a privilege given by the state, not a right, and that privilege may be hedged about with whatever limitations the state feels to be necessary, or it may be withdrawn entirely."[11] There was also great debate about whether pedestrians should be allowed to cross wherever they liked. Rules were put in place that required pedestrians to cross at crosswalks, for example, but these were then struck down in the name of supporting the rights of the pedestrians.[12] The majority of people were pedestrians and the usurpers of the street were the automobile drivers. They were termed "joy riders," "road hogs" and "speed demons" and their vehicles called "death cars" and "juggernauts."[13]

Nevertheless, by the 1930s there was general agreement by road users that the street was primarily a thoroughfare for the car. How did this rapid change in social opinion happen? And from our present-day perspective, with the introduction of AVs could this opinion as quickly reverse course?

Streets were already very crowded and prior to the automobile there were already debates about the use of the street. After the introduction of the automobile, the main groups of people taking positions on the use of the street were pedestrians, downtown business associations, safety reformers, police, traffic engineers, and street railways. The group that identified themselves as Motordom was an extremely powerful and well-funded group that invoked the "American ideals of political and economic freedom." They engaged the nascent tools of advertising and promoted the car

as "modern" and declared the "new motor age" to have begun.[14] This promotional approach provided them with a lever with which to influence policy and public opinion regarding roads. They fought their case in newspapers' editorial pages, courtrooms, engineering offices, legislatures and even schools. The organization of Motordom arranged themselves into a national hierarchy under a group called the American Automobile Association. In 1924 the organization was calling itself "organized motordom."[15] By 1930 the American Automobile Association had largely taken over the school safety initiatives.[16] They brought the engineers in to solve the safety problems of the streets and proclaimed that they could rebuild the city for the car. The group appealed to the public to 'let the market decide.' Although this discussion is mainly about the impacts in North America, similar concerns and developments were going on in Europe—for example, there was a *Salon de L'Automobile* in Paris by 1898 and it became very powerful.

In 1939, Motordom was responsible for one of the most monumental promotional events in history: the Futurama model at the World's Fair in New York. It displayed General Motors' "Highways and Horizons" visions of the city in 1960: a motor age utopian city, where everyone had a car and the city was free of accidents or congestion. It was an immensely popular exhibit and is widely referenced even today.

What Motordom realized was that the primary discussion about the road at the time was surrounding its use and 'misuse.' Norton, in *Fighting Traffic*, notes that by 1924 Motordom realized that the war over the street depended on them redefining the 'misuse' of the street by the car as in fact a primary and legitimate 'use.' Motordom used its substantial resources and savvy to go about ridiculing the slower and less efficient transportation modes as being old-fashioned. Norton further notes that, "Social constructivists have shown that users are 'agents of technological change' and in recent years they have examined how users change (and are changed by) the artifacts they use." Norton clarifies that, "misuse shapes artifacts as much as use, and that struggles between rival social groups to fix the meaning of an artifact in ways they prefer often take the form of struggles to define use and misuse."[17]

It the context of the automobile curtailing the rights of the pedestrian and other road users, a fight which has been drawn out for a century by now, Norton further states, "Through technological innovation, a society that prizes individual liberty can unintentionally curtail it. A city rebuilt (socially and physically) to accommodate cars cannot give street users the good choices a truly free market can

provide."[18] It is interesting to review these insights in light of the potential of the AV to reverse the hierarchy of the street and to give the pedestrian and bicycle back their status on the road. It may now be possible to conceive of a street that serves all users equally and, in building the next generation of streets, we can examine what a street that is built to accommodate multiple users may look like. Further, through technology, we may be able to adjust in real-time for the demand on the street, switching lanes from one direction to the other or allocating more lanes for bicycles as the need arises. The discussion of what a street should be may now begin again with a completely different viewpoint, and as such it is also worth looking at streets and their use and scale throughout history.

Pre-revolution Revolution: The Electric Streetcar

One of the relationships worth examining is that between the street railway or streetcar and the automobile; this is because of the potential similarities in the relationship between public transit and the AV today and between the streetcar and the automobile of the early 20th century. In fact, the automobile revolution is actually considered the second transportation revolution—the first was the electric streetcar (also known as street railway or trolley). The first reliable electric trolley line opened in

Richmond, Virginia in 1888 and within a year was adopted by two dozen other cities.[19] By the early 1890s it was the dominant mode of intraurban transit, replacing horse-drawn trolleys and tripling the speed of travel to over 25 km/h (15 mph). This transportation innovation brought a large amount of land into the city commuting limits and thus opened up urban development on these municipal fringes. Trolley lines were built radially out of the city fabric and were often built by developers wanting to sell housing developments. One of the most significant social impacts of the streetcar was that it gave industrial workers of the time the ability to move away from the factories. Social groups were able to choose where to live in the city and many chose to self-segregate into enclaves.[20]

However, the streetcar mainly disappeared once the mass-produced automobile entered the scene. While some authors blame the automobile companies for the intentional destruction of the streetcar as a transportation mode, the technology of the automobile was unarguably more suited to the American mindset and strongly supported the cultural aspirations of its citizens.[21] The American public loved their cars, which afforded them the freedom to travel wherever and whenever they wanted. It freed people from the timetables and crowded conditions of the streetcars. With the advent of the affordable automobile, developers realized that they no longer needed to build streetcars to sell their properties in the urban fringes and without this financial underpinning, trolley lines were no longer built. Traction companies could not borrow money for expansion because they couldn't raise fares enough to convince the market that it was a good investment.[22] During the 1930s Depression era, government intervention was required to take over streetcar operations when removing the trolley lines was deemed too harmful to communities. The streetcar, which was so highly influential in creating the form of the suburbs, quickly disappeared when the new technology of the mass-produced automobile appeared, leaving the traces of its existence in the urban form.

Street Scale

Moving down in scale from the urban to the scale of the street itself, there is a reciprocal relationship between transportation and the buildings on the street: streets provide public access to properties and so, in general, each property has a relationship to a street. From this perspective, we can understand that streets form an infrastructural network that links properties to the city by providing access to services and also by linking each individual property with other properties. This network is unlikely to change. Streets also provide a public conduit for delivering other services such as water, sewers, gas, hydro and telecommunications and this, too, is likely to remain consistent. However, streets have many uses and these uses are responsive to changes in technology. As a result, the makeup and division of the streets will change. As well what is located on the street—the street furniture—is likely to adapt in response to changes in how the street is used. Finally, and most importantly for the city fabric, the scale of the street has responded to transportation infrastructure in the past and this is again likely to change.

Pre-automotive Era (Walking and Horse and Carriage Technology)

Prior to the Industrial Revolution, streets were scaled for walking and sometimes for horse and carriage—the transportation technology of the day. The street was undifferentiated in terms of function across its sections. These factors resulted in quaint medieval towns with very narrow streets that are still much admired today owing to their human scale and walkability. An analysis of the appreciation of this urban form was undertaken by the Viennese architect Camillo Sitte in his influential book *Der Stadtebau nach seinen kunstlerischen grundsatzen (City Planning According to Artistic Principles)*,[23] published in 1900. His analysis, while derided as 'backwards' by Le Corbusier and the Modernists, remarkably still echoes current criticism.[24] Many others, such as Jan

Gehl, have written extensively on what makes a great street with regard to programming at the ground plane, activity and scale of shops, and while this is extremely valuable, the issue of scale and designing the infrastructure in relation to the built form is more relevant for this particular discussion.

Sitte laments the state of street design at the time and argues that city planning should not be "merely a technical matter" but rather an "artistic enterprise." His position is that mankind is enamoured with the spaces of the streets of the Greek, Roman, Middle Ages and Renaissance times and he attempts to figure out why. Sitte, however, determined that it was not only the scale of the street that pleased people; his assessment was that the public spaces of the streets and squares that people admire are like "urban rooms" and that the building facades on either side of the street in these pleasing street arrangements convey the impression of being like the walls of well-proportioned rooms.

Sitte claims that the Greeks and Romans believed that "there is little difference between the theatre, temple or house and a town square, although this might strike us as strange from our totally different viewpoint today."[25] He supports this by saying that the Roman author and architect Vitruvius did not include the Forum in the chapter on laying out public buildings in his *De Architectura*, but instead in a section of the book on the basilica (open Roman public court building) which includes discussion of theatres, palaestrae, colonnades and public baths—all the spaces which are open to the air but yet considered buildings. Sitte writes,

> "The close kinship of the forum with a space which is defined by being closed all around by architecture, and which is decorated like a festival hall with paintings and statues etc., emerges clearly from Vitruvius' description and, indeed, even more so from the design of the forum at Pompeii which substantiates Vitruvius completely. Vitruvius says "The Greeks lay out their forums in the form of a square surrounded by very spacious double colonnades, adorn them with columns set rather closely together and with entablatures of stone or marble and construct walks above in the upper story.""[26]

Thus, Sitte argues that public space should be designed as if it were an interior room of a building, with the proportion and considerations of the street façade as for the walls of a room. He celebrates the irregularity and the 'confinement' of the spaces.[27] To design in this way, he argues, the street viewpoint (perspective) is important. He applies the same argument to the streets, arguing that they should not be straight but should 'wander' and that they should be enclosed spaces—using arches, curves or jogs to facilitate this.[28] He argues for variety in the width of the

street for visual interest and to allow places to stop or put kiosks.

The scale of urban streets of this type was first codified by the Romans in around 100 CE when they set a standard for road widths of 4.5m (15ft) wide.[29] Emperor Augustus in 15 CE further mandated that the main road east–west—the *decumanus*—should be 12.2m (40ft) wide, that the main road north–south should be 6m (20ft) wide and the side roads—*vicinae*—should be 4.5m (15ft). And so began the role of standards in street construction and the differentiation of these standards according to road types. In this case the standards were to ensure the streets, which were public space, were of adequate size for their specific purpose and were not encroached upon by private citizens and their interests. After the decline of the Roman Empire, standards were largely ignored and the state of streets deteriorated. Medieval streets were generally winding and narrow and it was not until the Renaissance that street standards and the design of the streets were once again given attention. Leon Battista Alberti (1404–1472) was a key figure in this area. Alberti believed good city planning and architecture worked together and he promoted good health conditions and water supply along with efficient construction methodologies and harmonious design.[30] In the Renaissance, straight gridded streets became the ideal. The straight streets appealed to Renaissance architects because of their pure form and their potential to frame landmarks and scenery. At the request of the Doge of Venice in 1550, the architect Galeazzo Alessi (1512–1572) designed an early example of a straight street[31] which today is known as Venice's Via Garibaldi. The military at the time supported the initiative because it would facilitate control in times of social unrest or invasion.

Gridded street extensions in Europe became the popular urban form for new bourgeois suburbs in cities such as Turin, Berlin, Vienna and many others. Andreas Palladio (1518–1580) promoted segregation of street functions: in the city, pedestrians would be on the sides of the streets on elevated areas with porticos over the spaces to walk; carts and cattle could use the centre of the street. Outside the city gates, Palladio proposed a street of at least 2.5m wide with pedestrians in the centre and trees on either side. Cattle and carriages would be on the outside and a stone curb would divide the two functional areas.

By the mid-18th century, newly built roads were generally 5.5m (18ft) wide. The street section, which is the first modern street section and antecedent to our current streets, was first seen in 1765 in Britain and was developed for Westminster's street improvement programme.[32] It consisted of a cross section of the road, which was lowered, levelled and paved with paving stones, and a higher sidewalk, also paved and defined by curbs. The drainage is directed by sloping the paving stones in the roadway to collect water at the curb. By 1820, 200,000km (125,000 miles) of roads were built with this standard in England.[33]

Streets have gradually increased in width since then. The suburban development street section, used in the influential Park Village East development, and also the later Riverside, Illinois development, had a standard width of 9.2m (30ft) and a right of way of 15.2m (50ft).[34] This allowed for parking on the residential streets as well as lanes in each direction. Typical lane widths for arterial and highways are now 3.0m to 3.5m wide with width being related to design speed, although truck turning lanes can be as wide as 4.5m, and shoulders where required are approximately 2.5m.

Road Classifications and Street Widths

Today roads are typically scaled according to their functional hierarchy and the type and speed of traffic on them. The road hierarchy is a network typology that dictates the relationship of roads to other roads; the speed and width of the road is related to this typology. This network typology is extremely widespread in city fabrics built since the early 1900s. The concept of functional hierarchy is credited to Ludwig Hilberseimer and his *City Plan* (1927). Hilberseimer was concerned about the speed of traffic and its relationship to neighbourhoods and so he explored methods of organizing the city fabric in an orderly way to promote harmonious living. In *The New City* (1944) he proposes street classifications and widths:[35] "The width of a street should be determined by its function. It should not be decided upon arbitrarily but should be settled in relation to the number of vehicles the street is to serve."[36] Hilberseimer sets out his functional hierarchy as follows:

> [T]he functional organization of the street system would bring about a differentiation of traffic routes: from the residential lane intended only for pedestrians to the main highways-for automobiles only.
>
> We should have, in such a residential area, first lanes, then streets into which the lanes lead, then traffic streets into which the streets lead, and finally the traffic highways fed by the traffic streets. This traffic highway would, at convenient points, connect with the main highway.[37]

The organization of cities was discussed not only by Hilberseimer but also by his Modernist colleagues; they saw the city as disorganized and chaotic and thought that a progressive city for the new age should be more orderly and efficient in order to provide a better quality of life for its inhabitants. At the 1933 CIAM (*Congrès Internationaux d'Architecture Moderne*) IV meeting in Athens, it was agreed upon that streets should be organized to recognize the different functions of roads and the different speeds required for these functions. There were discussions of separating different speeds of cars on different layers, and of separating pedestrian and car traffic. Le Corbusier, in his documentation of the event, describes the ideal road network as one which "incorporates modern traffic techniques and is directly proportionate to its purposes and usage."[38]

Today we have a fully developed road network, which closely resembles what Hilberseimer envisaged in 1927. Arterial roads are typically 4 to 10 or more lanes wide (lanes being generally 3–3.5m wide) and carry traffic from freeways to more urban areas. These are the largest of non-highway roads. Collectors connect arterials to local roads and may access properties and local roads are residential and service properties directly.

The questions which we should ask at this point are: what kind of a network could emerge with the AV? How will it relate to the network typology discussed by the Modernists and carried out by traffic engineers, which is stamped across our cities? The control of the vehicle with AVs will be twofold: through software into which the street rules are programmed and also through some kind of network control, set up by cities and/or car companies to relay information to the cars. The physical form of the city will no longer determine control of the vehicle: speed bumps, for example, will no longer be necessary and could be replaced by a speed limit programmed into the mapping software the vehicle is using or picked up from the infrastructure. The scale of the lane will no longer have to increase with an increase in speed limit because the car will not wander in the lane. Lanes could also be blocked virtually rather than physically and street directions reversed instantaneously. These factors could play in to a reimagining of the relationship of speed and organization to the street network.

Urban Scale

Urban fabric varies over time and the fabric responds to the culture and technologies of each era. One can read the time period of the urban fabric by observing the scale and organization of the streets. The city grows and the urban fabric changes—generally, but not always—from the centre to the periphery. There are occasionally inconsistencies, such as Haussmann's Boulevards or slum clearing efforts from the mid-20th century, and these can also be clearly read from the fabric because they break with the scale and pattern of the rest of the immediately proximate urban fabric. While we do re-use and re-partition streets according to the priorities and transportation technologies of later times, the new fabrics to be built generally reflect contemporary societal priorities and technologies. For example, some of the more readable fabrics include, as previously referenced, the organically shaped streets from the Middle Ages with narrow widths similar to those established by the Romans. After the Renaissance we can observe an increase in rationalized street grids at a relatively small scale. In the early and mid 1900s we see hierarchical traffic arrangements with the development of freeways from the 1950s on.

Zoning

Intentional planning activities began in the 1800s in response to heightened concerns about pollution in the city from industrial activity. Cities were crowded and polluted and ideas of separating and decentralizing the city began to emerge. Tony Garnier (1869–1948), Patrick Geddes (1854–1932) and Ebenezer Howard (1850–1928) are credited with trying to take on these issues with their imagining of utopian towns, complete with new societal orders and new urban organizations to implement them. Garnier proposed the *'Cité Industrielle'* (Industrial City)—a project he worked on from 1901 until its publication as a book in 1917. This ideal city proposed zoning the centre into different areas, including industrial, residential, health-related, entertainment and civic zones. He created centralized pedestrian zones associated with residential areas which connected to vehicular streets around their perimeter. Garnier influenced Le Corbusier in this regard and his idea—of planning specific areas with specific functions—also influenced Howard. Garnier's ideas came to be highly influential in city developments across the Western world.

The Picturesque

Another significant movement from the 1800s which ended up heavily influencing the design of suburbs is the Picturesque. The movement idealized rural values and picturesque scenes of landscape and gained immense popularity; over one hundred pattern books for picturesque cottages were drawn up between 1790 and 1810. John Nash (1752–1835) was the first to be credited with applying the Picturesque to urban design problems.[39] He situated quaint cottages on winding lanes, ensuring that each had sufficient privacy and integrated with the landscape so that picturesque views were enjoyed throughout. Architects and designers including Fredrick Law Olmstead (1822–1903), Andrew Downing (1815–1852) and Calvert Vaux (1824–1895) were particularly interested in these English design trends, having similar problems with American cities, and visited England to see the work of Nash. They

brought these ideas back to North America in the form of parkways and parks.

The association between 'the country' or a life closer to 'nature' with health and the healthy family begins at this point. The terms 'the country' and 'nature' are used with respect to the specific social framework which existed at the time period. This framework included the inherited picturesque ideal as well as the notion of the nuclear family in a cottage situated in a highly constructed and designed 'nature.' The conditions in the city as a result of the Industrial Revolution were anything but healthy: increasingly overcrowded, poorly ventilated housing, and poor or non-existent drainage. Pollution was a major health concern—the air contained large amounts of dust, carbon gases and other toxic substances. The answer was seen as decentralization and movement into this idealized countryside.

Garden Cities

Ebenezer Howard was particularly influential in the move to introduce the country into the city (or to make the city more country-like depending on how one looks at it). Howard's *Garden Cities of To-Morrow* (1902)[40] is credited by Lewis Mumford as having done "more than any other single book to guide the modern town planning movement and alter its objectives."[41] Mumford also credits

Howard with having invented the idea of the greenbelt.[42] Howard's book and his dedicated effort to enact reform resulted in two towns built based on his principles of town planning (if not his ideology behind it): Letchworth (1903) and Welwyn Garden City (1920). Howard's ideology is discussed further in Chapter 10; in short, he was interested in creating a better life for people by having them live in healthier environments and saw moving people into the country in self-sufficient communities as key to this. His Garden Cities were connected to the city and each other by means of street railways (streetcars). These street railways out to the Garden Cities were extremely influential in the planning of American cities and can be seen in the fabrics of cities from the late 1800s and early 1900s. Howard's garden city movement was also influential in that it created the Garden City Planning Association in 1899; this organization is seen as providing a template for later city planning organizations.

The fabric and street network of the Garden Cities is one of the most influential factors on the post-war city: the streets developed by the architects who designed Howard's Garden Cities—Raymond Unwin and Barry Parker—were not the grid that Howard envisioned, but instead a version of the medieval type as promoted by William Morris, whose thinking Unwin and Parker followed.[43] This vision of a street arrangement

promoted what they saw as 'organic unity' and had a nostalgia for the traditional English village. Their curving street arrangements were designed to integrate with the landscape. Similarly, their buildings were not the iron and steel crystal palaces that Howard envisioned, but instead invoked traditional design using traditional materials, conveying the ethos of the Arts and Crafts movement.

The Garden City came to North America in 1924 through the City Housing Corporation, formed by Alexander M. Bing, a real estate developer and charter member of the Regional Planning Association. Bing hired Clarence Stein and Henry Wright who designed a smaller development of row houses in New York City called Sunnyside Gardens. With the success of this development, they went on to develop the larger Radburn in Fairlawn, New Jersey, 25km from New York City.

The Radburn development was based on a Garden City but modified for the American context, most significantly in its street arrangement. By this time, the car had become a widespread menace. The gridiron street arrangement of most cities was well suited to vehicular traffic and so no street was safe from the honking, exhaust fumes and endless vehicles. As a response to the negative aspects of cars, Stein and Wright deliberately arranged the residential streets to facilitate access only to the residences and not to be

Urban Scale 101

thoroughfares; they also invented the cul-de-sac. The Garden City's curving streets only served the residences and were meant to deter the car from residential streets. Their arrangement had the additional benefit that it reduced street areas and the length of utilities by 25% as compared to a typical gridiron development. The cost savings were said to have been invested in building parks. This development was hailed as a major innovation in town planning and a successful approach to dealing with the automobile.[44]

The resulting form of the subdivision, however, can also be thought of as a negative reaction to the car—a way to try to reduce the presence of the car and its danger, pollution and noise.

Modernists

Others, however, disagreed with the Garden Cities approach and thought the city should be improved rather than abandoning it for the suburbs. The members of CIAM, including Hilberseimer and Le Corbusier, were of this mindset. The Modernist school read, and was influenced by, the works of Howard, Sitte and others but they critiqued them too. Le Corbusier accused Sitte of senselessly initiating the 'donkey path':

> Man walks straight because he has a goal: he knows where he's going. He has decided to go somewhere and he walks straight there. [...] The donkey has laid

out all the streets on the continent, including Paris unfortunately [...][45]

Le Corbusier also critiqued the Garden Cities, saying they were "de-urbanizing" and railed against the "sterile isolation of the individual" that would result as well as the "slavery organized by capitalist society" that he thought would result from these innovations.[46] Le Corbusier was much more influenced by Garnier's plan for the Industrial City and adopted this segregated city planning for his own *Ville Contemporaine* (Contemporary City) and *Ville Radieuse* (Radiant City)—although Le Corbusier's Contemporary City had 3 million inhabitants in contrast to the mere 30,000 of Garnier.

Le Corbusier's own work was impractical but influential. He defines his ideas about transportation as 'organic' and he sees the city as an organism with the transportation routes laid out 'efficiently' on different levels. A 'river system' of 'classified traffic,' able to move in a continuous and coordinated flow, is one of the most important features of his city. Similar to Hilberseimer's theories, he believed in a functional hierarchy for urban transportation, only in his city, Le Corbusier planned to separate transportation vertically. In the Radiant City (1933) pedestrians could move anywhere they wished on the ground plane and vehicles were 5m above grade on viaducts. In the Plan

Voisin (1925), motor traffic operates on two levels according to speed, with higher speed traffic below. Pedestrian traffic is independent of car traffic and a subway system is also incorporated. Le Corbusier's traffic scheme modified into his road network, known as the system of 7 Vs, in 1945. This classifies roads as: V1 motorway, V2 main axis urban traffic, V3 interurban network, V4 commercial street (with characteristics of the neighbourhoods), V5 and V6 serve the residential and V7 is purely pedestrian. He radically exhibits the functional hierarchy proposed by Hilberseimer and puts this in section rather than plan. He values speed as a symbol of the advanced society and therefore insists that high-speed traffic must be separated from any other traffic that may impede it. He also, however, believes that the pedestrian should be free to go wherever they choose and be safe, and the only way of doing this is to segregate them completely.

The Modernists had an optimism regarding transportation technology and functionalism. At the same time, however, they, as well as Howard and many others, were deeply concerned by the living conditions of many workers who they viewed as being exploited by rampant capitalism and wealthy landlords in particular. It was the attempt to deal with the devastating effects of poverty and the poor conditions provided by the landlords that was behind the utopian and reformatory visions that the designers of the time were proposing. Ironically, it was only through the capitalist developers and company owners that any of these visions got put forward and built.

Regardless of whether they were built, however, the proposals put forward by Garnier, Howard, Hilberseimer, Le Corbusier and others have had huge impacts on urban development, planning and the resulting urban fabric, especially on the street networks. These intellectuals were attempting to deal with contemporary problems by using the new technologies of their times. The suburban pattern produced by projects which descend directly from the Garden City, for example, has had enormous impacts on the city since the 1950s. Yet within that pattern is an inherent contradiction: both the acceptance of the car by the construction of the highways and the rejection of the car as evidenced by the rebutting streets of the subdivision.

Freeway Era

The post-World War II Freeway Era was not so much revolutionary as the coming of age of automobile culture.[47] With the 1956 Interstate Highway Act, the freeway reached all corners of North America and accelerated decentralization of cities; as this decentralization occurred, cities became a mosaic of segregated areas. Belt highways also developed, the prototype of which is considered to be Boston's Route 128, completed in the early 1950s. These highways emerged from the development of bypasses to congested downtown areas and eventually fully encircled the city core, creating a 'belt.' At the interchanges of many of these highways, new concentrations of retail, business and light industry developed, which essentially became independent outlying urban centres.

The Freeway Era can be broken down into stages:[48] the bedroom community stage (1945–55), the independence stage (1955–1965) with suburban growth and the development of office park typologies, the catalytic growth stage (1965–1980) which involved the building of hotels, restaurants and offices and connecting highways, and the penultimate stage of the high-rise/high technology period of the 1980s and the development of high-rises in these suburban centres. The final stage was the mature urban centre as the social, cultural, recreational and civic functions 'filled in' to make them completely self-contained complex metropolises in their own right.

Conclusion

Although highly influential, the discussion here highlights the fact that transportation technologies are not the only determinant in the configuration of urban form. Socio-political context, available resources and public and private interests all have a large role to play. Another important observation is that a succession of transportation technologies typically leaves a much more significant mark in the expanding urban areas than in pre-existing urban fabrics. For example, although anterior to automobile introduction, older neighbourhoods were not fundamentally rebuilt to serve automobile infrastructure; instead, adaptations were made to allow for the circulation of automobiles, leaving the basic urban fabric mostly unchanged. Therefore, contemporary cities are often composed of different urban fabrics established at different moments in time and designed around a different set of transportation modes. Older city forms remain, around which newer urban designs develop.

Based on these understandings, we can anticipate that AVs will impact urban form in two different ways: firstly, by producing their own optimum infrastructure and urban design in areas of urban expansions; and secondly, by adapting existing urban fabrics without fundamental changes to the way they have been established. Furthermore, it is expected that cities that undergo massive expansion in the decades following AV introduction will develop specific AV-oriented patterns and design, while cities whose expansion has been stabilized will see their character change much less significantly.

The conspicuous characteristics of urban expansion as related to transportation technologies demonstrate that the spatial form and organization of the metropolis change after the introduction of a new urban transportation development.[49] It is this significant historic observation that underlies the study in this book—a question of what this form will be and, more importantly, *could* be. Furthermore, the expectation of urban expansion, especially in the form of sprawl, is a topic expected to raise concern.[50] Therefore, it is important to consider the effects of such models of development, the ways in which AVs might assist in the aggravation of its problems, and what can be done to mitigate any negative impact.

Notes

1. Ronald Kline and Trevor Pinch, "Users as Agents of Technological Change: The Social Construction of the Automobile in the Rural United States," *Technology and Culture* 37, no. 4 (1996): 765.

2. Peter D. Norton, *Fighting Traffic* (Cambridge, Massachusetts: The MIT Press, 2008), 1.

3. Kline and Pinch, "Users as Agents of Technological Change," 768.

4. Norton, *Fighting Traffic*.

5. The illustrated examples discussed in Chapter 5 look at urban form; in Chapter 7 the examples are at the scale of the street.

6. Peter J. Hugill, "Good Roads and the Automobile in the United States 1880-1929," *Geographical Review* 72, no. 3 (1982): 327–49.

7. Michael Southworth and Eran Ben-Joseph, *Streets and the Shaping of Towns and Cities* (New York: McGraw Hill, 1997).

8. Susan Hanson, *The Geography of Urban Transportation, Second Edition* (New York: The Guilford Press, 1995), 38.

9. Magistrate Costello, Philadelphia, Nov. 8, 1924, quoted in "City-Wide War Is Declared on Death Drivers" Public Ledger (Philadelphia), Nov 9, 1924 referred to in Norton, *Fighting Traffic*, 69.

10. Chicago Association of Commerce, "Report and Recommendations of the Metropolitan Street Traffic Survey," 1926, 26 as referred to in Norton, *Fighting Traffic*, 66.

11. Frederick B. House, quoted in editorial, *New York Herald*, August 23, 1923, reprinted in Stephen S. Tuthill, "The Attitude of the Motorist Toward Traffic Regulations," Oct. 2, 1923, *Proceedings of the National Safety Council, Twelfth Annual Safety Congress, Buffalo, Oct 1-5, 1923*, p. 811 as referred to in Norton, *Fighting Traffic*, 67.

12. Benison v Dembinsky, 241 Ilinois Courts of Appeals 530; see Myron M. Stearns, "Your Right to Cross the Street," *Outlook and Independent* 155 (May 14, 1930), 50-53, 80 (52) as referred to in Norton *Fighting Traffic*, 69.

13. Norton, *Fighting Traffic*, 3.

14. Ibid, 258–60.

15. Ibid, 92.

16. Norton, *Fighting Traffic*.

17. Ibid, 260.

18. Ibid, 261.

19. Hanson, *The Geography of Urban Transportation*, 34.

20. Ibid.

21. Peter O. Muller, "Transportation and Urban Form-Stages in the Spatial Evolution of the American Metropolis," in *The Geography of Urban Transportation*, eds. Susan Hanson, Genevieve Giuliano (New York: Guilford Press, 2004), 37.

22. Hanson, *The Geography of Urban Transportation*, 39.

23. Camillo Sitte, George Roseborough Collins, and Christiane Crasemann Collins, *Camillo Sitte: The Birth of Modern City Planning: With a Translation of the 1889 Austrian Edition of His City Planning According to Artistic Principles* (New York: Rizzoli, 1986).

24. Le Corbusier, *The Radiant City*, Translation 1967 (New York: Orion Press, 1933).

25. Sitte, Collins, and Collins, *Camillo Sitte: The Birth of Modern City Planning*, 5.

26. Ibid, 6.

27. Ibid, Chapter 3, 32.

28. Ibid, Chapter 7A, 67.

29. Robert James Forbes, *Notes on the History of Ancient Roads and Their Construction*, vol. 3 (Amsterdam: AM Hakkert, 1964).

30. Southworth and Ben-Joseph, *Streets and the Shaping of Towns and Cities*.

31. Ibid, 14.

32. Ibid, 18.

33. Ibid, 18.

34. Ibid, 26–34.

35. Ludwig Hilberseimer, *The New City: Principles of Planning* (Chicago: Theobald, 1944), 107.

36 Ibid, 111.

37 Ibid, 107.

38 Le Corbusier, *Charte d'Athènes. (The Athens Charter)* (New York: Grossman Publishers, 1973), 98.

39 Southworth and Ben-Joseph, *Streets and the Shaping of Towns and Cities*.

40 Previously published as *To-Morrow: a Peaceful Path to Real Reform* (1898).

41 Ebenezer Howard Papers. Hertfordshire County Archives, Hertford, England. Draft of an Unfinished Autobiography, Folio 17. as referenced in: Robert Fishman, *Urban Utopias in the Twentieth Century: Ebenezer Howard, Frank Lloyd Wright, and Le Corbusier* (Cambridge, Massachusetts: MIT Press, 1982).

42 Lewis Mumford, *The Highway and the City* (New York: The New American Library, 1964), 31.

43 Fishman, *Urban Utopias in the Twentieth Century*, 67.

44 Southworth and Ben-Joseph, *Streets and the Shaping of Towns and Cities*, 68.

45 Le Corbusier, *The City of To-Morrow and Its Planning* (1929) (Courier Corporation, 1987), 6–8.

46 Maurice Besset, *Who Was Le Corbusier* (Geneva: Editions d'Art Albert Skira, 1968), 152.

47 Hanson, *The Geography of Urban Transportation*, 42.

48 Hanson, these stages are proposed by Baerwald (1978), Erickson (1983), Harshorn and Muller (1989), 46.

49 Muller, "Transportation and Urban Form-Stages in the Spatial Evolution of the American Metropolis," 26.

50 Daniel Fagnant and Kara Kockelman, "Preparing a Nation for Autonomous Vehicles: 1 Opportunities, Barriers and Policy Recommendations for 2 Capitalizing on Self-Driven Vehicles 3," *Transportation Research Part A* 20 (2014).

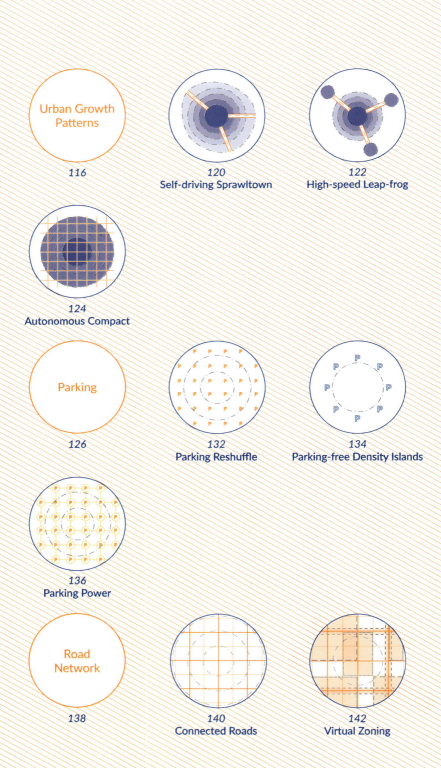

Chapter 5
Urban Scale Impacts

144
Movement Ecologies

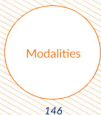

Modalities

146

150
Distributed Public

152
Door-to-door Mixed-mode

154
Private AV Commuting

Chapter 5
Urban Scale Impacts

Introduction

The introduction of AVs has the potential to change much about the way we move around and, as a result, affect where we move around *to*—our choice of where we live, work and otherwise spend our time—as well as the length of trip we are willing to take. Other significant factors are that cars no longer need to be parked near the user's destination and that the technology for AVs may provide more reliable public transportation for solving 'last mile' issues.[1] These changes in transportation technology have significant implications for the street and also on urban form. To analyze what these impacts may be, it is useful to look both backwards and forwards: back to the history of the impact of the automobile, which is well documented and in many cases lamented; and forward to speculate on the way people may use this new technology. By looking backwards and forwards it may be possible to see patterns and trajectories which, although not definitive, would lend credence to the speculations put forth here. The previous case studies demonstrated potential ways that people may use the technology in the future. The illustrated scenarios in the next chapters speculate on the urban form—first in its larger scale at the scale of the metropolis and then at the scale of the street. Each drawing has beside it the assumptions and logic that leads to that diagram. These drawings are meant to start a discussion about the future, not to provide an answer to what it will, or should, be.

Methodological Approach

The speculative drawings presented in this book have been generated in a structured way which consists of three processes: comparative research about historic changes; the establishment of a conceptual framework to look at these changes systematically; and then a process of drawing, based on speculations with these assumptions clearly detailed in the description for each drawing. While these are presented here in a linear fashion, they constituted parallel, iterative activities.

Comparative Research: Drawing on the Automobile and Before

As discussed in the previous chapter, the development of cities has been shaped by innovations in transportation technology; previous transportation paradigms and their impacts provide an historic context for speculating on the probable influences of new technologies, such as intelligent mobility and autonomous vehicles.[2] Similar transformations happened on the scale of the street. The spread of the automobile brought about a hierarchical network of paved roads, and geometric design standards were established for the dimensions and configuration of lanes and layout of intersections. A class of infrastructure elements responsible for controlling traffic, such as traffic lights, lanes and roadside signage, were gradually introduced. The character of streets and pedestrian movement was reshaped by fast-moving cars. As trucking gained an increasing share of ground freight transport, commercial vehicles such as shipping trucks became important determinants of road design. In addition, existing building forms adapted to the presence of the automobile, such as the insertion of the garage into residential space, and entirely new building types and programmes were also created, such as the parking lot, the parking garage, the gas station, the suburban shopping mall or the drive-in restaurant.

This work is grounded in the historical context of the impact of the automobile on both urban form and society in the 20th century, and positioned relative to these aspects. This approach has major advantages. Firstly, the existence of academic literature on the automobile helps to establish the conceptual lens through which different areas of its impact can be categorized and studied. Secondly, the comparative approach (followed through in the visualizations), allows for a registering of the similarities and differences that characterize urban form in the envisioned future scenarios. That is, while certain aspects of mobility are predicted to change as a result of new technology, other elements will remain familiar. For instance, while the movement and navigation of vehicles will likely undergo drastic changes due to the shift in decision making moving from human perception to that of sensors and computer algorithms, the spatial requirements and behaviour of pedestrians will remain unchanged. It is thus productive to visualize both 'before' and 'after' scenarios: this helps us to speculate on the future with conceptual rigour, and also allows our audience to better understand and inhabit the drawn space of the unknown by simultaneously being presented with the familiar.

The main limitation of the comparative approach lies in the extent to which the new technological paradigm is imagined according to the structure of the old. In the case of AVs in general, and this research in particular, this limitation can be considered acceptable since the current trajectory of technological innovation places AVs in the direct lineage of automobiles—or more accurately, at the convergence point between

Area of impact	Examples
Urban Form	Building form
	Urban growth
Mobility Infrastructure	Transportation systems
	Road infrastructure
Environment	Energy consumption
	Pollution
Society & Culture	Access to mobility
	Lifestyle
Economy	Freight transport
	Transportation industry

Table 5.1. The potential impacts of transportation technology: major areas and examples.

automobiles and mobile digital technology. To date, most innovations in the field of transportation have taken place in the realm of software, as opposed to the hardware-centric evolution of the automobile in the previous century. While this has spurred a new approach to transportation—mobility on demand—more radical change will come when the hardware again changes, this time into the autonomous robot-operated automobile.

While recent innovations, considered the first few steps towards intelligent mobility, are being added to otherwise conventional automobiles, there may be a point in this innovation process when referring to AVs as 'cars' will no longer do justice to their form and function. It is to be noted here, however, that this research is not centred on the vehicles themselves. Although it is likely that their physical form and social function will undergo radical changes, the work here has only marginally engaged with this subject, focusing instead on how a proliferation of AVs could impact the form and performance of urban spaces.

Framework

Once the inventory of the impacts of the automobile on the city was completed, it was studied in detail in order to establish a productive conceptual framework for speculating on the future impacts of AVs. While the

AV	**Urban Scale**	**Street Scale**
Urban Form	Urban growth patterns, Land use	Building typology, Programme
Mobility Infrastructure	Transportation systems, Movement patterns	Road infrastructure, Human interaction

Table 5.2. Simplified matrix of impacts of AVs on the built environment.

impacts encompass a variety of issues ranging from economic and political to social and cultural phenomena, as summarized in Table 5.1, this work is particularly concerned with the built environment and transportation technology. Hence, the in-depth, drawing-based exploration was limited to these two categories, referred to as 'Urban Form' and 'Mobility Infrastructure.'

It was also concluded that in both these categories it was helpful to separate the impacts of AVs according to scale; sub-categories of 'Street Scale' and 'Urban Scale' were identified. While street-scale impacts are understood as relevant in their specific form and revealing of the concrete inhabitation and experience of urban space by its various users and agents, urban-scale impacts are identified as more abstract, revealing systemic patterns and forces at play. Although arguably an oversimplification, this dichotomy of scales was pursued for clarity. Street-scale visualizations explore specific instances of building, infrastructure and movement; their urban-scale counterparts attempt to diagram their broader implications, as well as processes that are not evident at eye level. This chapter deals mainly with changes at the urban scale, and Chapter 7 with the street-scale changes.

Table 5.2 shows a simplified matrix of impacts, based on the combination of the two categories selected for further investigation, urban form and mobility infrastructure.

After this process of organization was undertaken for traditional automobiles, a corresponding matrix was generated on the possible impacts of AVs on urban form and mobility. This process took into consideration existing references made to such impacts in a variety of academic literature, reports and other media sources; it was followed by the development of a synthetic series of drawings that incorporate the referenced issues, as well as further issues identified in the process.

Table 5.3 presents a comparison between the automobile and AVs on the issues pertaining to urban form and mobility infrastructure, at the respective scales of the street and the city.

Responding to Scenarios: Speculative Diagrams

Following this step, a series of drawings were developed to speculate on and analyze specific instances of changes to the built environment, according to the roster of established impacts. While these drawings make proposals with regard to specific subjects, it should be noted that the work focuses on changes to built form and infrastructure, without in-depth consideration of, or value judgements on, real-world contextual issues, such as the price of fuel/energy, the social acceptance of new technology, or policy incentives or disincentives.

Generally speaking, the drawings are situated in a not-so-distant future, imagined as characterized by the proliferation of autonomous vehicles as a principal mode of urban transportation, having fully replaced human drivers. The visualized scenarios often take place in hypothetical urban environments developed according to the optimal infrastructure needs of AVs, since the focus of this research resides in envisioning changes to the physical urban fabric as a result of this technology. Suspending disbelief for a moment, the work therefore intentionally sidesteps contextualizing AVs in relation to other existing transportation modes, as well as the various political, economic and sociocultural forces that would shape the real-world manifestation of any new technology. Certain key issues, such as ownership models (for instance, personally owned AVs versus fleets of shared vehicles), are drawn on to the extent that these different models might result in radically different built environments. This also means that while the drawing sets are systematic in their speculation, their findings are by design incomplete, being intended as samples of a simultaneously rigorous and speculative mode of drawing. The social and cultural issues are dealt with further in Chapters 4, 6, 8, 9 and 10.

URBAN SCALE IMPACTS		Automobile	Autonomous Vehicle
Urban Form	**Urban Growth Patterns**	• Low-density suburban sprawl • Leapfrog and exurban development • Linear development along arterial roads • Decline of urban core • Multi-central urban structure	• Increased sprawl due to cheaper, faster and more convenient travel • Urban densification • High density exurban islands served by AVs
	Land Use	• Segregation of land uses • Parking as a major land use	• Changes in scale and incidence of parking
Mobility	**Transportation Systems**	• Hierarchical urban road networks • Interurban and regional highway networks	• Intelligent traffic management systems • AV-optimized road networks
	Movement Patterns	• Automobile-dependency • Long-distance commuting • Freight trucking • Increased mobility of certain services • Decline of public transport • Traffic congestion	• Increase/decrease in vehicle mile travelled (VMT) • Decentralization of public transit systems incorporating AVs • Reduced demand on road capacity and reduced congestion

Table 5.3. Comparison between the observed impacts of the automobile at the scale of urban systems, and corresponding possible impacts by AVs.

URBAN GROWTH PATTERNS

The development of cities and their increase in size and density is widely discussed in urban design and to date has had a significant relationship to transportation modes. Figure 5.1 presents the evolution of the relationship between transportation and urban form in North American cities, based on the seminal work of J.S. Adams[3] and Muller.[4] Displaying an idealized city developed around a single central core, the diagram presents to scale the growth of an urbanized area based on a hypothetical one-hour commute from any point in the city to the centre. The introduction of each new transport technology increases, in some cases exponentially, the distance travelled. The pattern is consistent—as each new transportation technology is introduced, it enables the expansion of the city limits. Yet one of the largest laments of urban planners in the late 20th and early 21st centuries is the 'sprawl' that has expanded the city limits. One of the key objections to urban sprawl is the assumption that it detracts from the life of the city by diluting density and as a consequence diminishes the city's levels of activity and vibrancy. In addition, sprawl also increases automobile dependence and therefore pollutant emissions as well as decreasing agricultural land.[5]

The diagram shown, however, continues the trajectory of transportation technology by further expanding the limits of the city. The addition of AVs to this speculative model shows further expansion of commuting distance.[6] This is based on three factors, none of which has yet been empirically quantified in research. The first factor is the potential ability of self-driving vehicles to travel safely at higher speeds, and the possibility of converted or purpose-built highway infrastructure that enables this. Vehicles that can travel safely at higher speeds would be able to travel longer distances faster if the appropriate infrastructure were in place. This would allow people to commute from farther locations, including those characterized by cheaper land prices.[7,8] Secondly, considering the probable increases in energy efficiency of AVs, commuting would become cheaper per unit of distance travelled (this is, of course, dependent on the power source and energy market prices). Thirdly, and potentially most significantly, the passenger could engage in other activities, such as rest, work or socializing, which may make longer commutes more tolerable.[9] It is difficult at this time to predict the extent of the urban expansion due to AV technology but there are

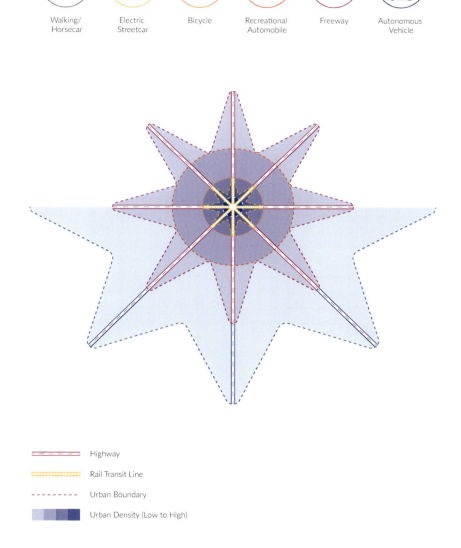

Figure 5.1. Evolution of transportation and urban form in North America based on the 1-hour commute. Adapted from J-P. Rodrigue, The Geography of Transport Systems (2015).

significant reasons, as discussed, as to why the expansion may happen. Taking a completely neutral view of the expansion of the urban realm, there may be factors that arise with AVs that decrease any negative aspects of this expansion: for example, if the AVs are also electric vehicles (EVs) then this could mitigate the pollution aspect of the expansion. In addition, if planners continue to design for dense developments rather than less dense suburbs, active walkable environments could still exist. However, what becomes particularly obvious in this study is that the constraint on the city limits will no longer be related to commuting distances. Cities—and those who plan them—will need to be more proactive in using other mechanisms to limit sprawl.

Extrapolated Urban Futures

The forms of cities are no longer only monocentric: other recognized urban development conditions have evolved.[10] Extrapolating from these typological conditions leads to several speculative future scenarios for urban growth and expansion with the introduction of AVs. Here the extrapolated speculations are connected with transportation and spatial planning—or lack thereof. Thus the interaction of transportation technologies, infrastructure and planning forces forms the new urban fabric. Which scenario ultimately occurs will be dependent on the planning forces and existing urban fabric of the place, but some simplified models are presented here for discussion and analysis purposes.

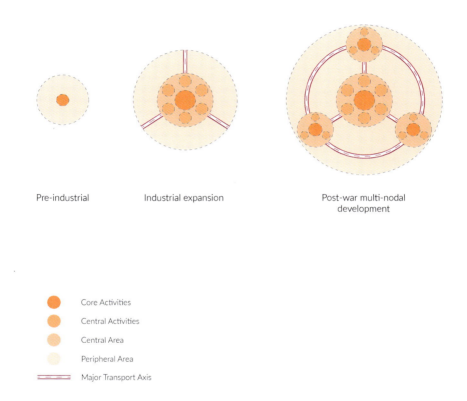

*Figure 5.2. Evolution of urban spatial structure.
Adapted from J-P. Rodrigue,* The Geography of Transport Systems *(2015).*

Urban Growth Patterns   119

Self-driving Sprawltown: Urban Edge AV Frontiers

As discussed earlier, one of the major impacts of the spread of the automobile and its road infrastructure was a low-density, multi-directional urban growth, which has resulted in vast areas of suburban sprawl. Suburban and exurban developments remain the most significant forms of urban growth in North American cities. An anticipated effect of AVs on urban growth is the exacerbation of further sprawl in indiscriminate directions, creating an overall effect of sprawl in multiple directions. The possible reasons for this, as discussed above, include higher travel speeds (commuting for the same amount of time, across a larger distance), increased energy efficiency per vehicle mile travelled (commuting across a larger distance at the same cost) and the improved quality of commuting time (working or relaxing while travelling). The ability of the car to negotiate a matrix of streets effectively owing to the increased efficiency of traffic prediction and vehicle interaction may also make the sprawl more evenly diffuse around the city and less likely to occur only near highways.

Highway along urban edge.

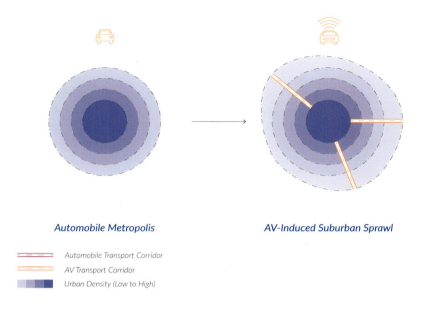

Automobile Metropolis   *AV-Induced Suburban Sprawl*

- Automobile Transport Corridor
- AV Transport Corridor
- Urban Density (Low to High)

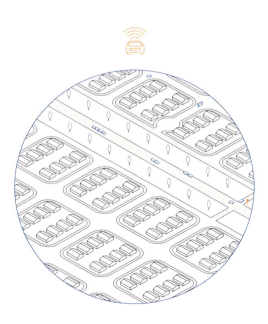

Suburban development along AV-optimized highway.

Urban Growth Patterns

High-Speed Leap-Frog: Exurban AV Enclaves

A related yet distinct pattern of post-war development has been the appearance of exurban communities. Spatially separate but functionally dependent on the metropolitan area, these exurban enclaves necessitate good transportation connections (which have been, with few exceptions, centred on the car). The proliferation of AVs and the associated improvements in the quality of time spent commuting, along with regulations regarding minimum urban densities, could see the appearance of higher-density 'islands' in outlying exurban areas, serviced by upgraded or newly constructed AV-specific infrastructure such as dedicated high-speed highway lanes for AVs.[11] Inter-urban commuting between the existing urban core and the AV enclave might take place using privately owned AVs, or using dedicated long-distance vehicles—such as interregional trains or other high speed shared autonomous transportation—which could be either publicly or privately run.

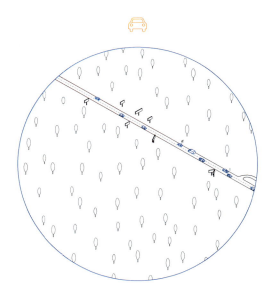

Road through exurban area.

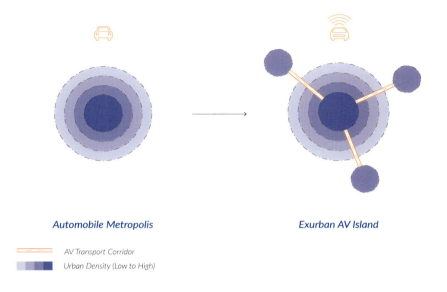

Automobile Metropolis *Exurban AV Island*

AV Transport Corridor
Urban Density (Low to High)

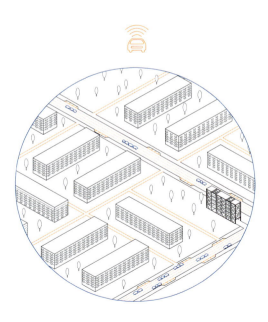

High-density development along AV-optimized arterial.

Urban Growth Patterns　　　123

Autonomous Compact: Shared-AV Densification

Another direction in terms of urban growth centres is the possibility of increased densities within existing urbanized areas. The current predominant model for such densification is the so-called transit-oriented development (TOD), under which areas near transit lines, and in particular transit stations, become the focus of urban development through planning and zoning. Given the nature of high-capacity transit lines, which require large investments and a spatially fixed infrastructure, TOD manifests in a linear form. On the contrary, the introduction of AVs, in particular shared autonomous vehicles, could allow for the possibility of a more distributed urban growth, through the more uniform distribution of mobility accessibility.

Shared Autonomous Vehicle (SAV) networks favour 'flat' cities (that is, cities that have an evenly distributed mix of work and residential buildings) and dense areas—this is because cars can be redeployed faster and service is quicker (see Fagnant and Kockelman for a simulation of this type of scenario).[12]

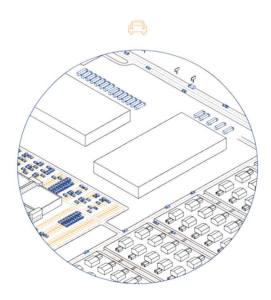

Low-density urban land uses.

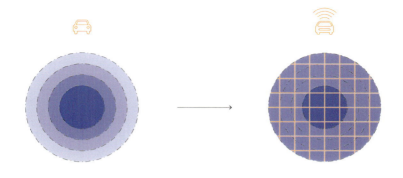

Automobile Metropolis   **Densified AV Transit Fabric**

AV Road Infrastructure
Urban Density (Low to High)

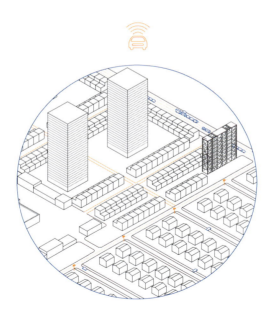

Car-free urban densification.

Urban Growth Patterns   125

PARKING

Besides restructuring the spatial organization of the city, the automobile had a major impact on urban land use in the form of parking;[13,14] the potential transformation of spaces currently used for parking is one of the first things remarked on about the impact of AVs on urban form. However, the possible impact on parking is intrinsically tied to the AV-ownership model and patterns of use as well as municipal street policy; this impact needs to be considered both spatially and temporally.

Spatially, a car most commonly requires a minimum of two parking spaces within the extents of a particular urban area: one at home, and another at a daytime destination. In reality, however, this number can be as high as eight parking spaces per car, ready at various urban destinations.[15] Consequently, parking often constitutes the single largest land use in urban centres. It is also considerable in other areas of the city, once all forms of parking, such as curb-side parking and residential garages, are accounted for.

Temporally, an average car spends about 90% of its lifetime parked and out of use. Furthermore, some studies indicate that up to 30% of downtown traffic is constituted of vehicles looking for parking.[16,17] The combination of these two factors accounts for the specific spatial patterns of parking, which manifests as large concentrations of parking space in surface lots and multi-storey garages, as well as a smaller scale distribution in residential areas. To serve the patterns of automobile use, and provide convenience, the amount of urban parking today is excessive, redundant and low in productivity. The introduction of AVs and a vehicle-to-infrastructure communication can have a major impact on parking in various ways, including the number and spatial distribution of parking spaces, as well as other novel functions coupled with parking, such as vehicle charging or even distributed energy networks.

Road Pricing and Parking: Symbiotic Relationships

One of the most common assumptions about AVs is that street parking will no longer be required in downtown areas and more of the street will therefore be available for pedestrians, cyclists and expanded sidewalk use. This is one possible future but there are others, depending on how proactive municipalities are in guiding their futures. If this apparently idyllic image does come to pass, it is a double-edged sword for municipalities since many rely heavily on parking income for their budgets. If parking income is no longer available then it is likely that municipalities will be forced to raise income through road pricing, a system currently used in many cities across the world such as London, Singapore, Stockholm and Milan. This may not seem to have immediate relevancy to the future of AVs, but the decision about how to move around a city is determined to a large extent on personal economics; if road usage charges are similar to or even higher than parking charges, then personal AVs will park near where their passengers are spending time to avoid road pricing charges. It is also worth mentioning that gas taxes, which are a significant source of income generation, will also dry up as cars are likely to be powered by electricity. As income from both parking and gas taxes may be highly disrupted in the future, it seems likely that road pricing in some form will be introduced to replace lost revenues.

There are many ways of pricing roads. London uses a 'cordon' model of pricing: once you pass a certain point moving into central London, the charge is triggered and then drivers may enter and leave the city centre as many times as they wish during the day without incurring additional charges. Called a 'Congestion Charge,'

this is a relatively unsophisticated model when looking at road usage generally, as it is used more as a deterrent from driving in the centre of London than to pay for road usage. As such, more sophisticated models of road pricing involving time or distances may be developed as technologies improve.

In the case of AVs, road pricing may also be used as a tool to discourage AVs from driving without passengers. In the cases of SAVs, the road pricing will be transferred directly to the passenger; however, if pricing is such that costs are incurred when the borders to the downtown areas are crossed (cordon pricing), SAVs working within those borders will avoid the cost and so will be incentivized to stay within those areas. It is easy to see how government policy in this regard will significantly impact the programmed behaviour of AVs.

Road pricing models that are based on time within a cordoned area could produce different road usage patterns for AVs, as they would discourage vehicles from staying in a certain area as well as reducing parking within that area. This may, however, increase vehicle kilometres travelled as the vehicles move in and out of the priced areas. In-depth modelling of AVs and SAVs with different road pricing models is necessary to determine likely outcomes and from the findings, optimal pricing structures could be chosen.

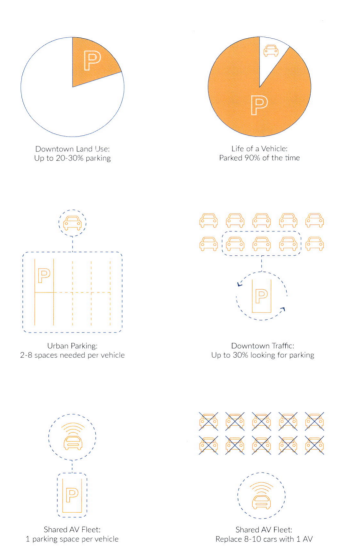

Figure 5.3. The space and time of parking and the city. Adapted from Rodrigue, J-P. **The Geography of Transport Systems *(2015).***

Programme

	Residential	Commercial
Onsite	*Driveway* *Residential Garage* *Underground Parking*	*Surface Parking Lot* *Multi-Storey Garage* *Underground Parkade* *Automated Parking*
Offsite	*Street Parking*	*(Paid) Street Parking*

Ownership

Figure 5.4. Parking typology by ownership and function.

Parking 129

Street Parking

In the absence of road pricing and rules prohibiting 'zombie' AVs (cars without passengers), a drop in the demand for street parking is probable. However, there is likely to be a significant increase in the necessity for zones for AVs to drop off and pick up passengers. One of the more significant problems which may arise is that of AVs idling and taking up curb space when passengers are not at their designated pick-up spots: if a passenger is delayed by a phone call or colleague at the office, this could entail their AV waiting an extra 10 or 15 minutes at the curb while they finish up their business. As such, the parking that will be needed is perhaps shorter term but still required. The difficulty arises from an empty AV paying for parking at any designated spot as this will require an automatic payment to be made directly from the AV to the city. If this is not resolved, or if AVs are not given sufficient parking spaces while waiting, they will likely circulate—similar to people looking for parking today.

Parkades

Within the current car parking paradigm, drivers are required to park their vehicle and leave it while they go about their business, creating the necessity for parking places in relatively close proximity to the popular destinations. Parking is thus competing directly with real estate for where most people want to go—downtown office areas, shopping areas, busy tourist attractions, etc. In the AV future, parking can be remote from the passenger's destination, if required at all. In the case of shared AVs, once a passenger has been taken to their destination, the car may then depart to drive other passengers and so parking is not required. If personally owned AVs are used, they may be dispatched to park at home or near the car's next task.

As we have seen from the streetside scenario, the freeing up of parking is not a given with AVs. In many cases, a cost of parking versus cost of driving analysis will determine whether parking locations and typologies change significantly: if road pricing is sufficiently high and/or zombie car driving is illegal in the jurisdiction, parking nearby may still be economic. As such, there is nothing to say that parkade use will change unless zombie cars are allowed to park at remote locations or the entire transport ecosystem moves towards shared AVs.

What may change significantly with SAV networks is that shopping malls and other unused parkades could be filled at night, as the SAVs will need to be stored when demand for them is low. It is, of course, possible that the vehicles could be stored on city streets; however, it seems likely that charging, cleaning and maintenance will be more efficient if there is a dedicated parkade to house them. In time, these parkades may be purpose built for AV cleaning, charging and maintenance. Even with personal AVs, it may be preferable to store them away from residences so that they can be charged more easily.

Potential Improved Parking Scenarios

Regardless of the caveats in the previous section, the decoupling of parking from other urban pro-grammes in combination with the ability of the AV to self-park offers the potential to restructure parking within the city. This gives rise to some exciting possibilities for urban design.

Parking Reshuffle:
Resize and Redistribute

In the case of SAVs, a significant reduction in the number of parking spaces is very possible: according to simulations by Fagnant and Kockelman[18] a shared AV can replace up to 12 conventional cars and eliminate 11 parking spaces. The introduction of SAVs would also reduce the need for separate daytime and nighttime parking for every vehicle.

Daytime and nighttime parking of privately owned automobiles.

Day/Nighttime Parking *Parking Reshuffle*

- Small-scale Residential Parking
- Large-scale Commercial Parking
- Medium-scale Automated Parking

Optimized carshare fleet and distributed automated parking.

Parking-Free Density Islands: Driving in Circles

Even with personally owned AVs and few SAVs, parking could be redistributed so that large-scale parking (surface lots and commercial garages) and small-scale parking (residential garages and curb-side parking) are both replaced by compact, medium size structures, optimally distributed in the city according to population density and daily commuting patterns. The possibility of relocating parking from the urban core to peripheral locations with lower land value is worthy of consideration in its own right. The exodus of parking from urban centres could result in parking-free islands of density, through the redevelopment of former surface parking lots and parking garages—or, where appropriate, the conversion of these spaces into public and/or green spaces, thus increasing urban amenities and liveability.[19]

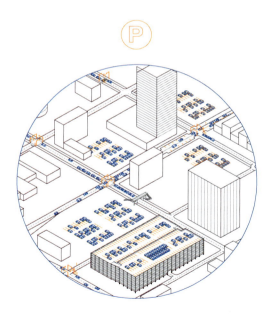

Urban centre with parking as a major land use.

Urban Centre Parking   *Parking-Free Density Island*

P *City Centre Parking*
P *Automated Parking Outside City Centre*

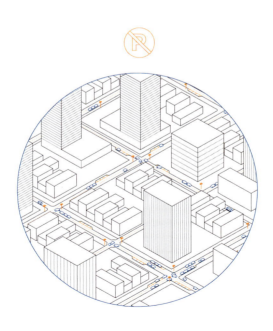

Urban centre without parking.

Parking   135

Parking Power: Vehicle-to-Grid Infrastructure Systems

The introduction of autonomous vehicles also presents the opportunity for parking to acquire a new function beyond the mere storage of unused vehicles. While it is to be seen what will become the dominant powering regime for future AVs, electric battery and hydrogen fuel cell technologies are certainly current contestants. This presents the opportunity for vehicles to be more than consumers of energy, but serve as temporary storage media (large batteries), and potentially produce power. Termed 'vehicle-to-grid power systems,' such models envision AVs serving as small-scale equalizers of the power grid, by drawing power from the grid during non-peak hours, and returning power during periods of peak demand.[20, 21] Logically, parking locations would be ideal sites where such connections to infrastructure could be deployed, hence the term "Parking Power."

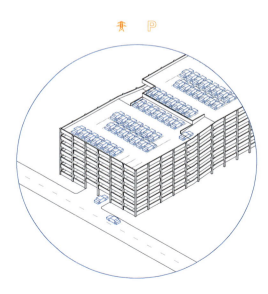

Multi-storey automobile parkade.

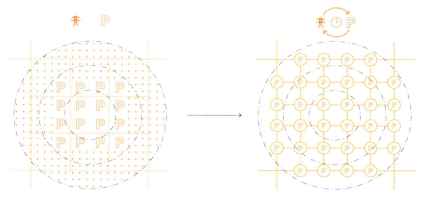

Parking vs. Energy Grid *Parking Power: Energy Grid Integration*

- P Mono-functional Parking
- P Electric Charging+Parking Station

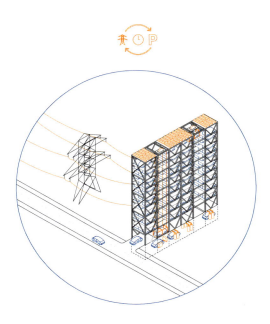

AV charging and parking station integrated to power grid.

Parking   137

ROAD NETWORK

One of the distinct features of road infrastructure systems, as opposed to other means of transport, is the highly hierarchical organization of road types. Figure 5.5 shows a basic network schematic according to speed and degree of direct access. One of the key issues with AVs is the behaviour of vehicles at points of intersection between different levels of road hierarchy. Currently, such interfaces are controlled by physical barriers and signage, in conjunction with drivers' knowledge of highway rules. With AVs, there is an opportunity for such interfaces to become increasingly 'virtual'—that is, rule-based. This virtualization also applies to the management of road transportation in its entirety, as a complex system. Current traffic management schemes rely on influencing the choice of agents through various incentives and control systems.[22] In a more integrated system, in which individual vehicles are able to participate in a self-organizing computation, there is potential for increased traffic efficiency through the reduced time required for decision-making and, where appropriate, the elimination of choice.

Intelligent Directions

The drawings that follow speculate on future scenarios regarding the way transportation infrastructure is conceived and operates.

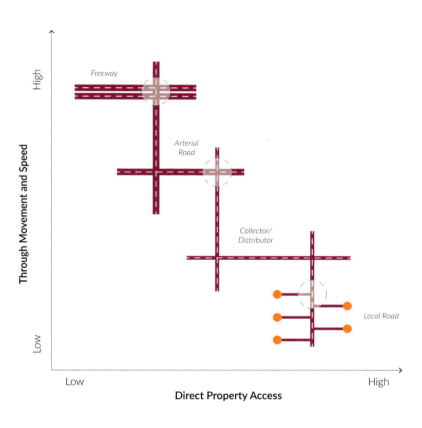

Figure 5.5. 20th century road network hierarchy.

Connected Roads:
AV Optimized Road Network

Upon the commercial implementation of AVs, they will begin to occupy the existing road infrastructure creating a need and/or opportunity to modify this infrastructure for the new technology. Within this context, there are multiple ways in which the existing road network can be made AV-ready. As the modification of infrastructure will be gradual, it will likely first affect highways and arterial roads in the form of dedicated AV-lanes, intelligent traffic beacons (see "Compass Pole," Chapter 7) and other devices. In this scenario, major roads would allow for efficient traffic flow through localized intelligent infrastructure; for the rest of the road network, AVs would rely more on their vehicle intelligence by navigating with a combination of autonomous sensory capabilities and offline map databases containing information on road space. In the case of growing urban regions, new infrastructure might be constructed already optimized for AVs. Upon the further unrolling of new infrastructure elements, or in the case of newly constructed roads, the entire road network could be characterized by a network of communicating infrastructure intelligence.

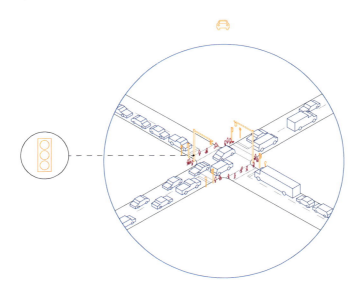

Typical intersection with traffic lights.

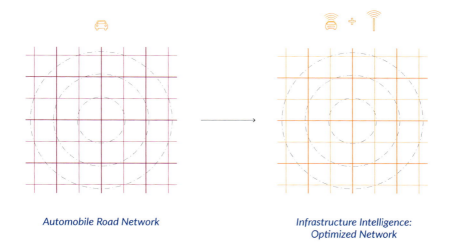

Automobile Road Network

Infrastructure Intelligence: Optimized Network

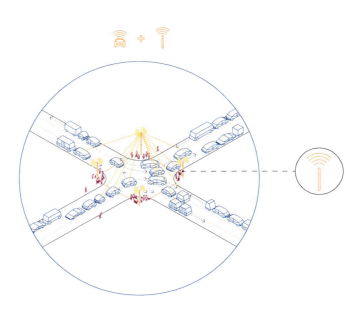

Automated intersection with traffic control beacons.

Road Network   141

Virtual Zoning:
Intelligent Infrastructure

A key aspect of the combination of vehicle and infrastructure intelligence would be the reduced necessity for the various physical elements of road infrastructure, some of which could be replaced by virtual databases stored in the vehicles or in the 'vehicular cloud.' In the case of a fully AV traffic flow, virtual control mechanisms would eliminate the need for physical control elements such as highway barriers, traffic lights and signs (except for those targeting pedestrians, which would be somewhat more difficult to entirely eliminate). Furthermore, the possibility of a virtual infrastructure would also allow rules to be more temporally flexible, without making changes to physical signage and barriers. For instance, speed limits on a road could change throughout the day in a matter of hours or minutes according to traffic flow, or there could be a switch between one-way and two-way traffic. Access for certain kinds of vehicles could be similarly regulated in this manner, for example only allowing trucks to pass at certain hours or having pedestrian- and bicycle-only areas at set times of the day[23,24] (also see "Unblock the Block" in Chapter 7).

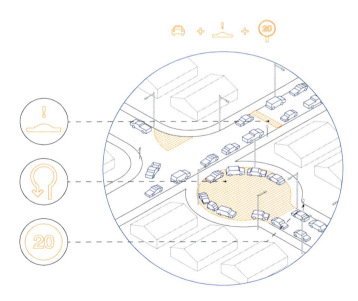

Physical zoning and fixed traffic rules.

142   Chapter 5 Urban Scale Impacts

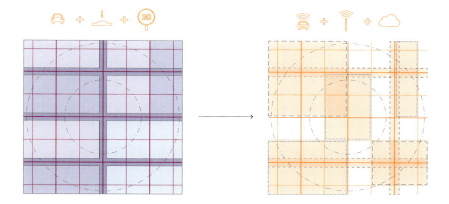

Rigid Zoning:
Physical Barriers and Signage

Flexible Zoning:
Infrastructure Intelligence

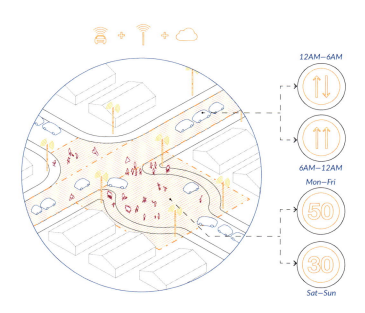

Virtual zoning and time-based traffic rules.

Road Network   143

Movement Ecologies: Responsive Traffic Flow

Another aspect of infrastructure intelligence is the possibility of two-way communication between vehicles and infrastructure. Unlike today's intelligent transportation systems, which still rely on human oversight for control, urban transportation in the future will likely consist of autonomous elements that are capable of sensing their environment while being simultaneously interconnected via digital networks and intelligent infrastructure. This will result in more complex interaction between software, hardware and humans, creating an assemblage of biological and machinic agents—so-called 'movement ecologies' on an urban scale. This will allow for coordination between the aforementioned 'top-down' responsive zoning of roads according to traffic flows and the parallel 'bottom-up' decision making by individual vehicles.[25,26]

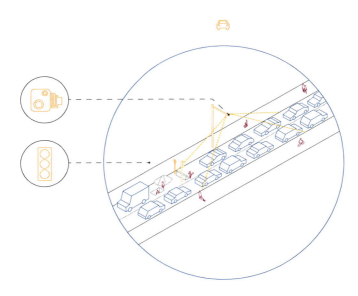

Traffic congestion.

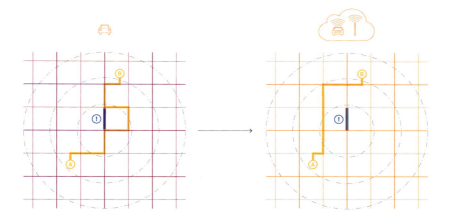

Conventional Route Planning: Path of Least Resistance

Real-Time Route Planning: Path Optimization

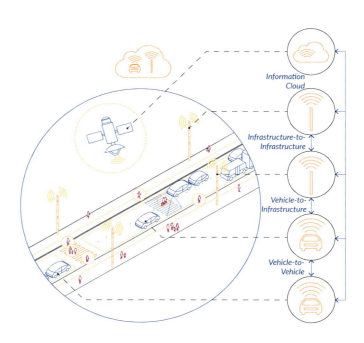

Inraction between AVs and intelligent infrastructure.

Road Network

MODALITIES

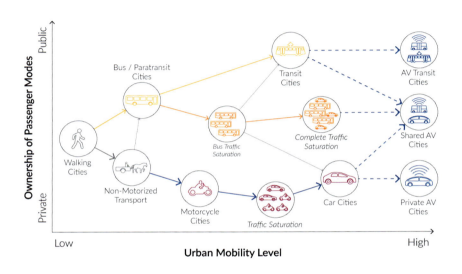

Figure 5.6. Urban transport development paths.
Adapted from J-P. Rodrigue, The Geography of Transport Systems (2015).

The relationship between the evolution of urban form and historically dominant modes of urban transportation can follow several paths (see Figure 5.6 for examples). Rodrigue describes it as a path-dependent process, which moves from low to high levels of mobility, and follows three main pathways based on ownership.[27] On one end of the spectrum are cities with public transportation ('Transit Cities'); on the other, car-dependent cities dominated by privately owned vehicles ('Car Cities'). In between the two is a third path consisting of cities with both public and private transportation ('Hybrid Cities').

Based on possible new ownership structures with the future proliferation of AVs, Figure 5.6 also speculates on the continuation of the three transportation pathways identified by Rodrigue for achieving even higher levels of mobility within each context. Evolving from Transit Cities, 'Transit-AV Cities' would be characterized by the continued importance of public transportation, enhanced by including AVs in the transit fleet (for instance, to replace or introduce community-scale shuttle services in areas where currently public transit is not economical). On the other hand, Car Cities would evolve into 'Private AV Cities,' characterized by the continued importance of private vehicle ownership and relatively high number of vehicles. Thirdly, and perhaps most importantly, all currently dominant transportation models,

especially current Hybrid Cities, have the potential to evolve into 'Shared AV Cities.' This type would become dominated by shared autonomous vehicles, and possibly feature the inclusion of AVs in the existing transit services as well.

In addition to differences according to dominant transportation modalities, cities also vary in terms of their movement patterns. As shown in Figure 5.7 (redrawn after Rodrigue[28] and Bertaud[29]), four major types can be identified according to the degree of organization of major traffic flows (organized vs. disorganized), and the complexity of urban structure (monocentric vs. polycentric).

Generally, "cities with a higher level of reliance on public transit tend to be monocentric with a higher level of organized flows, while cities depending more on the automobile tend to be polycentric with a more disorganized structure of flows."[30] Figure 5.8 shows this by combining the matrix of movement patterns with the three dominant modality paths and their counterparts under a proliferation of AVs, as identified in Figure 5.6.

Modalities and Choice of Modes

The diagrams that follow discuss development of cities based on their mobility decisions.
In urban environments with

Modalities   147

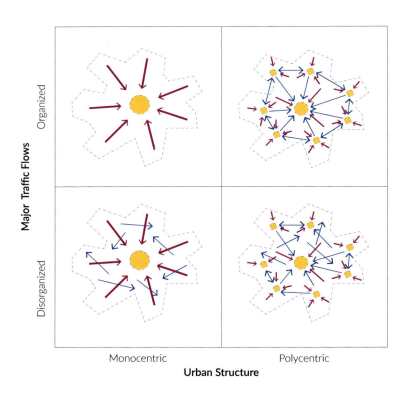

*Figure 5.7. Urban movement patterns.
Adapted from J-P. Rodrigue,* The Geography of Transport Systems *(2015), and A. Bertaud
"Metropolis: A Measure of the Spatial Organization of 7 Large Cities" (2001).*

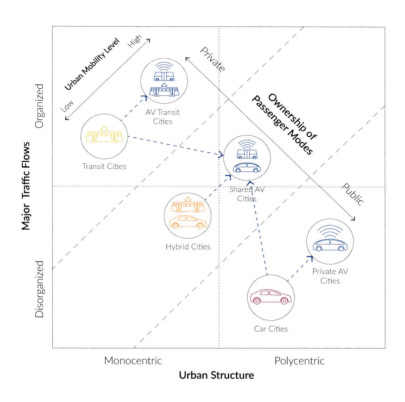

Figure 5.8. Urban movement patterns and modes of transport.

Modalities

Distributed Public: AV-Integrated Transit

developed transit networks, AV technology presents the opportunity to expand and complement existing mobility modes and services. In general, traditional transit services are able to operate efficiently and maintain economies of scale by relying on either spatially fixed infrastructure (such as rail, subway or streetcar services), and/or on itineraries fixed in the short term (days/months) and only subject to changes in a larger temporal frame (years), such as bus services. Autonomous vehicle technology, by being scaleable from a single passenger pod to a city bus without a proportional added cost of drivers, allows for new models of distributed public transit networks, made up of a range of vehicles in terms of size and route flexibility.

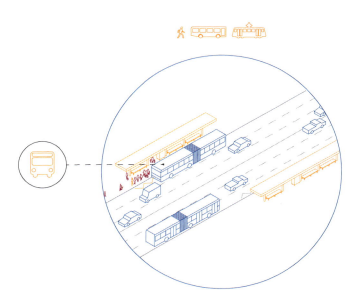

Typical urban bus exchange.

**Transit City:
Movement via Public Transit**

**AV-Transit City:
Modal Integration**

- Walking/Cycling
- Bus Transit
- Rail/Rapid Transit
- Flexi-Shuttle
- Fixed-Route AV Shuttle

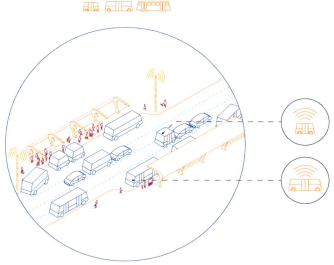

AV transit shuttle exchange.

Modalities 151

Door-to-Door Mixed Mode: Shared AV Cities

Urban settings with an evolved integration of public transit and automobile use, such as exemplified in the park and ride model, present the opportunity for the integration of SAVs into the transit system. This would be particularly effective in areas too low in density for public transit to function efficiently but which could be served conveniently using shared vehicles. The evolution of the hybrid model into what is termed here "Door-to-Door Mixed Mode" is also interesting in terms of potential business models and ownership structures. For instance, shared vehicle schemes can have multiple tiers ranging from a private vehicle to a carpooling situation; the schemes themselves could be offered from a range of providers, from private companies to services owned or subsidized by the government for certain geographical areas or socio-economic groups. The scenario thus suggests new models of multi-modality, but also poses questions regarding the binary of personal and public transport.

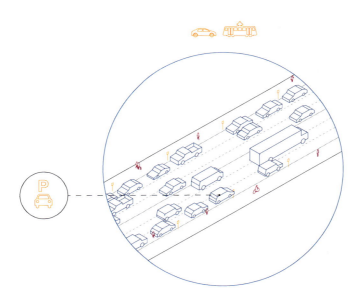

Urban arterial road with kerbside parking.

152   Chapter 5 Urban Scale Impacts

Hybrid City:
Driving to/from Transit

Shared AV City:
Distributed Transit

.... Walking/Cycling
———— Driving
▦▦▦▦▦ Rail/Rapid Transit
———— Shared AV

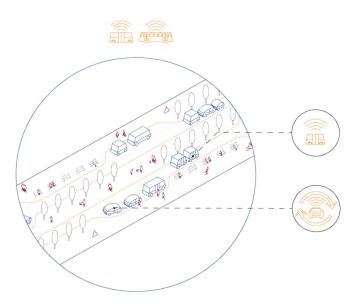

Urban street with drop-off zones and reclaimed lanes.

Modalities   153

Private AV Commuting: Live/Work/Play Nomadism

In cities characterized by high levels of automobile dependency—in reality, the majority of North American urban areas—the advent of autonomous vehicles can arguably have the biggest impact. The model of shared AVs is highly significant here, capable of dramatically reducing the amount of traffic. At the same time, it is valuable to consider the other extreme, that of continuing private vehicle ownership. The impact in this case may be in the quality of the commuting experience. While the automobile in its different forms already allows for the mobility of various types of functions (for example, limousines or ambulances), vehicle automation would greatly expand the possibilities of new combinations of living, working and playing in the context of the private automobile. As explored in the previous section on urban expansion, the increased convenience of commuting, a so-called 'Live/Work/Play Nomadism,' might alter the way in which the space and time of the 'car' is conceived and programmed with activities.

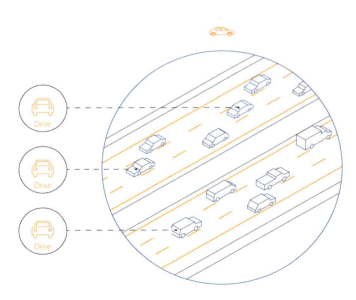

Automobiles on a typical twin carriageway.

Car City:
Driving Between Live, Work, and Play

Private AV City:
Live—Work—Play Nomadism

——— Driving

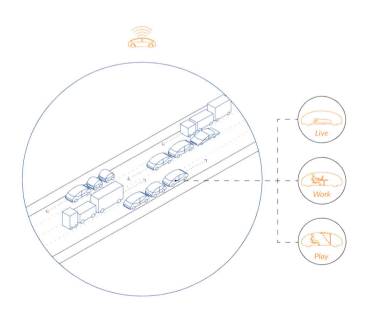

Platoons of AVs on an intelligent highway.

Modalities   155

Notes

1   'Last mile' meaning the last mile of a trip by public transportation—often from a more high capacity mode to a more local route which often has poor service due to less demand. It is this part of the trip that often discourages people from taking transit—also see Chapter 5.

2   Peter O. Muller, "Transportation and Urban Form-Stages in the Spatial Evolution of the American Metropolis," in *The Geography of Urban Transportation*, eds. Susan Hanson, Genevieve Giuliano, Third Edition (New York: Guilford Press, 2004), 62.

3   John S. Adams, "Residential Structure of Midwestern Cities," *Annals of the Association of American Geographers* 60, no. 1 (1970): 56.

4   Muller, "Transportation and Urban Form," 29.

5   Ibid, 38.

6   Wolfgang Gruel and Joseph M. Stanford, "Assessing the Long-Term Effects of Autonomous Vehicles: A Speculative Approach," *Transportation Research Procedia* 13 (January 1, 2016): 18–29.

7   Stelios Rodoulis, "The Impact of Autonomous Vehicles on Cities," *Journeys*, (November 2014): 17.

8   Paul Godsmark et al., "The Coming of the Next Disruptive Technology" (The Conference Board of Canada, 2015), 33.

9   Joseph Coughlin and Luke Yoquinto, "Autonomous Cars and the Future of the Commute," http://www.slate.com/articles/ technology/future_tense/2015/05/ autonomous_cars_and_the_future_of_the_ commute.html.

10   Muller, "Transportation and Urban Form," 42–50.

11   Robert Bruegmann, "Driverless Car Could Defy the Rules of Sprawl," *Bloomberg*, February 21, 2012, https://www.bloomberg.com/view/ articles/2012-02-21/driverless-car-could- defy-rules-of-sprawl-commentary-by- robert-bruegmann.

12   Daniel Fagnant, Kara Kockelman, and Prateek Bansal, "Operations of Shared Autonomous Vehicle Fleet for Austin, Texas, Market," *Transportation Research Record: Journal of the Transportation Research Board* 2536 (January 1, 2015): 98–106; Daniel Fagnant and Kara Kockelman, "The Travel and Environmental Implications of Shared Autonomous Vehicles, Using Agent-Based Model Scenarios," *Transportation Research Part C: Emerging Technologies* 40 (2014): 1–13.

13   Martin V. Melosi, "The Automobile Shapes The City" (The University of Michigan Dearborn & Benson Ford Research Centre, 2005), http://www.autolife.umd. umich.edu/Environment/E_Casestudy/E_ casestudy.htm.

14   Donald Shoup, *The High Cost of Free Parking* (London: Routledge, 2017).

15   Godsmark et al., "The Coming of the Next Disruptive Technology," 17.

16   Fagnant and Kockelman, "The Travel and Environmental Implications of Shared Autonomous Vehicles," 9.

17   Shoup, *The High Cost of Free Parking*.

18   Fagnant and Kockelman, "The Travel and Environmental Implications of Shared Autonomous Vehicles," 8.

19   Peter Wayner, "How Driverless Cars Could Turn Parking Lots into City Parks," *The Atlantic*, August 5, 2015, https:// www.theatlantic.com/technology/ archive/2015/08/driverless-cars-robot- cabs-parking-traffic/400526/.

20   AnnaLisa Meyboom and Sara Costa Maia, "Persuasive User Interfaces to Match Plug-In Electric Vehicle (PEV) Charging to Renewable Availability and off-Peak Power Demand" (University of British Columbia TIPSlab, 2014), http://www. tipslabubc.com/images/documents/ TIPSlabPersuasiveInterfaces.pdf.

21   JA Peças Lopes et al., "Smart Charging Strategies for Electric Vehicles: Enhancing Grid Performance and Maximizing the Use of Variable Renewable Energy Resources," in *EVS24 International Battery, Hybrid and Fuel Cell Electric Vehicle Symposium*, Stavanger, Norveška, 2009.

22 Mohammad Mirshahi et al., "Active Traffic Management: The Next Step in Congestion Management" (Federal Highways Administration, US Department of Transportation, 2007), http://international.fhwa.dot.gov/pubs/pl07012/.

23 Ted Gregory, "The Future of Speed Limits in Chicago," *Chicago Tribune*, January 5, 2014, http://articles.chicagotribune.com/2014-01-05/news/ct-future-speed-limits-20140105_1_variable-speed-limits-traffic-sensors-atm.

24 Bidoura Khondaker and Lina Kattan, "Variable Speed Limit: A Microscopic Analysis in a Connected Vehicle Environment," *Transportation Research Part C: Emerging Technologies* 58 (2015): 146–159.

25 Mario Gerla et al., "Internet of Vehicles: From Intelligent Grid to Autonomous Cars and Vehicular Clouds," in *Internet of Things (WF-IoT), 2014 IEEE World Forum* (IEEE, 2014), 241–246.

26 Godsmark et al., "The Coming of the Next Disruptive Technology," 28.

27 Jean-Paul Rodrigue, Claude Comtois, and Brian Slack, *The Geography of Transport Systems* (Abingdon, Oxon: Routledge, 2016), https://people.hofstra.edu/geotrans/.

28 Ibid.

29 Alain Bertaud, "The Spatial Organization of Cities: Deliberate Outcome or Unforeseen Consequence?," 2004, https://escholarship.org/uc/item/5vb4w9wb.

30 Rodrigue, et al., *The Geography of Transport Systems*.

Chapter 6
Urban Theories and Autonomous Vehicles

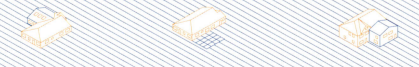

Chapter 6
Urban Theories and Autonomous Vehicles

The street is not only a contested space in terms of its functionality but also in terms of who claims design autonomy over it. These two contentious issues are interrelated since whoever has design authority over the street decides who gets to use it. The issues become further interrelated by the question of why the space of the street is contested: is it simply because there are many demands on the street and only limited space, or is it because the current process of designing the street and choosing which groups are prioritized is problematic?

In terms of how we choose who designs the street, it is not a straightforward process. We elect groups of people and those people hire staff who carry out the design of the street or, at a minimum, set the priorities for street design to be implemented by consultants. However, in any given city or jurisdiction, certain disciplines carry more sway over the design. This is a discussion which has been had by the notable urban theorist Jan Gehl, who points out that those who have data have a stronger voice because they can quantify the problem and the solution clearly. Gehl advocates

for counting pedestrians and cyclists with equal zeal to counting cars. This gives both quantifiable evidence and a voice to underrepresented pedestrians and cyclists, thereby changing design decisions.[1] We can also look to the example of the preliminary design of a large interchange which is landing in an urban area: for example the case of the redesign of the Brunette Avenue/Highway 1 interchange in New Westminster, British Columbia. The preliminary design process involved the traffic engineer articulating what was necessary for free flow conditions at the interchange and determining the interchange configuration based on that modelling. That modelling, done in isolation of all other disciplines, determined the alignment and the road design of the interchange, and also limited the urban design decisions that could be made. In this instance, the traffic engineer had the loudest voice and the interchange was configured overwhelmingly to favour the concerns of the traffic engineering discipline. Should the bridge engineer or the urban design group (including landscape architects in this case) have had the larger voice, the interchange design would have been significantly different, favouring instead the values put forward as primary concerns by these disciplines.[2] These examples illustrate the critical issue of disciplinary authority over the street.

While disciplinary authority will perhaps soon be an historic way of looking at how we divide knowledge, we will have the legacy of the system for a long time. In the opinion of the author, we are moving towards a 'post-disciplinary' state where people will still have deep and valuable expertise. However, the areas of their expertise may be better thought of as deep spheres of knowledge which are positioned relative to other people's spheres; the artificial linear boundaries drawn between disciplines will fade as many spheres take over.

However, the current situation being what it is, in order to position the inevitable re-designing of the street for autonomous vehicles within a broader design discussion, it is worthwhile considering what contemporary theorists in different disciplines have to say about the design of the street and which design theories may be beneficial in designing the new AV city. Various disciplines claim expertise on design of the street: engineering, transportation planning, planning, urban design, landscape architecture and architecture. These professions have differing approaches to the design of the street, all based on social and cultural concerns. These approaches, or theories, are articulated in their specific professions' writings on the theory of design of the street. Some of the disciplines are more interested in logistics and measurable outcomes, others more in the social and cultural concerns about design and public use. This book focuses more on the social and cultural theories but it is relevant to understand where the interests of different disciplines lie, and what those interests are. The first part of this chapter discusses the positions of the various professions in relation to the design of the street; the second part focuses more on cultural design theories. Further discussion of theories is also to be found in Chapter 9, relating to technology and the city.

Which Professions Govern Design of the Street?

Architecture

The role of the design of the city as a whole has always been in flux, and the design of the street with it. As discussed previously, some of the orchestrators of the Garden City and the suburban organization of the streets were architects, as were the designers of visionary city projects such as Le Corbusier and Frank Lloyd Wright. Architects have also contributed to design of the street in special projects—Sir Christopher Wren redesigned the street system of London after the 1666 fire, and both Alberti (c.1470) and Vitruvius (c. 27 BCE) included comments on design of the street in their treatises. However, in contemporary society the architect is not recognized as the designer of the street. Some say the architect left the field after Modernism when the discipline, made up of baby boomers, became suspicious of architecture as an "inevitable coalescence of power and established regimes of authority"[3] and moved to smaller scale efforts. Others assert that planners claimed jurisdiction over the city much earlier.[4,5,6] One might also argue that the architect's obsession with form has relegated the architect to the confines of the building; the increasing complexity of the building project today has likely reinforced this neglect of the project of the city. In any case, architecture as a discipline has been increasingly marginalized in the design of the city and its streets as other disciplines move in. This is highlighted by Dana Cuff and Roger Sherman in their introduction to *Fast-Forward Urbanism*[7] in which they state:

> architecture has, to a large extent, abandoned the city [... and] the city's principal players—be they developers or policy-makers—have come to see architecture as irrelevant. In the latter case, it is more accurate to say that the city has abandoned architecture.[8]

Cuff and Sherman call on architects to once again engage with the city and help solve some of the very difficult problems that come with issues such as mass movement to cities, natural disasters and human-caused disasters as a result of terrorism or wars.

It should be emphasized, however, that architectural theories on design are potentially highly valuable as the space of the street becomes more contested: architectural theory as the origin of 'design thinking' focuses on solving complex cultural and social problems which also include technological aspects. Architectural design solutions generally question all constraints; solutions are synthetic and propose spatial and object configurations that are multifunctional or provide simultaneous solutions to several problems. On occasion, these approaches are highly celebrated[9]—but rarely are architects asked to design the streets of a city. As mentioned, architecture today is primarily applied to buildings but it has the potential to create solutions to the problems of the highly contested space of the street. This assertion is what led to the development of the field of Urban Design.[10] As such, there is a flux in these two professional areas[11] and it is difficult to draw discrete professional boundaries. However, in any case it is clear that the disciplinary skills of the architect—the ability to imagine the future in multiple forms and the potential of a design approach which incorporates a broad range of cultural and social concerns—are a powerful

162   Chapter 6 Urban Theories and Autonomous Vehicles

tool for designing the future, no matter in which discipline we deposit this 'architectural' design knowledge.

Engineering

I would argue, however, that the history of street design in North America does not show a 'ground-losing' trend by architects but rather the exclusion of architects from the infrastructure design process from the beginning.[12] Granted, the history of infrastructure design in North America dates from around the late 1800s so it is not a particularly long one; but, as previously discussed in Chapter 4, we have inherited the idea of requiring a military to build infrastructure from the French tradition. The military and its engineering offspring have dominated the design of roads since their beginnings.[13,14] Engineers generally focus on the social concerns of safety, functionality and efficiency; through this focussed expertise, they have maintained a firm hold on the field in the name of public safety and efficiency. This was demonstrated when engineers were the ones called in to solve the safety problems caused by the automobile upon its introduction in the street in the early 1900s.[15] While extremely skilled in optimizing roads for transport efficiency and safety, dealing with matters of social and cultural concern outside of safety and efficiency are not in the realm of the engineer's expertise. As such, if any social or cultural issues are brought to the space of the street,

other disciplines generally take on these concerns. This collaboration between disciplines takes many forms and hierarchies of decision-making.

Engineers are likely to continue to take a primary lead on design of streets for AVs but will need to work to a much greater extent in collaboration with design disciplines. The ability of the engineer to problem-solve is invaluable when confronted with problematic conditions and, similar to the original role of the engineer as 'arbiter-in-chief' of the street space, the role of solving the problems of the new AV street using technology is still in the firm hands of the engineer. However, engineers are increasingly realizing that the biggest problems to solve are not with the technology itself but with the social aspects—namely the way the human interacts with the technology.[16] Two major aspects relating to AVs are the ways in which people engage with the technology—pedestrian/AV interfaces, for example—as well as how to mediate the contested space of the street and all of the social implications of doing so. It is these challenges in particular that will increasingly require intense collaboration with other disciplines.

Transportation Planning

In order to deal with the challenges of transportation decision-making in the complex public context, there has now developed a specific discipline called transportation (or transport) planning. The origins of transportation planning came about in the 1940s, when "it was apparent that if certain relationships between land use and travel could be measured, these relationships could be used as a means to project future travel."[17] Analytic models were developed in the 1950s and in 1954 the National Committee on Urban Transportation was created, which for the first time documented comprehensive procedures for transportation planning.[18] This is a multidisciplinary profession that primarily deals with the planning of all forms of transport routes including streets, highways, bike lanes and public transport. It involves multiple stakeholders and looks at analysis and planning of the different modes of transport. The field of transportation planning is primarily concerned with a rational planning model that defines measurable goals and objectives, primarily relating to environmental performance. The field includes planning decisions, as well as engineering modelling of transport modes and routes, and aspects of behavioural psychology as it relates to people's choices regarding modes of transport. This field has been active in modelling and simulating networks of shared autonomous vehicles[19,20] and will continue to play an important role in predicting volume impacts from autonomous transportation decisions on all modes of transport.

Planning

The discipline of planning itself dates back to the National Conference on City Planning in Washington, D.C. in 1909.[21] Its role includes the administration of legislation, data analysis, project management and public consultation.[22] Current conversations in planning are very much centred on data-driven design and include discussions of sustainability and the health impacts of planning decisions. From its inception, the discipline clearly understood the organizing power of new infrastructures of hydroelectricity and automobiles and their ability to spawn communities, as outlined by the Regional Planning Association of America (formed in 1923 and lasting 10 years). In its modern-day form, the discipline of planning focuses to a large extent on the administration, bureaucracy and code-writing for the building forms of the city. Urban design as a specialized focus in planning has now developed into a discipline in its own right. Thus, those in planning who are dealing with design of the street are more likely to be in the professional area of urban design than that of planning.

Urban Design

In *Urban Design* (2009), Alex Krieger suggests that urban designers should take on infrastructure:

> Apart from the occasional efforts to "architecturalize" infrastructure, as in the various mega-

structure proposals of the 1960s (a source of fascination today), neither planners nor designers have played a significant role in transportation or other urban infrastructure planning. Thus, it has become another sphere for an urban designer to attempt to address at both the pragmatic level of calibrating demands for mobility with other social needs and in advancing new (or reviving 125-year-old) ways in which city form and transportation systems may be integrated.[23]

By implication this suggests that, as of 2009 when the book was published, urban designers had not taken on transportation or other infrastructural planning. Urban design has its own professional internal debate on what the field entails, a debate which has been ongoing since the birth of the profession in 1956 at a conference on the topic at Harvard University.[24,25] In the founding conference on Urban Design in 1956, José Luis Sert, the organizer of the conference and Dean of the Harvard Graduate School of Design, asserted that the field "is that part of city planning which deals with the physical form of the city" and that it is "the most creative phase of city planning, in which imagination and artistic capacities play the important part." Secondly he stated that the purpose of the conference was "to find the common basis for the joint work of the Architect, the Landscape Architect, and the City Planner... Urban Design [being] wider than the scope of these three professions."[26] In

general then, the field sits between the design disciplines (of architecture and landscape architecture) and planning and takes up design at the scale of the city. As such, it is surprising that this is not the field which would have the mandate of the design of the street.

In the last number of years, the profession has been criticized by Charles Waldheim (Harvard Graduate School of Design) and others for being too focused on the cultural nostalgia of "New Urbanism."[27] New Urbanism, while having nothing explicitly problematic about its list of goals, focuses on walkable cities with a range of housing types and business. The critique of New Urbanism is that it looks to a traditional and privileged model of what a city should be rather than addressing the messy, sprawling, and often underprivileged metropolises of the world today. As such, it is hard to imagine how the theorists of New Urbanism will discuss the AV as it is hardly relevant in the New Urbanist model of the walkable community: why would one need an autonomous vehicle if one can walk? Contemporary theorists in urban design have proposed new disciplinary models which address issues of the complexity of the city as a plurality with many divided parcels, owners and opinions.[28] Other current theorists, such as Mark Shepard, Dana Cuff, Roger Sherman and Scott Lloyd, deal more with technology and infrastructure and the city (looked

Which Professions Govern Design of the Street?   165

at in more depth in Chapter 9). It is likely that the city of the AV will be influenced by these types of ideas—but only if the discipline engages not just at the theoretical level, but also operationally with the scale of the street and the interactions of technology, public space and the street.

Landscape Architecture

Landscape architects have a history of designing streets and, more importantly, designing landscapes with streets that support the larger intent of a project. As mentioned in Chapter 4, Frederick Law Olmstead designed Parkways as well as street configurations for new subdivisions which are still relevant today. Landscape architects are also asked to design road cross-sections, probably more than any other profession. However, it is landscape architecture's more current theories and thinking which make it the most likely disciplinary framework to engage with designing the new AV landscape.

Current theories in this discipline are highly engaged with the issues regarding the incorporation of ecologies (natural and artificial) and infrastructure, whereas most discussions of the street outside the discipline do not consider environmental concerns or ecological thinking even though they are increasingly a concern in city design. As Pierre Bélanger points out so succinctly:

Fordist modes of production and Taylorist principles of efficiency have oversimplified the ecology of urban economies and underplayed the social role of urban infrastructures, by way of marginalizing and suppressing the living, biophysical systems. At the center of this ecological divide are the historic practices of engineering and planning that operated well into the twentieth century, under the tenets of efficiency and control through centralization.[29,30]

Landscape architects have suggested in a series of recent manifestos[31] that their discipline should be the one to oversee urbanism, due to its ability to incorporate environmental concerns and ecological thinking. Ian McHarg originally presented this idea in 1956 at a conference on Urban Design but the idea was not carried forward and planning essentially took over the stewardship of urban design for another 50 years.[32] However, there is substantial merit to this argument, which will be elaborated on in the next section, even though to date limited application has been demonstrated.[33] This may change with the increasing need for designers to participate in the design of the increasingly contested space of the urban environment, much of which is the space of the street.

It seems critical that ecological concerns be brought to the issue of the street at multiple scales. In particular, there is great potential to address the new AV-networked city within the current thinking that considers the environment of the city as a landscape which incorporates natural and artificial systems. In this case what is being referred to is a more literal discussion of ecology, but it is the metaphorical discussion introduced by this discipline which is also critical.

Cultural Theories for Design of the AV City

An innovation in landscape architecture theory evolved in the 2000s, moving landscape architecture from a more pastoral documentation of culture and role as historic protector of the environment to a more active design strategy, shaping large infrastructural systems and integrated urban environments. The call for this innovation can, amongst others, be found in the publication of Strang's "Infrastructure as Landscape"[34] (1996), events such as the Landscape Urbanism conference of 1997 (Graham Foundation, Chicago) as well as in James Corner's *Recovering Landscape* (1999) where he laments the "sentimentality and conservatism" of the current profession and calls for the discipline to engage with the opportunities of using landscape to evolve the built environment.[35]

The supporters of the Landscape Urbanism approach posited that architecture and urban design were not adequately taking on the condition of the contemporary urban city. Their position stated that architecture in the Modernist period, in its zeal for machine-like buildings and universal housing, proposed over-scaled environments incompatible with human occupation and devoid of community and human interaction.[36] Architecture's subsequent swing to the post-Modern relegated it to the production of images that spoke to multiple audiences but which, in fact, served mobile international capital and relegated architecture to producing form within the bounds of the property line. Planning was likewise heavily criticized for having abandoned design in favour of policy, procedure and public consultation.[37] Urban Design, as previously mentioned, was more interested in promoting small-scale walkable communities and was reluctant to engage with the design of the larger city. Landscape Urbanism stepped in with the mandate to address large-scale sites and larger-scale issues with a detailed knowledge of ecological systems.

The resulting movement developed over the course of a decade and its manifesto was documented in *The Landscape Urbanism Reader* (2006).[38] The basis of Landscape Urbanism is the idea that landscape architecture has a "capacity to theorize sites, territories, ecosystems, networks, and infrastructures" and in particular that its "thematics of organization, dynamic interaction, ecology and technique point to a looser, emergent urbanism, more akin to the real complexity of cities and offering an alternative to the rigid mechanisms of centralist planning."[39] It is easy to see from this concise description how the application of this type of thinking may be relevant to the design of the new AV city. A shared autonomous vehicle (SAV) network, for example, is not an isolated system; in order to generate understanding of the network dynamics, the behaviour of the network will be heavily influenced by urban characteristics such as accumulations of business or housing in certain areas which affect demand locations and wait times at peak hours.[40] Cities which are more segregated will have longer wait times at morning peak hours, for example, due to the time necessary for cars who have already made a trip to return to the residential area. While network design theory can discuss different parameters that may influence an increase or decrease in travel and wait times, in this case it is the urban form itself that is causing the wait times. A more holistic design methodology will document these characteristics and their interrelationships, apply them to the metaphorical ecosystem of the SAV and its relationship to urban form, and thereby generate insights of where an intervention in urban policy may be applicable.

It should be noted, though, that this type of application of the theory is not a conventional use. Landscape Urbanism has mainly been applied to large-scale sites in suburban and peripheral urban areas as a theory to inform the design of the landscape.[41] What is being suggested here is that the ideas behind the theory are applied to the infrastructure of the AV city across the city as a whole and not just on one land parcel: for example, planning the infrastructure and routing for a network of automated transit shuttles or a series of parking facilities for AVs outside the city centres. These are usually planned by transportation planners or engineers but there are invariably many other transportation networks and societal factors involved which may also be interrelated, drawn and understood, with design action resulting from the understanding of the larger urban system—in short, an approach more akin to Landscape Urbanism.

Infrastructural Systems

The media through which Landscape Urbanism was proposed to operate can be defined as infrastructural systems and the public landscapes. It was this adoption of the infrastructural systems that incorporated the manmade into the natural and blurred the distinction between the two. Whereas landscape architecture had always been about creating infrastructural systems through the manipulation of the land, it had never been explicitly put forward as such. The idea of moving 'landscape' as a concept from its role as a visual representation of nature and a generator of the pastoral to an active manipulator of forces and a large-scale working machine is a process that is still ongoing. Strang outlined the basis of this infrastructural idea at the time of its introduction, stating "Designers have most often been charged with hiding, screening and cosmetically mitigating infrastructure, in order to maintain the image of the untouched natural surroundings of an earlier era. They are rarely asked to consider infrastructure as an opportunity, as a fundamental component of urban and regional form."[42] He goes on to identify the potential for infrastructure to be used for multiple purposes in contrast to the tendency to engineer for a single use and he remarks upon how different that approach is from a design approach which engages biological materials (plants, soil, etc.).

Strang also points out that infrastructural systems are very complex and in many ways similar to biological systems—except that human systems are not resilient. This may be even truer and increasingly problematic when we shift to an AV network whose collapse could paralyze a city entirely. Strang also stresses that human systems should incorporate biological systems rather than neutralize them—an idea which is now accepted as a clearly desirable design approach—and rejects the separation between nature and man-made. He further speculates, "It is not only imaginable

but probable that the current shift to a predominantly technological environment has provoked a (similarly) profound spiritual crisis—one that can be relieved by reconsidering the relationship between urban settings and natural processes."[43] This is likely to be exacerbated by the introduction of even more technology into our lives through the significant contribution of the AV.

Strang considers infrastructure to be the result of bringing technology together with nature; he is convinced that linking "technological developments with the organic principles of nature" provides an opportunity for designers.[44] He believes nature and infrastructure together should be a major determinant of urban form and he calls for architects, landscape architects, engineers and biologists to carry this out. Strang is a proponent of multidisciplinary design projects and runs a multidisciplinary firm. However, his examples and discussion are still very general in form, expressing an idea and a desire but not a clear path to get there or any particular projects to support the case. He is, however, one of the first to begin discussing designing the landscape and infrastructure together as one operational component and is quite clear that he envisions these two concepts should be brought together—just not so clear on how to do this.

System Non-Boundaries

Another factor which supports the idea of thinking of infrastructural systems as landscape is the ability to approach the design issue from a position of the system boundaries and not the geographic boundaries the systems cross. As Landscape Urbanism evolved, the view of the city was changing—it was seen as a dynamic system, in flux and responsive. It was also evident that the traditional notion of the city with a downtown and suburbs was no longer relevant; instead we can see cities becoming multiple centres which are connected by a circulation system which comprises various networks—transportation, communication, production, consumption and waste management. The political boundaries are irrelevant to some of the networks but provide boundaries and gradients to others, depending on what those networks are and how they are tied to these organizational structures. As Charles Waldheim says in his 'manifesto' for landscape urbanism, "contemporary landscape urbanism practices recommend the use of infrastructural systems and the public landscapes they engender as the very ordering mechanism of the urban field itself, shaping and shifting the organization of urban settlement and its inevitably indeterminate economic, political and social futures."[45]

The theory of infrastructure as an organizational tool is very strongly positioned to take on the design of the new AV city. The issue that arises is that the organizational framework for the new AV city will likely exist mainly in software. When we look at the concepts illustrated in this book such as 'Unblock the Block,' 'Road Network Hierarchies' and 'Intelligent Directions,' what we see is that spatial organization of traffic flows does not need to be the 'hardware' of the road but can now be embedded in the software providing directions to the AV. Whether this software is explicitly provided as infrastructural wireless directions to AVs or coded within the proprietary mapping systems of the AV is yet to be determined. It would be highly advantageous to a city to be able to adjust its instructions to AVs live so that they could block off affected streets when there are events such as races or parades, or even emergency incidents. If this were to be done, cities would have to take on another software control system which brings its own caveats and costs. It is possible that less affluent cities will simply produce maps which give information to programmers on restrictions on parking, speed limits at various times and no entry areas, for example. Street signs will in either case be unnecessary, and since they are costly to a municipality will likely end up as sentimental wall decorations.

Part of the impetus for this transformation of landscape architecture, and the basis of some of the largest projects completed within these theoretical bounds, was the recognition that landscape architects are called in to remediate sites.[46] The remediation strategies are often landscape strategies with a biological basis. In these cases, the design work is truly intended as an infrastructural intervention. As Reyner Banham puts it, "A new generation of architects and landscape architects were suddenly asked to operate on a landscape that was neither wholly natural nor machinic."[47] It is perhaps these projects that are some of the strongest demonstrations of the principle.

Other projects, such as the Trinitat Cloverleaf Park by Enric Batlle and Joan Roig, involve the integration of transportation infrastructure and public space.[48] Here, the design task was to stitch a highway into an urban fabric, while allowing both to function simultaneously. In this case there are two major requirements: transportation efficiency and the maintenance of a public space that contributes societally to support recreational functions. In most projects, these two needs are in direct conflict: transportation efficiency requires efficient flow-through at a minimum and, preferably, at speed; a good public space requires the ability to walk as desired and an environment free from excessive noise and air pollution. As Alex Wall and James Corner point out:

> [T]he design of transportation infrastructure is central to the

functioning of the urban surface. The importance of mobility and access in the contemporary metropolis brings to infrastructure the character of collective space. Transportation infrastructure is less a self-sufficient service element than an extremely visible and effective instrument in creating new networks and relationships.[49]

It is these types of complex design problems, with conflicting requirements, that call out for an architectural design approach at the scale of the landscape. Landscape architecture in its new manifestation offers this as well as two other benefits: the use of time in design and the knowledge of ecological systems.

Space-Time Frameworks

The use of time in design is an aspect that is specific to landscape architecture. Waldheim, Corner, Allen and others propose that landscape is a medium that "is uniquely capable of responding to temporal change, transformation, adaptation and succession."[50] They conceive of landscape "as an analog to contemporary processes of urbanization and as a medium uniquely suited to the open-endedness, indeterminacy, and change demanded by contemporary urban conditions."[51] Thinking about the city and its infrastructures demands an open-ended, staged approach since city building is a time-consuming and expensive undertaking. Both infrastructure and city building benefit from a design process that explicitly speculates on changes and possibilities over time. Drawing these potential futures is important in order to interrogate and understand them fully. Like a natural ecosystem, the city grows and develops in complex and seemingly unpredictable ways, driven by forces which may not be immediately obvious but are more likely to become so when the future is drawn.

Biological Complexity

The biological complexity of an infrastructural system can be thought of in many forms, from pipes and networks under the street to networks themselves to worldwide digital networks. The forthcoming AV ecosystem and its interconnection to worldwide digital networks, as well as to the urban form of the street, is perhaps the largest example of an interconnected ecosystem with immense complexity. Even within the system of the AV itself, there is already extensive research which uses neural network technology for AV navigation.[52] The complexity of the network and interrelationships between vehicles themselves will very quickly simulate a biological complexity.

These types of networks and interrelationships between the factors are well served by the theoretical approach which has underlaid projects by the firm Field Operations. Stan

Allen, one of the principals of the firm, introduces his book by quoting from Michel Serres:

> Stations and paths together form a system. Points and lines, being and relations. What is interesting might be the construction of the system, the number and disposition of stations and paths. Or it might be the flow of messages passing through the lines. In other words, a complex system can be formally described.[53]

Allen is interested in thinking about the city as a complex dispersed field: he considers the city as a field—and sometimes, when referring to Tokyo, as a three-dimensional field. He looks to complex, more bottom-up organizing structures such as flocking and crowd behaviour as a way of understanding organizing forces and structures within the city. Allen is not looking at form but instead looking to organizing structures and forces to inform design. It is easy to see how this type of theorizing can be applied to the AV city when looking at the 'last mile' issue in public transportation, for example. One of the significant challenges with public transportation is how people move from their home to the closest transit station. This is a particularly significant issue in less populated areas, where bus routes are often infrequent and badly served, and it is often necessary to walk some distance. An autonomous on-demand shuttle or SAV service could easily remedy this problem. If this type of system was to serve transit users well, then the benefit of the public transit to the directly adjacent property changes and likewise does the benefit to further properties. This flattens out the density of the development around the transit. It may also make transit more attractive in the process, but that would require a larger analysis of value to the traveller.[54] Mapping these types of influences and visually representing the interrelationship of forces is key to understanding what they are and how to design for them.

Interfaces

The key space for designers, however, may not be the 'neural network' of the AV system or how it relates to its sensors, but instead the interface between the infrastructural systems and the people who navigate them. This is clearly an example of a complex problem that needs to be addressed, not by solving a technological issue, but instead by looking to understand the social and cultural relationships of people both to the space of the street and to its other users. Several of the examples in the following chapter are pertinent to this discussion, such as the considerations of how to design intersections for the AV landscape: how can an approaching AV predict the movements of pedestrians? Google has algorithms to predict bicycle, pedestrian and other vehicle movements[55] but predicting a bicycle movement is not

as complex as predicting those of pedestrians: the wheel movement of bicycles ensures that rapid changes in direction are not possible, but a pedestrian can move suddenly and quickly in any direction. So, will pedestrians always have to "apply to cross the street"[56] (as Jan Gehl puts it) by pressing a button to indicate their desired direction—or is there a better way?

Another example of the potential challenges posed by the new relationship between AVs and pedestrians is that pedestrians will have the ability to cross the street at any point because they know the AVs will stop. This will result in traffic coming to a standstill. While this may be a positive turn of events in the realm of the walkable city, it will result in gridlock if allowed to proliferate. At some point, when everyone accepts that the hierarchy of the street has been overturned, there will be a desire to improve through-flow. This will clearly not be a technological problem but rather a social/technological interface problem. Several design approaches are possible which include (from most physical to least physical): designating a hierarchy of streets so that there are more streets where pedestrians are given priority ('pedestrian mainly') and others which are deemed 'AV mainly' streets where cars are given priority; road design to allocate AV-only zones and limit crossings to specific locations; clearly marking pavements to facilitate group

Cultural Theories for Design of the AV City   173

crossing; media campaigns to support vehicle courtesy zones; and/or fines which are enforced by in-AV-cameras. These are examples of design problems where collaboration between multiple disciplines is necessary and where design approaches become critical.

Ecological Urbanism: The Evolution of Landscape Urbanism

Since the Landscape Urbanism manifesto, there have been many critiques and discussions of the theory and its aspects. One of the most significant of these is outlined in the eponymous *Ecological Urbanism*,[57] which suggests that design is the key to balancing the conflicts between ecology (natural ecosystems) and the overt consumption of urbanism. It is not a completely separate theory from Landscape Urbanism but rather a theory that emphasizes and elucidates an aspect of particular interest within its parent theory. Waldheim, in "On Landscape, Ecology and Other Modifiers to Urbanism,"[58] refers to Ecological Urbanism as "critique and a continuation by other terms of the discourse around landscape urbanism."[59]

Ecological Urbanism brings several things to the fore that Landscape Urbanism did not significantly address: it more thoroughly discusses the interrelationship of systems and includes people as a driver and a force to be accounted for within

its theoretical framework. Where Landscape Urbanism is mainly talking of systems (infrastructural, landscape, ecological) and the idea of the landscape as an interconnecting system between buildings, Ecological Urbanism looks at multiple systems and infrastructures, some of which interrelate, as well as people and real-world scenarios of dense urban living which are not always situated in affluent 'first world' settings.

Ecological Urbanism outlines the manifesto of this theoretical framework and does a good job of pointing out what the problem is and how we should think about it; however, it does not point to any examples of how to implement this in a project. It does sum up what the issues are and it proposes that designers are the ones to address these issues. But, as with Landscape Urbanism, the field is very young and the book is a manifesto of sorts. It is worth noting that projects which land under these theories are not yet common and this is likely due to the need for interdisciplinary collaboration on large infrastructural projects, which take many years to come to fruition. The theories are currently still ahead of the implementation.

Infrastructural Ecologies

Some of the synergetic aspects of the ecological urbanism theory are well represented by Hillary Brown in *Next Generation Infrastructure.*[60]

Brown looks in a more practical way at issues of infrastructure and ecologies and thinks infrastructure systems should be "multipurpose, interconnected and synergistic."[61] She calls these "infrastructure ecologies," which she defines as co-located services that cost-effectively share flows of energy and resources in a closed-loop system.[62] As a simple example, Brown looks at the renewable energy park of the township of Hempstead, Long Island. The energy park is located at the Town of Hempstead's Conservation and Waterways headquarters. It is a prototype municipal facility featuring wind and solar power, ground-source heating and cooling, electric-vehicle charging, a fuel cell, a net-zero energy office and aquaculture facility. When networked, all of these components constitute an "infrastructural ecology." Brown points out many valuable aspects to the synergetic design of infrastructure and her approach demonstrates an aspect of Ecological Urbanism; it does not, however, go as far in the involvement of society, the city and natural systems as the theory of Ecological Urbanism.

Society | Nature

Ecological Urbanism insists that the social factor of the human be taken into account in a sustainable society. Sanford Kwinter is an architectural theorist who writes about philosophical issues related to design, architecture, and urbanism. Kwinter points out that ecological efficiency does not equal sustainability and warns against narrow or indoctrinated thinking on both ecological and sustainability issues.[63] Kwinter starts his discussion by pointing out that the dichotomy between city and nature is a social construction, largely fabricated by the Industrial Revolution. He argues that the transformation of territory is rooted in this "archaic and false opposition" and that today's economic and biospheric crises are a result of this false opposition. In other words, if we thought of city and nature as an interrelated continuum then we would not be having a climate crisis.[64] He clarifies,

> There can be no "ecological thinking" that does not place human social destiny at the heart of our posture towards our environmental context. We may well learn over the next years that cities, even megacities, actually represent dramatically efficient ecological solutions, but this fact alone does not make them sustainable, especially if the forces of social invention remain trapped in tyrannies that only ecological thinking on an ecumenical scale can free us from. For ecological thinking too has its counterfeit and debased forms, and many 'sustainability' discourses remain more oppressive than liberatory, more stifling than inventive.[65]

Kwinter postulates that the origin of both our understanding of nature today and current thinking on ecology is based on a movement from the 1970s called 'Deep Ecology.' Deep Ecology included humans within its idea of the larger ecosphere and did not dissociate humans from nature. Once humans are placed within the framework of the larger ecosphere, then the system is continuous and humans are one part of it—influencing it, but also relying on it. This conceptual framework does therefore not allow 'nature' or the 'environment' to be seen as external aspects which can be exploited.

Another theory of the time, the Gaia hypothesis formulated by James Lovelock, was more radical and presented the natural biosphere almost as an autonomous entity—a super organism.[66] This theory looks at the earth as an open but bounded system in which the environment and the life within it are in a coupled state where a change in one results in a change in the other—living organisms affects the environment and the environment affects the organisms.[67] Both the Gaia and Deep Ecology theories try to bring the human into the ecological discussion, a discussion which can be seen as having a clearly different viewpoint from the human— almost a self-interested personality. It may be beneficial to think of AV networks as self-interested systems interrelating to the larger 'biosphere' containing people and 'nature.' In fact, the algorithms which will likely control such systems will have optimization goals which may be independent of both societal interests and nature; their purpose will be to maximize their efficiency on an agent-based level, and to serve the interests of those who control them at the system-wide level.

Urban Form Approaches

Kwinter has a few other points which help clarify the theory of Ecological Urbanism and its theoretical underpinnings. He brings to our attention a reminder that rationalizing and/ or modernizing urban areas is a highly problematic undertaking, and design of a city must take this into account.[68] He notes that the fabric of the city—i.e. the circulation corridors of the city—in some places is an outcome of social activity; if one thinks of the definition of infrastructure as that which supports human activity,[69] then the design of the circulation corridors has to support the social fabric. Looking more to city form, Kwinter states:

> Current ameliorative development in cities targets the archaic physical structures and the archaic social life forms that adhere to them. Two examples among hundreds are the destruction of Beijing's Hutongs and the proposed redevelopment of the Dharavi slum quarters in Mumbai. It is an unexamined and possibly dangerous proposition that the solution to the new demographic and economic pressures is to fully rationalize and modernize our existing urban habitats; indeed, the opposite

may be the case. Take for example the proposed Dharavi redevelopment (as a model for very rapid capital-intensive development taking place in India, China, Brazil and other giant economic territories). Among the great singularities of India is the intensity of its local commerce, the vastness and ubiquity of its social markets, which are virtually coextensive with its metropolitan fabrics.[70]

Kwinter's viewpoint on Ecological Urbanism insists on the integration of the social and creative as part of the ecology. He warns against entrenched, dogmatic and uncreative thinking about the problems of ecology and sustainability, and calls on the design community to serve as an "organizing centre for the variety of disciplines and systems of knowledge whose integration is a precondition for connecting them to clear political and imaginative and, most important, formal ends."[71]

Ecosophy

Underlying the theories of Ecological Urbanism, and providing an important theoretical framework for consideration of the AV city, is the concept of 'existential ecologies.' This idea was put forward by Félix Guattari and includes "everything that is required for the creative and dynamic inhabitation and utilization of the contemporary environment"[72]—or to paraphrase, the social and cultural aspects of our environment as rooted in the

natural. Guattari was something of a polymath who wrote *The Three Ecologies* in 1989. He was, amongst other things, an ecological philosopher and even ran for political office on an environmental ticket. Guattari's viewpoint was that a traditionalist environmental perspective does not adequately represent the complex relationship between humans and the natural environment. The two ideas of human systems (culture) and natural systems (nature) are too binary and oppositional and therefore counterproductive to the urgent issue of environmental stewardship. Guattari proposed 'ecosophy' as a better approach, which treats ecology as a study of complex systems including human thought and culture, social relations, and the natural environment all on an interrelated continuum. This idea is also linked back to the 'deep ecology movement' from where the term ecosophy originated.

Guattari's three ecologies are the 'social, mental and environmental' and all three combine in his ecosophy. He argues that the techno-sciences are crucial to the survival of the planet but that in order to re-orient the techno-sciences to this purpose, capitalist structures and the concept of subjectivity have to be reconsidered. In effect, the requirement that we denounce the dominance of the economic regime of capitalism means that we have to change the way we, as a society, think about things. He calls upon architects,

Cultural Theories for Design of the AV City   177

educators, artists, designers, media people—anyone, in fact, who can influence people's psyches—to produce 'wedges' (defined as "procucing an interruption or making openings that can be inhabited by human projects leading to other ways of feeling, perceiving or conceiving"[73]) in order to provoke people to think differently. Guattari discusses subjectivity in this way and recognizes that our philosophies should change and constantly renew, rather than remain stuck in one repetitive theory.

We can see the influence of his thinking on the Ecological Urbanism movement and, in fact, we could say his theories are the basis of the movement. Guattari also proposes that the movement should constantly be questioning itself and evolving and, so far, we can see that as well. In the case of the focus of this book, and as the technological complexity and interrelationship of the natural and unnatural accelerate, the ideas of ecosophy and the re-alignment of the techno-sciences are ever more critical.

Future Ecologies and Urbanisms

Chris Reed and Nina-Marie Lister comment that in the field of science, ecology has, in the last few decades, reinvented itself. Formerly a field which mainly held to classical determinism and reductionist Newtonian concerns about order, certainty and stability, it has evolved to offer a

more contemporary understanding of dynamic systems and related phenomena of adaptability, flexibility and resilience.[74] They point out that many other disciplines are adopting complex adaptive systems theories: business with management theory and network organization, engineering with systems design and, of course, computer engineering with AI and machine learning. We have also pointed out in this chapter the adaptive network analysis for transportation engineering. As Reed and Lister write, "Increasingly these concepts of ecological thought are found useful as heuristics for decision-making generally, models or metaphors for cultural production broadly, and for the design arts in particular."[75] They argue that landscape architecture is placed between ecology and design of the built environment and is therefore uniquely placed to use ecological models.

But ecology is now used by many theoreticians and researchers as a metaphor or a broader idea for the behaviour of a system with political, economic and/or social implications; sometimes they have even redefined the term to include these realms. Reed and Lister also refer to Guattari and credit him with the basis of the idea, supporting this with a quotation from *The Three Ecologies*:

> Ecology must stop being associated with the image of a small nature-loving minority or with

178   Chapter 6 Urban Theories and Autonomous Vehicles

qualified specialists. Ecology in my sense questions the whole of subjectivity and capitalistic power formations.[76]

Reyner Banham had a similar idea in *Los Angeles: The Architecture of the Four Ecologies,*[77] his urban and architectural design history of Los Angeles. Banham writes of a combination of "geography, climate, economics, demography, mechanics, and culture" which is only made evident via movement on the city's characteristic roads and freeways; these constitute four organizational 'ecologies' for metropolitan Los Angeles: Surfurbia, the Foothills, the Plains of Id and Autopia.[78] His book was mainly a re-imagining of LA as a significant city for urban considerations; it became in many ways a model for the future as it reinvented the history of LA in people's minds.

Reed and Lister titled their book *Projective Ecologies* because, unlike ecologists who can only observe their models of ecosystems, designers can create and speculate on systems. Their work is influenced by landscape ecology, human ecology, urban ecology, applied ecology, evolutionary ecology, restorative ecology, deep ecology, the ecology of place and the unified theory of ecology. They think that this theory will encompass interdependencies and complexities that exist in our environments.

Conclusion

Disciplinary theories are frameworks to understand and elucidate how we approach problems in our domains. They bring cultural and social values and knowledge to inform decision making in the field. When examining the theories of the disciplines surrounding the AV and the city, it is clear we need an approach which acknowledges the health of the environment, societal goals, systems that spread beyond boundaries, changes over time and complex networks. Such a framework can be found in landscape architecture and the evolution of its Landscape Urbanism/ Ecological Urbanism theories. These theories, however, will need to adapt further to incorporate more fully the digital networks as an integrated force on the transportation network and, therefore, the urban form. Economic, political and policy forces, while acknowledged, are not explicitly dealt with and these are again invisible forces with a wide-reaching influence. While Kwinter does warn us against normalizing development which negates social relationships, there is a lack of theoretical discourse on integrating policy with social patterns beyond the narrow and normalizing concept of 'the neighbourhood.' Future theoretical frameworks could take this on more strongly in the context of the new AV city and its increasingly intense international competition for brain power and capital investment.

Conclusion 179

Notes

1   Jan Gehl, *Cities for People* (Washington, DC: Island Press, 2013).

2   This interchange design is currently in public consultation phase.

3   Michael Sorkin, "The End(s) of Urban Design," in *Urban Design* (Minneapolis: University of Minnesota Press, 2009), 171.

4   Alex Krieger and William S. Saunders, eds., *Urban Design* (Minneapolis: University of Minnesota Press, 2009), ix.

5   American Planning Association, "American Planning Association History" accessed December 9, 2017, https://www.planning.org/history/.

6   Richard Marshall, "The Elusiveness of Urban Design," in *Urban Design* (Minneapolis: University of Minnesota Press, 2009), 44–47.

7   Dana Cuff and Roger Sherman, *Fast-Forward Urbanism: Rethinking Architecture's Engagement with the City* (New York: Princeton Architectural Press, 2011).

8   Ibid, 15.

9   "Audi Urban Futures Awards." Audi Urban Future Initiative, audi-urban-future-initiative.com/facts/big-bjarke-ingels-group. Accessed September 24, 2017.

10   Alex Krieger, "Where and How Does Urban Design Happen?," in *Urban Design* (Minneapolis: University of Minnesota Press, 2009), 114.

11   Marshall, "The Elusiveness of Urban Design," 49.

12   Pierre Bélanger, *Landscape as Infrastructure* (New York: Routledge, 2017), 50–63.

13   The Army Corps of Engineers, "The U.S. Army Corps of Engineers: A Brief History," US Army Corps of Engineers, accessed January 5, 2018, http://www.usace.army.mil/About/History/Brief-History-of-the-Corps/Improving-Transportation/.

14   Peter D. Norton, *Fighting Traffic* (Cambridge, Massachusetts: MIT Press, 2008), 202–4.

15   Ibid, 103–48.

16   Chris Urmson, Director Google Self Driving Car Project, "The Future of Autonomous Driving," keynote lecture delivered at TRB Conference, January 13, 2016. Also available online at https://www.youtube.com/watch?v=A2IlbgKuf6Y. Urmson points out that the solution of the technical problem of the Level 4 self-driving car is a much easier problem to solve than the people problem of bringing people's attention back to the road in case of emergency. As such, they are skipping Level 3 autonomy and not releasing the technology until Level 4 is reached.

17   Edward Weiner, "Roots of Urban Transportation Planning," in *Urban Transportation Planning in the United States: History, Policy, and Practice* (New York, NY: Springer New York, 2013), 19–30.

18   Ibid.

19   Daniel Fagnant, Kara Kockelman, and Prateek Bansal, "Operations of Shared Autonomous Vehicle Fleet for Austin, Texas, Market," *Transportation Research Record: Journal of the Transportation Research Board* 2536 (January 1, 2015): 98–106.

20   Gereon Meyer and Susan Shaheen, *Disrupting Mobility: Impacts of Sharing Economy and Innovative Transportation on Cities* (New York: Springer, 2017).

21   American Planning Association, "American Planning Association History."

22   American Planning Association, "Choosing the Planning Profession," accessed September 24, 2017, https://www.planning.org/choosingplanning/.

23   Krieger, "Where and How Does Urban Design Happen?," 124.

24   Ibid, 114–30.

25   Marshall, "The Elusiveness of Urban Design," 44–45.

26   Krieger, "Where and How Does Urban Design Happen?," 114 quoting Sert.

27   Charles Waldheim, "On Landscape, Ecology and Other Modifiers to Urbanism," *Topos* 71. June (2010): 22.

28   See for example: Brent D. Ryan, *The Largest Art: A Measured Manifesto for a Plural*

29   *Urbanism.* (Cambridge, Massachusetts: MIT Press, 2017).

29   Pierre Bélanger, *Landscape Infrastructure: Urbanism beyond Engineering* (Wageningen University, 2013), 276.

30   Bélanger, *Landscape as Infrastructure.*

31   Charles Waldheim, *The Landscape Urbanism Reader* (New York: Princeton Architectural Press, 2006); Pierre Bélanger (New York: Routledge, 2017), *Landscape as Infrastructure*; Mohsen Mostafavi and Gareth Doherty, *Ecological Urbanism* (Baden: Lars Müller Publishers, 2010).

32   Krieger, "Where and How Does Urban Design Happen?," 125.

33   Krieger and Saunders, *Urban Design*, 126.

34   Gary L. Strang, "Infrastructure as Landscape [infrastructure as landscape, landscape as infrastructure]," *Places* 10, no. 3 (1996): 9–15.

35   James Corner, *Recovering Landscape: Essays in Contemporary Landscape Architecture* (New York: Princeton Architectural Press, 1999), 1–26.

36   Reyner Banham, *Theory and Design in the First Machine Age* (Cambridge, Massachusetts: MIT Press, 1960), 9–12.

37   Charles Waldheim, "Landscape as Urbanism," in *The Landscape Urbanism Reader* (New York: Princeton Architectural Press, 2006).

38   Charles Waldheim, *The Landscape Urbanism Reader* (New York: Princeton Architectural Press, 2006).

39   James Corner, "Terra Fluxus" in *The Landscape Urbanism Reader* (New York: Princeton Architectural Press, 2006), 23.

40   Fagnant, Kockelman, and Bansal, "Operations of Shared Autonomous Vehicle Fleet for Austin, Texas, Market."

41   Brent D Ryan, "Hard Urbanism," *Journal of Urban Design* 20, no. 3 (2015): 321.

42   Strang, "Infrastructure as Landscape," 11.

43   Ibid, 15.

44   Ibid.

45   Waldheim, "Landscape as Urbanism," 39.

46   Projects by West8, Hargreaves Associates, Corner/Field Operations and DIRT Studio.

47   Reyner Banham, *Theory and Design in the First Machine Age* (Cambridge: The MIT Press, 1980).

48   Waldheim, "Landscape as Urbanism," 45.

49   Alex Wall and James Corner, "Programming the Urban Surface," in *Recovering Landscape* (New York: Princeton Architectural Press, 1999), 233–49.

50   Waldheim, *The Landscape Urbanism Reader*, 39.

51   Ibid.

52   Dean A. Pomerleau, "Efficient Training of Artificial Neural Networks for Autonomous Navigation," *Neural Computation* 3, no. 1 (1991): 88–97.

53   Stan Allen, *Points and Lines: Diagrams and Projects for the City* (New York: Princeton Architectural Press, 1999).

54   See an analysis of current technologies on agent based modelling on transportation and land use: Miller, Eric J. "Modeling the demand for new transportation services and technologies," *Transportation Research Record: Journal of the Transportation Research Board* 2658 (2017): 1–7.

55   Zhu, Jiajun, Michael Steven Montemerlo, Christopher Paul Urmson, and Andrew Chatham. "Object detection and classification for autonomous vehicles." U.S. Patent 8,195,394, issued June 5, 2012.

56   Jan Gehl, "Cities for People" (Vancouver, BC, January 24, 2011).

57   Mostafavi and Doherty, *Ecological Urbanism.*

58   Charles Waldheim, "On Landscape, Ecology and Other Modifiers to Urbanism," *Topos* 71, no. June (2010): 21–24.

59   Ibid, 24.

60   Hillary Brown, *Next Generation Infrastructure* (Washington, DC: Island Press, 2014).

61 Ibid, 17.

62 Ibid, 18.

63 Sanford Kwinter, "Notes on the Third Ecology," in *Ecological Urbanism* (Lars Müller Publishers, Baden, 2010), 103.

64 Ibid, 94–105.

65 Ibid, 103.

66 James E. Lovelock, "Hands Up for the Gaia Hypothesis," *Nature; London* 344, no. 6262 (March 8, 1990): 100.

67 Ibid.

68 Kwinter, "Notes on the Third Ecology," 99.

69 Merriam-Webster dictionary defines infrastructure as 1. 'the underlying foundation or basic framewor< (as of a system or organization)' and in 3. as the system of public works of a country, state, or region; also : the resources (such as personnel, buildings, or equipment) required for an activity. "Definition of INFRASTRUCTURE," Merriam-Webster, accessed January 3, 2018, https://www.merriam-webster.com/dictionary/infrastructure.

70 Kwinter, "Notes on the Third Ecology," 99.

71 Ibid, 105.

72 Ibid, 104.

73 Verena Andermatt Conley, "Urban Ecological Practices: Félix Guattari's Three Ecologies," in *Ecological Urbanism* (Lars Müller Publishers, Baden, 2010), 139.

74 Chris Reed and Nina-Marie E Lister, *Projective Ecologies* (Harvard University Graduate School of Design Cambridge, MA/New York, 2014): 15.

75 Ibid.

76 Ibid, 13.

77 Reyner Banham, *Los Angeles: The Architecture of Four Ecologies* (Harmondsworth, Eng.: Penguin Books, 1973).

78 Ibid.

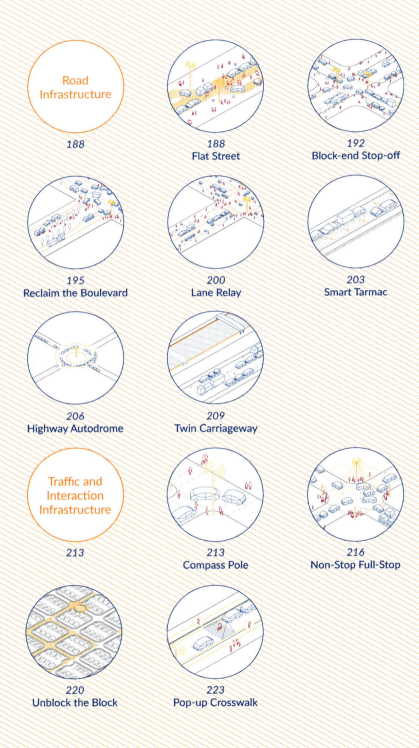

Chapter 7
Street Scale Impacts

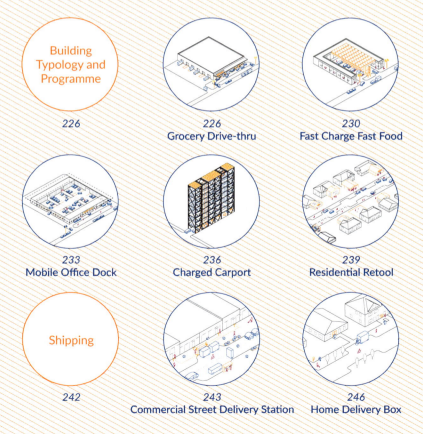

Building Typology and Programme

226

226
Grocery Drive-thru

230
Fast Charge Fast Food

233
Mobile Office Dock

236
Charged Carport

239
Residential Retool

Shipping

242

243
Commercial Street Delivery Station

246
Home Delivery Box

Chapter 7
Street Scale Impacts

Overturning Hierarchy

The impact of the automobile on the public space of the street during the past century has been in most cases devastating. It precipitated a paradigm shift by altering the dominant mode of occupation of open urban space from walking to driving. Prior to the mass production of the automobile in the early 20th century, the road was considered a place for walking. The automobile was an unknown interloper whose presence was considered noisy and dangerous. It was only through the extensive lobby effort of the automobile clubs, known as 'Motordom,' that the car was given priority in the street.[1] However, with the introduction of AVs, it is now possible for these priorities to be reconsidered. While AVs will continue to utilize many existing elements of the streetscape as we know it today, they also have the potential to provoke changes in the form and function of the street and its infrastructure, and in various other elements of the built environment. At this point in history, when we are about to have a radical change in transportation technology, it may be beneficial to claim back some of the roadway which has been sacrificed to the worship of the car. This presents an opportunity to re-shuffle the hierarchy of the road and reprioritize the space of the street.

It is interesting to note that the technology of the AV may, in any case, completely reverse the hierarchy of the street. One of the reasons we, as pedestrians, do not cross the street is the danger of being struck by an oncoming car—the reasons for being struck might be driver inattention, the driver's inability to see us, or the inability of the vehicle to stop in time. As pedestrians, if we are sure that the approaching car is an AV then we will, in time, come to trust that an AV will sense us and stop. Once pedestrians develop this trust—and all cars on the road are AVs—there is no longer a reason not to walk out into the road. The only reason an AV may hit us is if it does not have the distance required to stop. Barring this, pedestrians will be safe to walk willy-nilly across any road or highway. This fact is another destabilizing element which needs to be considered upon the introduction of AVs. While AV makers can make cars more or less 'aggressive' in personality, the prioritizing of pedestrian safety over the vehicle will turn our understanding of the space of the road on its head.

One of the biggest challenges of the entry of the AV into the urban realm will be the interaction between pedestrians and AVs. Intersections may no longer need traffic lights if cars use vehicle-to-vehicle (V2V) technology to communicate or if the communication between cars is facilitated by infrastructure—but how does anyone know where the pedestrian wants to go? A pedestrian can never be guaranteed to be connected to a digital network and therefore cannot be tracked through GPS or Wi-Fi signal. Even if smart phones are tracked, one cannot guarantee that all people will carry one. Privacy is also a significant issue with tracking pedestrian movement. As such, the infrastructure is not guaranteed to know a pedestrian is in the vicinity unless the pedestrian is scanned via image recognition cameras or interacts physically with the infrastructure in some way. Furthermore, the direction that the pedestrian wants to go is unknown. Unlike a bicycle that (should) give warning of a change in direction, a pedestrian can quickly pivot and move much more erratically; if a pedestrian is standing at a light, it is hard to know in which direction they wish to travel.

Secondly, the current mode of interaction between a pedestrian and car is communication between the pedestrian and the driver of the car. In many cases a pedestrian makes eye contact with a driver and indicates through body positioning their intent

to cross. Similarly, a driver communicates to a pedestrian to go ahead or indicates when they intend to move by inching the car forward. While the ability to read body language may one day be programmable, it is not possible to rely on this. Some researchers, such as Kent Larson at MIT Media Lab, have developed methods to indicate to pedestrians that they have been 'seen' with the use of 'eyes' attached to the AV and specific LEDs running along the side. Other opportunities to track pedestrians can be seen in V2V technology where one car passes on information on pedestrians to other vehicles in the area, thus enabling cars who cannot 'see' the pedestrian to have information on their location. Drawings which look at these issues are addressed in the Flat Street, Compass Pole, Pop-up Crosswalk and Non-Stop/Full-Stop drawings. While these drawings are only preliminary ideas of how the pedestrian–AV interaction may be addressed, they serve as starting points for future discussion.

Drawing Configuration

The drawings in this section are analytical comparisons between buildings and infrastructures associated with the automobile as we currently know them, and those envisioned in the future context of the dominance of AVs. The drawings address aspects of urban form, comprising building typology and programme, as well as

ROAD INFRASTRUCTURE

Flat Street

mobility infrastructure, consisting of road infrastructure, traffic control devices, and the related interaction of vehicles and pedestrians.

While somewhat specific in their formal representation of buildings and infrastructural elements, the drawings—similar to their urban scale counterparts—aim to be read as diagrams that visually communicate various issues pertinent to AVs at the scale of the street. The drawings and their associated annotative descriptions are intended to be complementary, working together to address key issues rigorously yet speculatively, while also allowing for further questions to be raised.

The sensing and navigation capabilities of AVs offer the opportunity to re-imagine the way people and vehicles share space and interact with one another. Contrary to the automobile's gradual overtake of pedestrian space in the 20th century, AVs could allow for the safe coexistence of mixed modes of mobility. In fact, as discussed in the introduction to this chapter, the priority of personally powered transportation over AVs is almost a guaranteed fait accompli, since AVs will always yield to the more vulnerable pedestrians and bicyclists. The road portion travelled by cars then becomes a 'courtesy zone' which pedestrians and cyclists must agree not to impede. Having said this, it would still be possible for an authority having jurisdiction to decide to give priority to the automobile traffic by enforcing laws which prevent pedestrians from entering into the roadway and impeding traffic; in this case, laws of this kind will be easily enforceable since all the vehicles on the road will be equipped with multiple on-board cameras.

But assuming a desire for an equality of the street, we can look to an earlier example of this in the concept of the 'Woonerf' ('living yard'), a low-speed residential zone conceived in the Netherlands in the 1970s.[2] This type of street makes it difficult for cars to navigate and so drivers are forced to reduce their speed, while paving and other treatment indicates that this is a pedestrian zone first and a space for cars second. In the case of AVs, this concept can flourish without the necessity for obstacles and different paving to denote pedestrian priority: it is coded into the AV to obey the posted speed limit and automatically cede right of way to bikers and pedestrians.

The drawing "Flat Street" envisions just such a pedestrian-friendly urban street: instead of completely banning automobile traffic, the conventional separation of vehicles and pedestrian traffic is relaxed, enabled by remote-sensing and responsive capabilities that allow AVs to track pedestrians and other vehicles in real-time. In this drawing, AVs are allocated a visually marked right of way in the street's cross section which maintains orderly and efficient vehicular flow while providing the

visible order still needed by pedestrians; pedestrians, cyclists and small personal vehicles (which could be autonomous or manual, such as an electric or manual bike) are able to occupy the full surface of the street. The image also depicts a designated zone for drop-off and pick-up which keeps the single flow-through traffic lane clear, somewhat similar to the next drawing "Block-end Stop-off."

Flat Street

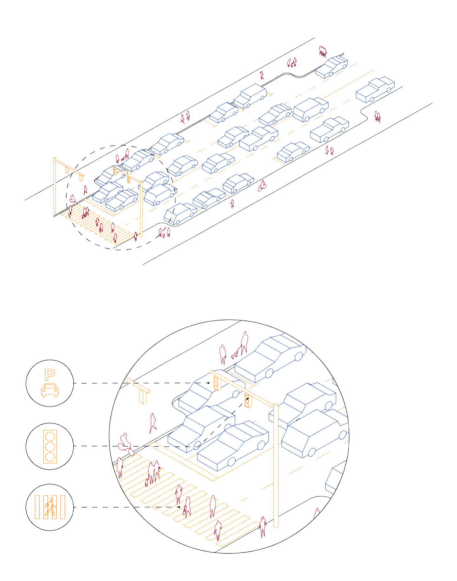

Current street section with multi-lane traffic, on-street parking, and sidewalk.

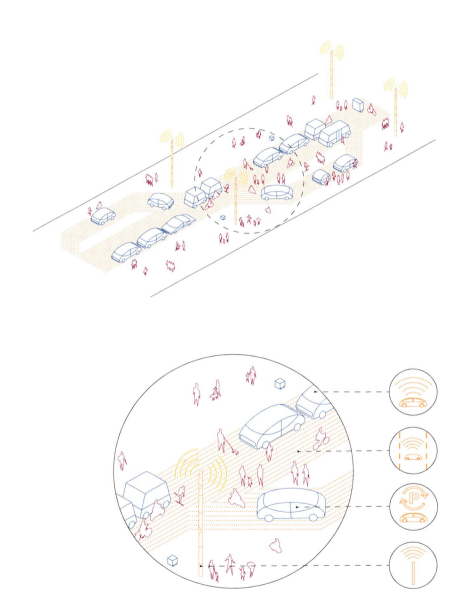

Flat Street: street space shared between different users.

Road Infrastructure

Block-end Stop-off

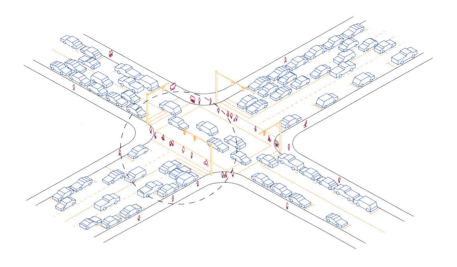

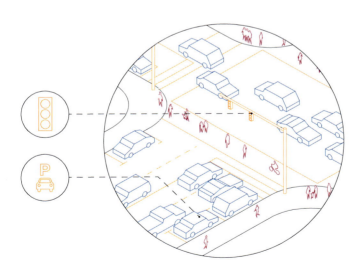

Typical curb parking condition.

Chapter 7 Street Scale Impacts

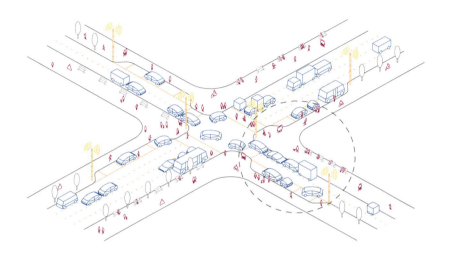

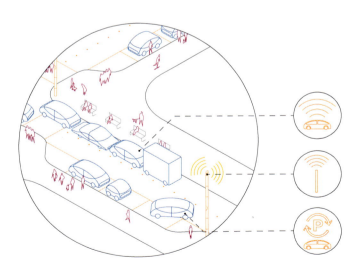

AV pick-up/drop-off stations near the intersection, with expanded mid-block sidewalk.

Road Infrastructure

Block-end Stop-off

Over the past few years, car-sharing services have undergone a dramatic increase in many major cities of the world. For many consumers, the flexibility and low cost of these services are making owning one's own vehicle less desirable, threatening the auto-maker industry with a paradigm shift in driving behaviour. In this trajectory, the introduction of fleets of shared autonomous vehicles could be truly transformative, allowing for a fleet of intelligent vehicles to be optimized in size for a particular geographic area and population. For example, a computer simulation in which 3.5% of formerly human-driven trips within the service area are replaced with SAVs indicated that the population affected could be served with just 10% of the vehicles compared to self-owned personal vehicles.[3]

What might be required of road design to adjust to such a cultural shift? It would likely help to organize both cars and passengers if there are designated 'stop-off' zones. The advantage of designating a 'stop-off' zone is that pedestrians waiting for pick-up by roaming AVs know where to find their cars and the cars are authorized to stop there. It also allows the cars to move out of the traffic flow rather than impeding other vehicles. Standardizing such an area would be beneficial to all involved

as they would be recognizable and predictable spaces of the street with amenities such as Wi-Fi and seats to accommodate waiting passengers.

A saving in street parking is a potential result of this shift: since AVs are capable of driving themselves to remote parking locations after dropping off their passengers, and since vehicles in an optimum-size SAV fleet would rarely be stationary, it is reasonable to anticipate that street parking spaces can be converted to other uses. If much of the block can be given over to pedestrians and street-front café use, it would transform many streets into more dynamic spaces for people. In busy downtown areas there may be a question of how much of this parking could revert to additional pedestrian space as more space may be required on the block for pick-up and drop-off, but in many cases in a city the scenario is likely to be feasible.

"Block-end Stop-off" examines this possibility with a focus on organizing drop-off zones at each end of the block. Most street parking space is given over to pedestrian use, with the exception of the designated zones where AVs would drop off and pick up their passengers. This facilitates stores and restaurants using the excess lanes as amenities and gives more space to pedestrians mid-block.

Reclaim the Boulevard

The coming of autonomous vehicles is often hailed as the opportunity to reclaim the road from cars and provide more space for pedestrians, cyclists and other modes of more sustainable transport. The theory advanced is that cars will be more efficient both in their use of the road space and their flow-through.[4] Depending on policy decisions and future pricing of AVs, this may come true; however, roads are often very inefficiently allocated as it is. For example, straight six-lane roads (three lanes each direction) often have a lane allocated for parking at non-peak hours, in effect reducing the road to four lanes (two each direction). If people are allowed to turn left out of the left lane (with no dedicated lane) then this effectively becomes a two-lane road (one each direction). Jan Gehl claims that a one-lane through road with effective turning lanes where turns are allowed is just as effective as a three-lane road. Even without AVs, this increases the road allocation for other users as well as making the road more efficient for all.[5]

Using this design approach, and assuming the roadway is freed up by more efficient AVs and/or a reduced number of cars, the question of how to reclaim the road arises. Three scenarios for a three-way through road are shown in the illustrations.

In Scenario 1, the sidewalk is expanded by up to two lanes in some cases. Drop-off areas are accommodated mid-block and turning lanes for left and right turns are facilitated at intersections off the main street. The disadvantage of this option is that the lanes 'jog' at two points—one just across the intersection—which may be considered to create less safe conditions for human-driven cars. AVs, however, will have no difficulty with these conditions.

Scenario 2 shows the expansion of the sidewalk as well as the insertion of the boulevard. The boulevard can be planted or used for walking as the crosswalks connect to the boulevard. While walking in the boulevard may seem like a strange idea, in congested urban areas where there is limited grass, it is not uncommon for dogs to be walked in the boulevard in order to find some grass.[6]

Scenario 3 shows all the allocated space being provided to the boulevard. In this example, the boulevard is intended to provide more functions—it can be a space for walking but also provide a drop-off zone—thus facilitating other uses of the sidewalk and reduced congestion. This option would be more suitable for situations in which ample sidewalk is already provided.

Reclaim the Boulevard: Edge

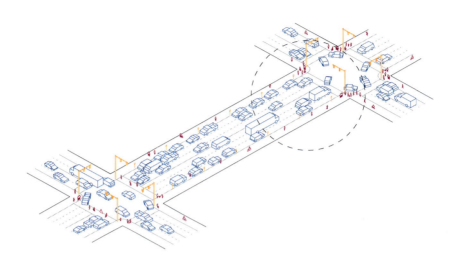

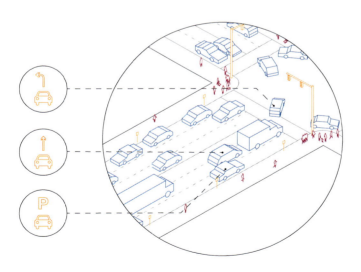

Street allocated to cars.

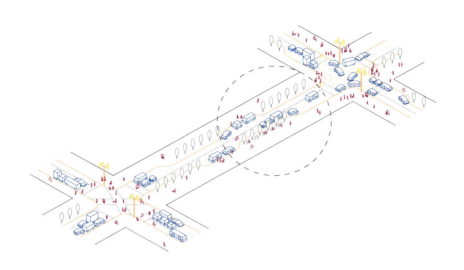

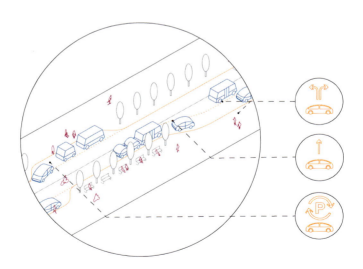

Street reallocated to walking boulevard on perimeter.

Reclaim the Boulevard: Centre

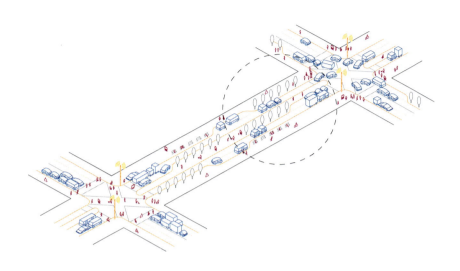

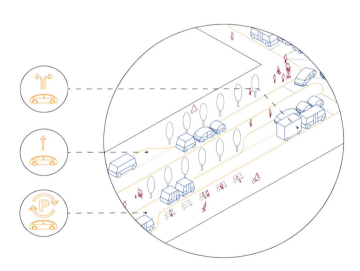

Street reallocated to walking boulevard in centre and perimeter.

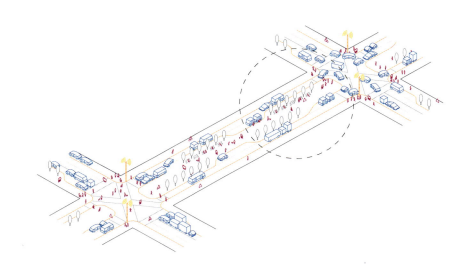

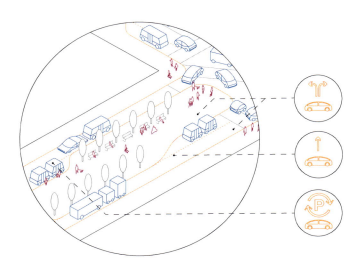

Street reallocated to walking boulevard.

Road Infrastructure

Lane Relay

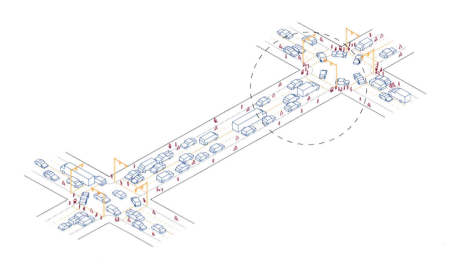

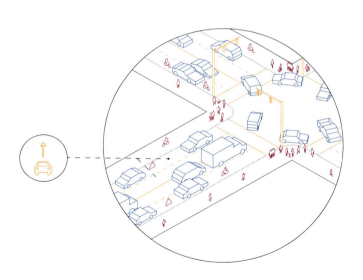

Lane allocation by vehicle type.

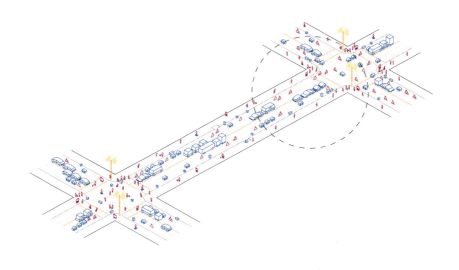

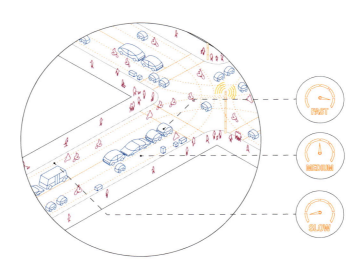

Lane allocation by vehicle speed.

Road Infrastructure 201

Lane Relay

The second discussion with reclaiming roads has to do with alternate modes of transport. Even if automobile demand for road space decreases, other emerging modes are increasing. Autonomous delivery vehicles are one such innovative technology; it may be beneficial to take part of the street to facilitate these vehicles rather than have them use already cluttered sidewalk space. With the use of AVs there is expected to be a decrease in the size of vehicles ('right sizing') due to reduction in crash protection requirements. This will facilitate the proliferation of light electric vehicles in a multitude of formats. These alternative vehicles are sometimes now in competition with bicycles for bicycle lanes. An increase in lane size for bicycles would facilitate the multiple uses of the space by both cycles and light electric vehicles.

In analyzing future modes of transport and delivery and attempting to allocate these space demands, it becomes clear that perhaps the best way of organizing the street is not by mode but rather by speed. Ironically, it will be the person who is a little unstable on the bicycle who will need more weaving room than the steady unwavering autonomously guided vehicles. As such, the 'fast lane' which will be occupied by the AVs need not be any wider than the widest vehicle itself (in this case a truck of approximately 2.5m depending on local standards). The next lane, which can facilitate medium-speed cyclists and other light electric medium-speed vehicles, could also be 2.5m wide but in this case to facilitate passing and two people biking side by side. The inside lane closest to the sidewalk could facilitate the slower delivery pods and this could be 1m (or less) wide. Alternatively the delivery pods could be facilitated on a wider sidewalk, perhaps on the outside of the street furniture; rebuilding curbs, though, is an expensive process for a municipality when compared to painting striping on lanes.

Smart Tarmac

One of the original impediments to the dominance of the automobile in personal transportation was the necessity for an extensive network of paved roads suitable for cars to drive on. Asphalt, concrete or composite pavements, along with various lane markings and occasional embedded elements (such as reflective lights) have for a long time remained unchanged, primarily serving the purpose of sustaining vehicular traffic. While this primary function will continue to be a necessity with AVs, there are a multiplicity of areas in which pavement can become more performative, including aspects that are directly related to autonomous vehicles. The drawing "Smart Tarmac" explores some of these. Firstly, various methods have been identified to aid the road navigation of AVs, including visual, electronic or magnetic markers (for examples, see Durrant-Whyte, 25–30;[7] also UC Berkley's Robotics Lab[8]). Such embedded markers can also become programmed transmitters or sensors, broadcasting further information about the road to vehicles, and thus function as part of the infrastructure intelligence. Moreover, the pavement could also participate in vehicle charging and energy generation, as shown by research on the inductive charging of vehicles in motion,[9] as well as special paving elements with integrated solar panels.[10]

Once embedded with sensors and lights, it is easy to anticipate a road that includes low temperature defrosting cables that auto-defrost the road, creating safer roads for pedestrians and automobiles and permitting biking all year round in snowy climates. This would also serve the purpose of allowing cars to charge in all weather conditions with inductive roadway charging—something that might be an impediment if snow or ice interrupted the contact.

The road with many sensors could also transmit its status to whoever may be interested; if ice or snow is accumulating, this information could then be sent to cars or infrastructure to alert them to adjust speed. If damage occurred to the sensing or lighting this could also be relayed to the authority having jurisdiction to inform them that maintenance is required.

Smart Tarmac

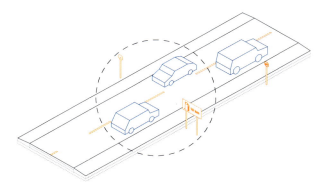

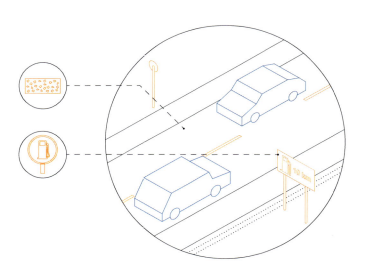

Typical road pavement and traffic signage.

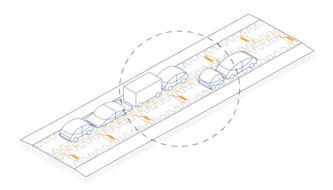

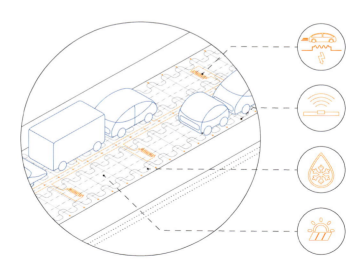

Intelligent road pavement infrastructure with inductive charging, pavement heating and sensor devices.

Road Infrastructure 205

Highway Autodrome

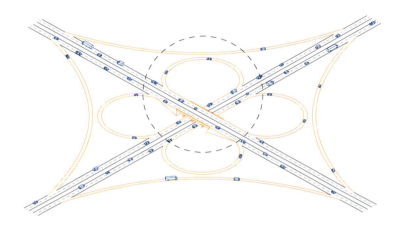

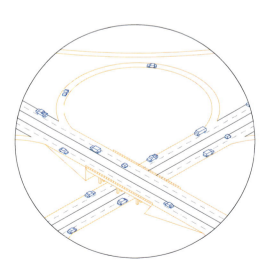

Traditional cloverleaf highway interchange.

206   Chapter 7 Street Scale Impacts

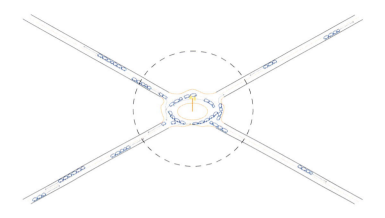

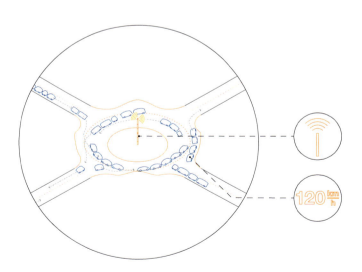

Space-efficient high-speed interchange with extreme superelevation.

Road Infrastructure

Highway Autodrome

The basic objectives of the geometric design of roadways are their optimization for efficiency and safety. Currently, this process of optimization needs to take into consideration both the physical capabilities and limitations of automobiles as well as those of their human drivers, such as reaction time and cognitive decision-making abilities. It is predicted that the shift from traditional vehicles to AVs will significantly increase the level of precision, predictability and speed of response of vehicles, in turn allowing for modifications and improvements to road geometry.[11] Through their various sensors and with the aid of precise navigation systems, AVs will be able to drive on narrower lanes at higher speeds, or safely negotiate turns and intersections with reduced curvature radii. When infrastructural intelligence is added to this mix—an interchange which can give hierarchy and direction to its automobiles—this speed and efficiency can be increased, perhaps exponentially.

Taking these developments as a premise, the drawing "Highway Autodrome" re-imagines the traditional highway interchange as a high-speed switch: optimized in size while allowing vehicles to maintain high speeds due to the banked cross-section (superelevation) of the intersection, similar to race tracks and velodromes. Moreover, it is imagined that the former sectionally stratified type can become an articulated topography negotiated by entering vehicles with the aid of vehicle-to-vehicle and vehicle-to-infrastructure communication. As such, the vehicles in the image are shown to be organized in so-called 'platoons,' which are strings of vehicles spaced close together and moving synchronously.

Twin Carriageway
(a.k.a. Hydroponic Expressway)

One of the major impacts of the post-war expansion of automobile culture has been the construction of inter-urban, regional and national road networks, resulting in the particular infrastructure landscape of multi-lane highways, interchanges, bridges, tunnels, etc. While this extensive network is very likely to continue to be utilized with the emergence of AVs as a major form of transportation, there are also numerous possibilities for alterations to make the infrastructure more efficient while lowering its environmental impact. Simultaneously, in those areas where roads will continue to be built in the future, there is the possibility for highways to be designed in consideration of the capabilities of AVs. The drawing "Twin Carriageway" studies the cross-section of a typical dual carriageway and presents two scenarios for the introduction of autonomous vehicles. In the first scenario, which may occur during the incremental introduction of AVs into traffic, the carriageway would be 'twinned' so that separate lanes exist for human-driven cars and AVs, the latter of which are capable of travelling safely at higher speeds in self-organized 'platoons' (see above).[12] Thus, similar to today's HOV or bus lanes, high-speed AV lanes would be used exclusively by self-driving cars, while AVs would also be able to occupy other lanes.

In the second scenario, further on in the roll-out timeline of AVs, it is imagined that AVs are capable of driving reliably and safely on narrower lanes, allowing for more lanes on the existing cross-section and also making the wide median between opposite direction lanes unnecessary. Since AVs driving in closely spaced platoon formations would also require less total road space, the drawing shows one half of the former highway decommissioned and re-utilized for other purposes—in this case, intensive linear agriculture.

Road Infrastructure

Twin Carriageway

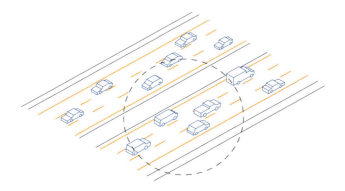

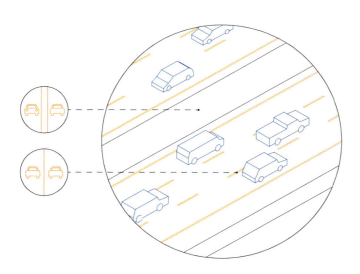

Traditional dual carriageway.

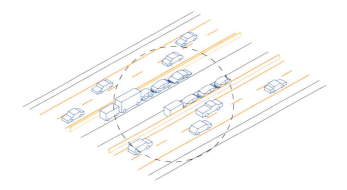

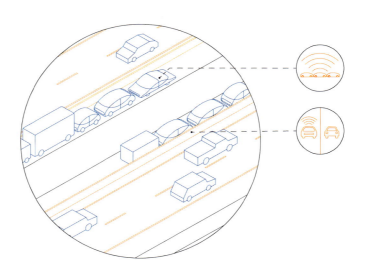

Carriageway with separate high-speed AV lanes.

Road Infrastructure 211

Hydroponic Expressway

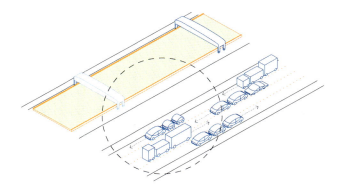

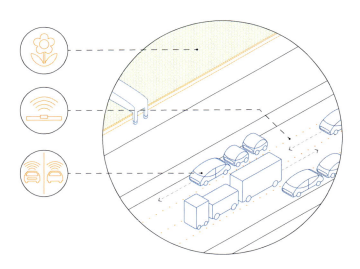

AV-highway with reversable lanes, and agricultural production in freed up lane space.

212 Chapter 7 Street Scale Impacts

TRAFFIC AND INTERACTION INFRASTRUCTURE

Compass Pole

The traffic light celebrated its one hundredth birthday in 2014, but it may very well soon be extinct.[13] In a world of autonomous vehicles the nature of traffic control infrastructure is set to change radically. Equipped with dozens of different sensors, including GPS, LIDAR, radar, infrared and visible light cameras, AVs will not only constantly monitor their position in relation to the street and other vehicles, but might also directly interact with intelligent infrastructure installed along the roadway, embedded in the pavement, located along the street and at traffic intersections. Such infrastructure will not only monitor but also control traffic for optimum flow.[14] It may also pass information to facilitate V2V communication and provide up-to-date local network information. It could even be used as a node in a local communications network passing all manner of information including entertainment or citizen generated content. Access to apps which interact with the poles could be set up by the city 'app store.' For further discussion, see Chapter 9.

Based on a scenario of intensive infrastructure intelligence, the drawing

"Compass Pole" presents a scheme for a singular, multi-functional piece of intelligent street furniture, which synthesizes and augments the functions of various discrete elements of the streetscape. Rendered as a simple vertical pole, this 'traffic beacon' contains receivers and transmitters for communicating with vehicles and other traffic information systems,[15] built-in street light fixtures, digital and holographic screens for display and interactive content, and can also be equipped with micro energy-generation features such as solar panels. These programmes can be incorporated into the Compass Pole in a modular manner, depending on the number of functions the pole is required to perform. The drawing is in part inspired by Douglas Coupland's 'V-pole' design.[16]

Compass Pole

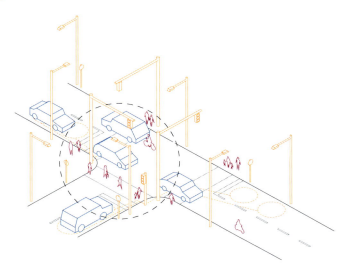

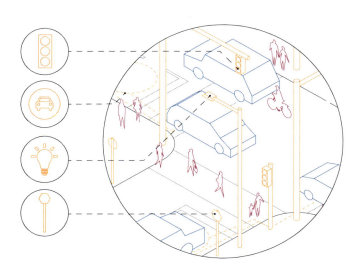

Traditional intersection infrastructure, including traffic lights, sensor circuits embedded in pavement, street lights and road signs.

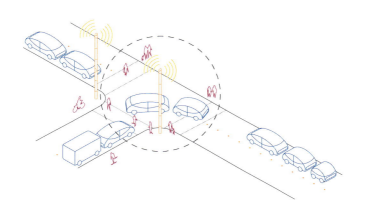

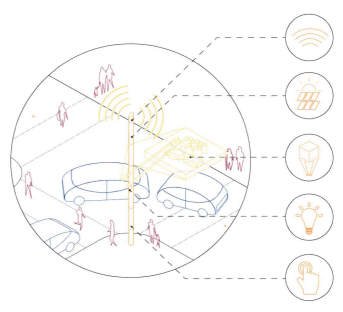

AV intersection consisting of multi-functional traffic beacons.

Traffic and Interaction Infrastructure

Non-Stop/Full-Stop

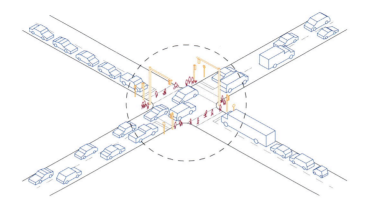

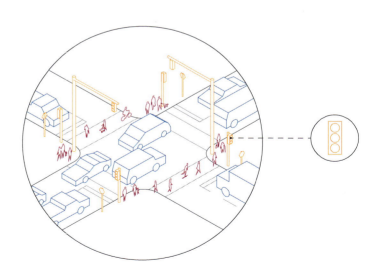

Traditional four-legged intersection.

216　　　Chapter 7　Street Scale Impacts

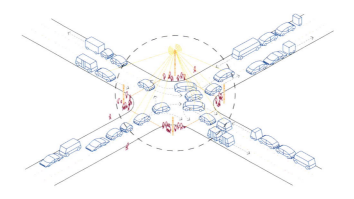

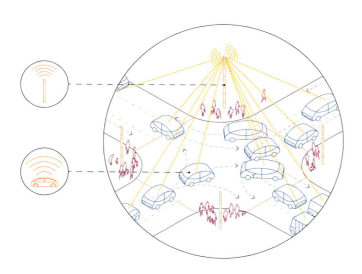

Intersection with automated traffic management: automated vehicle navigation.

Traffic and Interaction Infrastructure

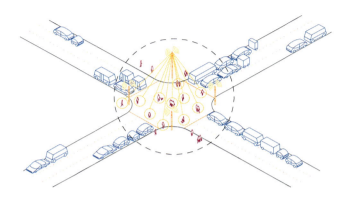

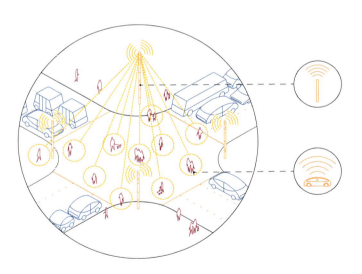

Intersection with automated traffic management: pedestrian–infrastructure interaction.

Non-Stop/Full-Stop

Taking inspiration from the computer simulations designed at the Autonomous Intersection Management (AIM) project at the University of Texas,[17] the drawing "Non-Stop/Full-Stop" illustrates a typical urban intersection controlled not by traditional traffic lights but by a "traffic intersection manager"[18]—a computer installed at the intersection that directly communicates with each approaching vehicle. As the vehicle approaches, it is prioritized and then instructed to change its speed and direction in order to facilitate the most efficient flow through the intersection. The result is a continuous flow of traffic in both directions, as well as a reduction in congestion and associated fuel emissions. (See also the drawing "Compass Pole.")

The question arises, then, of how to deal with pedestrians and bicyclists within this highly directed interchange? In this proposal, pedestrians and bicyclists are sensed and wait for their turn. At this point all vehicles are stopped and pedestrians, cyclists and other slower traffic cross to their respective desired destination.

Unblock the Block

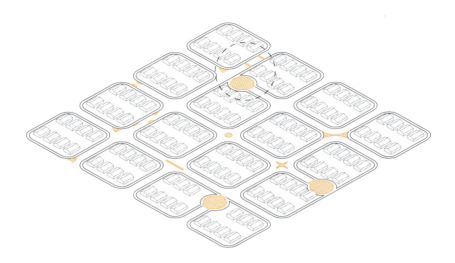

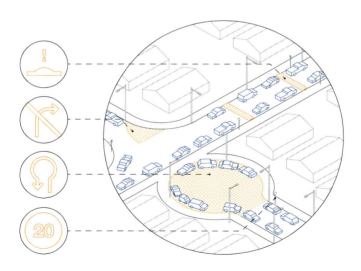

Residential neighbourhood with ensemble of traditional physical traffic control devices.

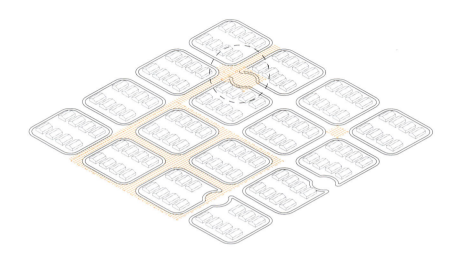

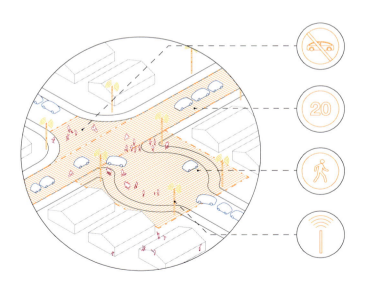

'Virtual control' scenario using intelligent infrastructure.

Unblock the Block

With the proliferation of automobile culture and urban landscapes dominated by cars, a variety of physical elements have been developed to control driver behaviour and access to restricted areas. Unlike traffic lights and signage, which indicate rule sets that drivers must follow, elements such as speed bumps, traffic circles or diverters direct and regulate traffic by their mere physical attributes. Bollards are a ubiquitous and expensive accessory to urban life. Removing bollards from the urban fabric would in itself produce a remarkable change in the city streetscape.

While the North American suburban fabric has developed in conjunction with the automobile, it often did so in a way to limit and mitigate the dangers of moving vehicles. This can be seen in the cul-de-sacs and the circular suburban layouts throughout the post-war North American suburb. In urban areas this has resulted in varying degrees of disconnectivity and inaccessibility in the street network, exemplified by the 'different but similar' types of cul-de-sac or no through roads, which originated before the automobile era but are widely used in modern street planning for limiting and calming traffic. The drawing "Unblock the Block" adapts the functions of traditional physical traffic control devices in a scenario in which AVs operate in conjunction with

intelligent infrastructure. Whether from cloud-based mapping and navigation services or from local traffic beacons (see "Compass Poles"), AVs would navigate the urban environment based on 'invisible' or 'virtual' barriers and rules, controlling various elements such as access or speed on a temporally flexible basis (such as prompting vehicles to slow down near a school during school hours). The advantage of virtual rules is that AVs are programmed to follow traffic rules and are capable of operating according to complex or temporary rules. Simultaneously, the absence of inflexible physical barriers allows for more accessible and flexible urban spaces.

Pop-up Crosswalk

Similar to "Flat Street," the drawing "Pop-up Crosswalk" illustrates AV–pedestrian interaction, but in this case on a roadway where continuous automobile traffic remains a priority. There are two variations of vehicle intelligence and infrastructure intelligence shown in the drawings, through the example of a pedestrian crossing.

In the first scenario, a pedestrian is shown crossing the street at a random location. AVs are programmed to monitor pedestrian movement in a defined 'buffer zone' along the road—a particular area of the sidewalk or street edge closest to the vehicle lane. When the intention of crossing is deduced from a pedestrian's trajectory, an AV is shown to project a temporary crosswalk. This behaviour is inspired by visualizations carried out by Mercedes-Benz on its experimental self-driving car.

In the latter case, that of intelligent infrastructure, a pedestrian crossing is shown which is both familiar and different: visible traffic lights exist only for the benefit of pedestrians, who are able to signal their intention to cross at the intersection. (See also "Compass Pole" and "Non-Stop/Full-Stop.")

Pop-up Crosswalk

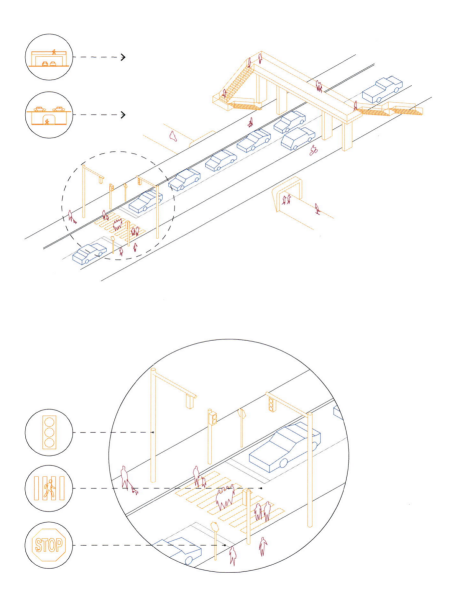

Traditional pedestrian crosswalk with traffic lights.

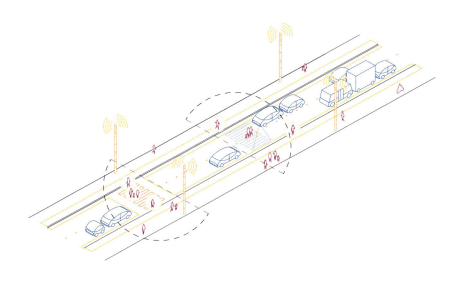

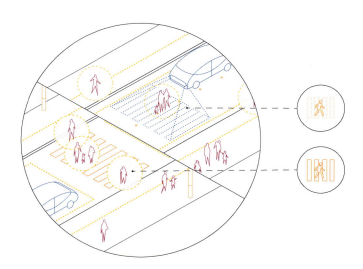

Crosswalk scenario in the case of vehicle intelligence and infrastructure intelligence.

Traffic and Interaction Infrastructure   225

BUILDING TYPOLOGY AND PROGRAMME

Grocery Drive-thru
(a.k.a. Dispatch Hub)

The package delivery service is a phenomenon which has radically changed character in recent years. The emergence of internet shopping is one of the most important disruptive economic drivers in retail and the competition in this area will determine the survival or demise of many corporate interests. Delivering these goods is an increasingly important part of who has market share—the demand of consumers for goods is dependent in large part on the speed of delivery available. This in turn has created a need for innovation in delivery methods, including the introduction of drones and robot delivery. The future AV is part of this ecosystem but its exact role, as yet, remains undefined in form or function. Requiring neither driver nor windshield, we can foresee a large box on wheels, wired into the economic system and dispatched via efficiency algorithms. These AVs could belong to companies dispatching goods locally, to large distributors operating from offshore, or to car-share companies who are servicing customer orders while they are at work or at home. In terms of our built environment, the modification to buildings

and parking lots to accommodate this new shift in delivery modalities is also of significance. Parking lots could potentially be reduced in size or even eliminated altogether for grocery (and other) stores as more customers choose to have their purchases picked up or delivered by AVs.

Although quite a rarity today, older supermarkets in North America were designed with a pick-up area for more convenient loading of the groceries into the car by an attendant. Although nowadays one carries one's own groceries to the car in a cart, it used to be that the customer was spared the trouble of hauling and lifting the groceries to the car; instead, they drove around to the pick-up area where the attendant would identify the groceries with a matching tag number and load the groceries into the trunk. Inside the store there were conveyor belts installed to transport one's groceries from the till to the pick-up areas.

More recently, supermarkets are offering online grocery shopping which can be ordered from anywhere that has Wi-Fi. This reduces the store even further to little more than a warehouse and a loading area. In this case the store can save significant amounts of money by locating itself away from high density areas where real estate is expensive. The disadvantage to the customer is that the AV must travel further from the store to the home, using more energy. This matters less if the store arranges the delivery and a personal AV is not used so the cost accrues to the store and not the customer.

Some commentators predict that the rise of AVs might also bring about their use for completing errands and transporting goods, and pointedly describe neighbourhoods "patrolled" by "driverless ice cream trucks, food trucks, vending machine trucks and Google Streetview cars all day long."[19] Yet the strangeness of the presence of autonomous vehicles performing unforeseen tasks should not hinder the consideration of other potential efficiencies that might result from their implementation. "Grocery Drive-thru" reimagines the traditional supermarket or big-box store, typically needing large amounts of parking and product display space, as a compact digitalized warehouse, optimized for the storage of groceries (or other goods) and the assembly and loading of custom orders into pick-up AVs. A further implication of this scenario is what is termed the "Internet of Things," an assemblage of intelligent machines with the ability to "exchange their sensor inputs among each other in order to optimize a well-defined utility function,"[20] which will redefine human interaction with everyday objects. One's fridge could thus monitor its contents, order replacement food from the grocery store, and arrange for its delivery via an AV—whether that be a private AV belonging to the same household, or a specialized delivery vehicle with compact storage space. (For a version of this idea, see IDEO's "The Future of Automobility."[21])

Building Typology and Programme   227

Grocery Drive-thru
(a.k.a. Dispatch Hub)

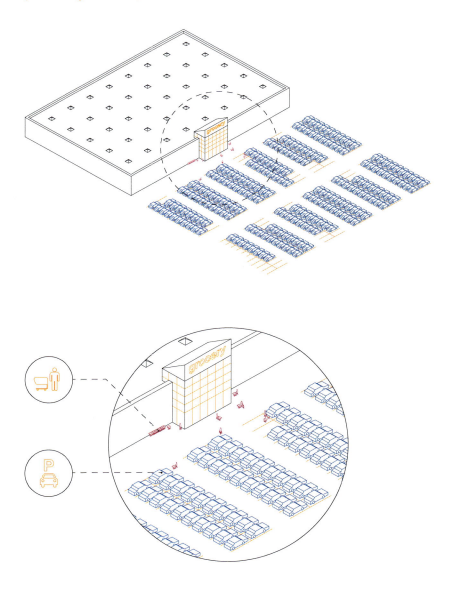

Traditional big-box store with surrounding surface parking.

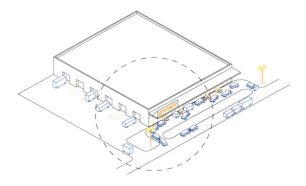

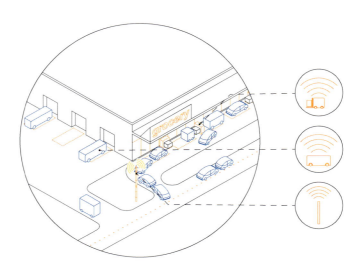

Grocery dispatch hub with automated goods loading from freight trucks and into consumer vehicles.

Building Typology and Programme

Fast Charge Fast Food

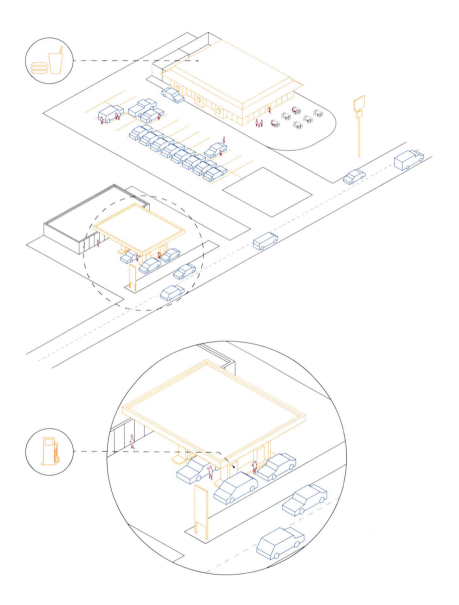

Typical gas station and drive-in restaurant.

230 Chapter 7 Street Scale Impacts

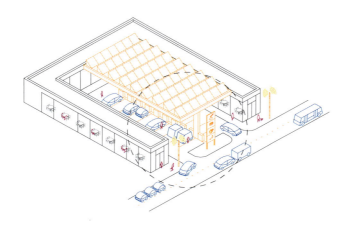

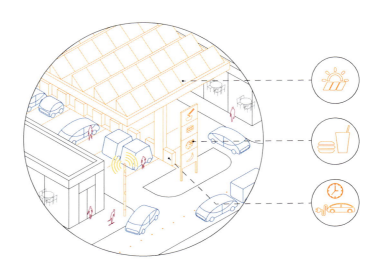

Fast-charging station combined with fast-food service.

Fast Charge Fast Food

It is predicted by many that autonomous cars will likely be electric vehicles (EVs), powered by rechargeable batteries. In fact, autonomous vehicle technology is seen by some as the breakthrough for EV technology for various reasons, including less complex technology, increased safety, lower service cost and reduced emissions.[22] While battery technology is under constant development, currently EVs have a limited travel range after which they need to be recharged. At present there are variations on charging technology, including alternating current (AC) charging and direct current quick charging (DCQC), as well as 'battery swap'—the replacement of the drained battery, usually located in the bottom of the car, with a fully charged one. The drawing

"Fast Charge Fast Food" conceptualizes a quick electric charging or battery swap scenario in an urban context using the gas station and the drive-in restaurant building types as precedents. The two requirements—refilling the fuel tank and purchasing food—are based on a combination of expedience and accessibility by car, and are combined advantageously. One can order take-out food during the 5–15 minute time slot needed for fast charging, and either eat at the provided seating area or on the go in their self-driving vehicle. Since the disappearance of the vast car-dependent landscapes of North America is unlikely in the foreseeable future, this scenario offers a new type of service and social space. Similar to "Charged Carport," the building is drawn to include a solar panel canopy—a new

Mobile Office Dock

spin on the gas station precedent. One of the disruptive aspects of autonomous vehicles is the possibility for passengers to engage in various activities while being transported, in combination with increased comfort and privacy. For instance, a commuting vehicle can serve as one's mobile bedroom or office space. "Mobile Office Dock" takes this latter case as the inspiration for a scenario of hyper-mobile white-collar workers adapted to working on the go in AVs that double up as their office cubicle. The drawing depicts a building type that accommodates AVs and provides them with a basic infrastructural framework. These buildings could also include access to cafés, coffee shops, washrooms, kitchen facilities, meeting and co-working space, electronic services such as printing, and

vehicle charging. Compared to the traditional suburban office park type, surrounded with surface parking, the vehicle in this scenario remains integral to the minimal furnishing of the shared space which might resemble a kind of conditioned open-plan warehouse. Similar to existing types of shared workspaces, space in a Mobile Office Dock could be rented either short- or long-term, based on the needs of users. The cafés and coffee shops could be configured so that they serviced the general public as well as the mobile office patrons.

Mobile Office Dock

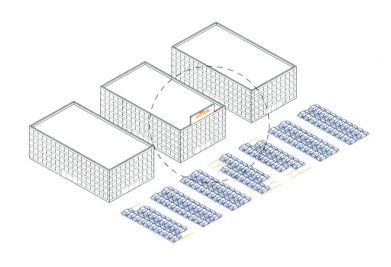

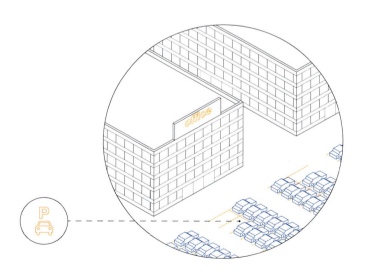

Typical suburban office park.

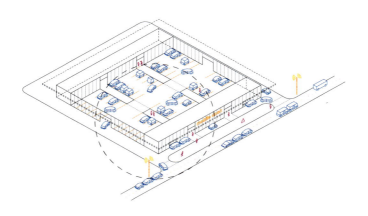

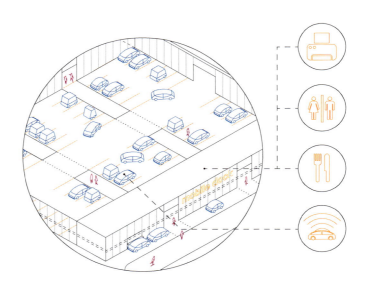

Shared workspace infrastructure for mobile AV offices.

Building Typology and Programme

Charged Carport

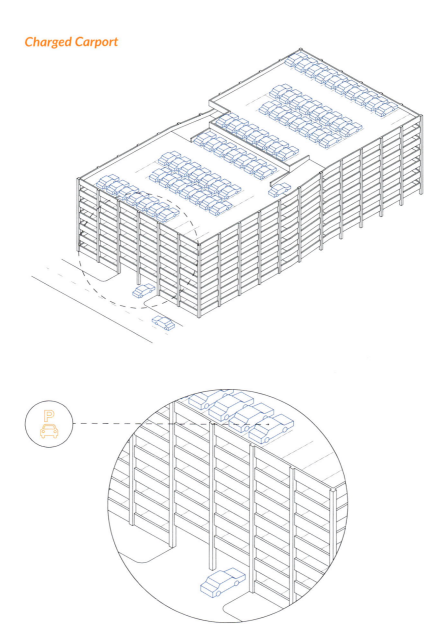

Traditional ramped urban parking garage.

236   Chapter 7 Street Scale Impacts

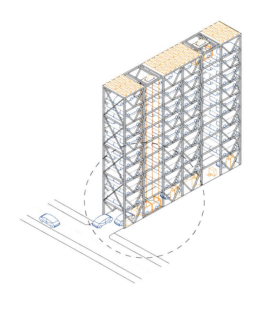

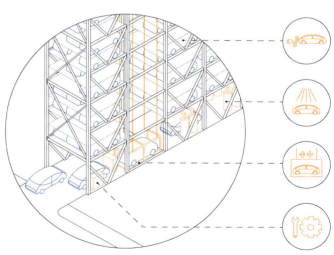

Charging and service station for shared-AV fleet.

Building Typology and Programme 237

Charged Carport

At present surface parking lots and parking garages constitute a major land use and building type in North American urban centres, due to the necessity and desirability of the proximity of parking to destinations. According to some estimates, an average of 30% of traffic in central business districts is generated by vehicles seeking to find a parking space close to the occupants' final destination.[23] It is also an established fact that an average car is parked and unused for as much as 90% of its lifetime.[24] In a world of intelligent mobility, self-driving vehicles will be able to pick up and drop off passengers where desired, and drive themselves to parking locations.[25] This fact in itself destabilizes the future of the urban landscape, which to date has been highly parking-oriented: one only has to think of Los Angeles and its extended parking, or even European squares that are now covered with parked vehicles.

Inhabiting this future further, if we look at the consolidation of parking at more remote stations, we note that the form of parking structures could transform from mere storage to include new functions associated with intelligent mobility. Taking the interaction between vehicles and the city one step further, the Charged Carport building type can be also envisioned as part of a vehicle-to-grid power system, in which parked vehicles are charged with alternate energies while they are plugged in— essentially making the parkade into a giant battery for renewable energy. The entire garaged fleet of cars can begin charging when alternative energies are online and cease charging when the energy is offline. Further, parking vehicles could return surplus electricity to the grid during peak demand hours. Part of this system, the structure itself, can be a platform for energy generation (see also: "Parking Power" in Chapter 5).

Inspired by existing compact parking structures in dense urban environments such as Tokyo or Hong Kong, "Charged Carport" also envisions a new building type that combines the storage of vehicles, storage of energy, electric charging and servicing. In comparison to a large, monofunctional parking garage, it presents a structure entirely free of human occupants and thus scaled to vehicles, serving as both a parking and charging space for unused vehicles and also equipped with the cleaning and maintenance functions that would be necessary for intensively used SAVs. Not only would such parking structures be more compact but they could be smaller in total capacity as well, since a shared vehicle fleet could dramatically decrease the number of cars in use in the city.[26]

Residential Retool

The significance of the automobile in North American culture is laid plain by the predominance of the garage in 20th century housing design in North America. Not only is the garage a large use of land, sometimes accommodating two or even three cars, but in many cases it has been built on the front face of the house as land tracts have contracted and squeezed the garage out in front of the rest of the house.

The garage plays a large role in the culture of the suburban family, often providing storage space for equipment and tools and functioning as a workshop as well as a storage area for the vehicle. The garage and the lawn are significant identifiers of North American suburban life: while the other programmes in the house are fairly consistent across housing types, it is those two things that really act as symbolic signifiers of North American culture and could even be seen as representative of the American Dream. It is a testament to the impact of the AV that visual signifiers of culture on such a massive scale will be so directly affected by the technology.

The question then becomes, what is the impact? If the garage is no longer of use, it is likely that resourceful citizens will find an alternative use for it, such as densifying housing, or even

remove it and use the land area for lawn. With baby boomers ageing and more families having to take on larger responsibilities for caring for older parents and relatives, the possibilities which emerge here are a fortuitous coincidence: garages can be converted into 'granny suites' and allow parents to stay nearby while providing some semblance of autonomy. Along similar lines, the spaces could be rented out to generate income.

In areas where zoning is less strict, it may be beneficial to rethink the integration of services or commercial ventures: from doctors' offices to nail studios, the garage in the front of the house could be converted to a commercial use. The space is easily visible from the street and therefore lends itself to signage. Its positioning closer to the street also facilitates entry without incursion into the more private areas of the house making it ideal for a business. This may be particularly suitable for busier streets or corner lots where, in the past, corner stores may have been located.

Building Typology and Programme 239

Residential Retool

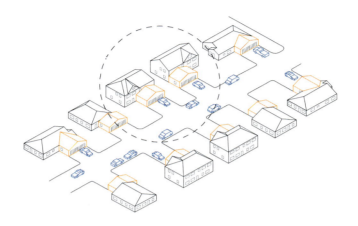

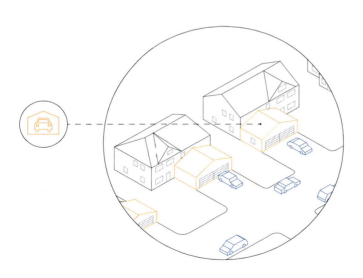

Detached housing with driveways and garages.

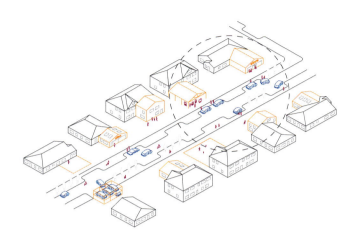

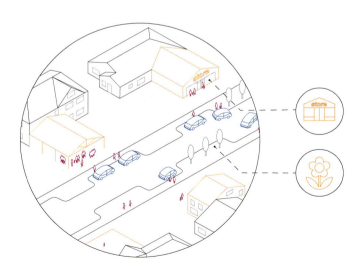

Renovated housing with SAV network pull-outs and reallocated space.

SHIPPING

The exponential growth in online shopping means that there is already a demand for AV technology. As is often the case with new technologies, larger companies have more resources to put towards capital investment and can engage more easily with the technology. Companies have already invested significantly in looking at this technology and innovative autonomous delivery technologies are being developed at a rapid pace in order to get things to consumers ever cheaper and faster.[27] Large shipping companies like Amazon, Uber, FedEx, Google and Domino's, are working quickly to develop autonomous shipping capability both in the form of drones and delivery robots and AVs in various forms and sizes.[28,29] There is a strong financial incentive to do so since salaries for drivers are a significant factor in the cost of package delivery. The Starship individual sidewalk delivery robot is being developed by Skype founders Ahti Heinla and Janus Fris,[30] and Google has requested a patent for an autonomous delivery truck with compartments that can be unlocked by a customer with a unique code.[31] Boston Group has extremely sophisticated human-form robots to tackle the last 100m delivery issues; these robots are capable of addressing stairs and other obstacles on the way to the porch.[32]

These innovations will cascade down to smaller businesses and could see them moving forward in two possible ways. Smaller businesses may opt to buy their own small delivery vehicle, such as Starship, and dispatch it from inside the store on an as-needed basis. Alternatively, they could subscribe to an on-demand service which would provide automated dispatch and delivery services for local companies. The delivery service could offer features such as client confirmations of shipping and coordinate timing of delivery to the customers. Also, if multiple shipments need to be dispatched at a 'rush hour' then they would have access to a larger fleet of dispatch vehicles when required.

Customers who are more environmentally conscious may prefer to order from local businesses as shipments from global dominant firms need to be delivered from warehouses which are many miles away, increasing energy consumption and supporting global markets rather than local communities.

Infrastructure could change to support these types of shipping requirements at businesses and as a result, receiving deliveries at home and at places of business may change form too. Some of these infrastructures are schematically shown in the following drawings.

Commercial Street Delivery Station

The main challenge for shipping with AV technology is the last 100m from the vehicle into the shop or home. While larger stores are likely to have staff that can unload from the vehicles, with small businesses staff may not be able to leave the shop making unloading problematic: one can think of a small convenience store owner or even a crew from Starbucks who are busy in their stores. Some local deliveries may be serviced by small agile sidewalk-based delivery vehicles. Store design may start to incorporate a delivery 'robot door' which allows the robot to enter the store directly and thus prevents staff from having to leave the store. A similar feature may be used for home deliveries too (see below).

For a larger range, a more robust vehicle may be desired, in which case loading becomes an issue. More roadside loading zones may be required due to increased numbers of online deliveries; this may be easily accommodated if street parking is less in demand. A better solution, though, might be to have a shipping distribution centre at the curbside where store owners can come out when convenient and load the facility with a packed custom delivery box; the delivery vehicle can then remove the boxes robotically and deliver them on a route tailored according to where the day's deliveries are

required. At the other end, it may deliver to another box or a customer may unlock the box in the van and retrieve their goods.

*Commercial Street
Delivery Station*

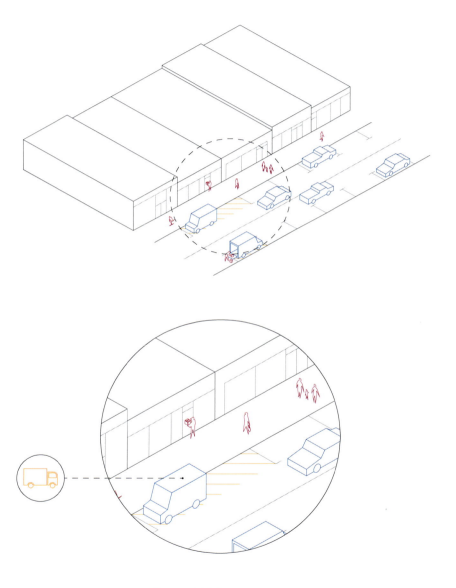

Commercial delivery zone area.

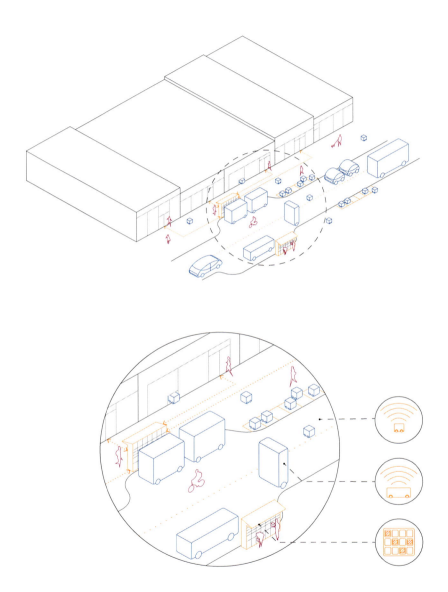

Commercial delivery zone areas with automated shared delivery boxes.

Shipping

Home Delivery Box

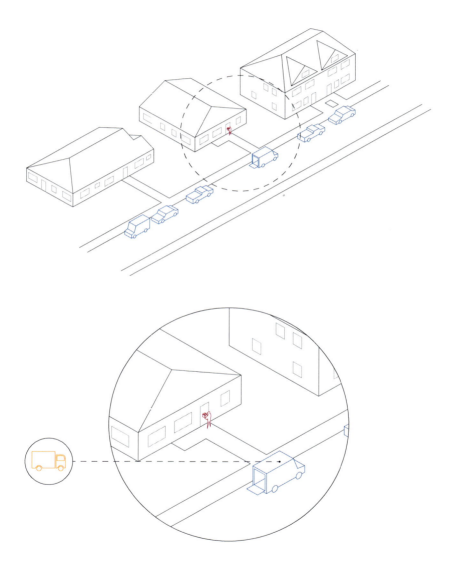

Conventional door-to-door delivery.

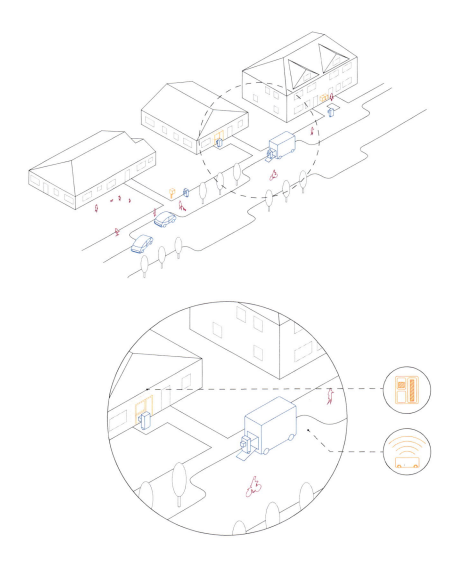

Driverless automated shipping to Home Delivery Box.

Shipping 247

Home Delivery Box

The simplest home delivery method is one where a robot delivers the package and leaves it on the doorstep, sending an email or other digital correspondence to the customer to indicate it has been delivered. For delivery articles requiring more security, the delivery vehicle could wait outside the home until the customer has come and unlocked the vehicle with a secure code. The disadvantage to this is that it ties up the delivery vehicle until the customer comes out and retrieves the package.

As another option, a community 'delivery box' may be possible. These are already used by postal services to centralize mail delivery, saving time for the delivery company. It doesn't save time for the citizen, who must go to the centralized place to pick up the mail, but it does facilitate opportunities to meet one's neighbours and, if expanded in programme, could become a small community hub where local posters are placed and books shared.

In other situations, a mailbox similar to a country mailbox with a flag on it to indicate that contents have been delivered could be used. The robotic delivery vehicles could place packages within these home delivery boxes in the same way they do for commercial delivery hubs.

Finally, it may be possible that a 'robot door' could be installed in the home and that the robot could enter the home through the door and leave the package.

Notes

1 Peter D. Norton, *Fighting Traffic* (Cambridge: MIT Press, 2008).

2 Koninklijke Nederlandse Toeristen Bond ANWB, *Woonerf: A New Approach to Environmental Management in Residential Areas and the Related Traffic Legislation* (ANWB, 1980).

3 Daniel Fagnant and Kara Kockelman, "The Travel and Environmental Implications of Shared Autonomous Vehicles, Using Agent-Based Model Scenarios," *Transportation Research Part C: Emerging Technologies* 40 (2014): 8.

4 Burkhard Bilger, "Auto Correct—Has the Self Driving Car Arrived at Last?" *The New Yorker*, November 13, 2013, https://www.newyorker.com/magazine/2013/11/25/auto-correct.

5 Lene Herrstedt, "Traffic Calming Design—A Speed Management Method: Danish Experiences on Environmentally Adapted Through Roads." *Accident Analysis & Prevention* 24, no.1 (1992): 3–16.

6 Yaletown in Vancouver is one example.

7 Hugh Durrant-Whyte, "A Critical Review of the State-of-the-Art in Autonomous Land Vehicle Systems and Technology" (Sandia National Laboratories, 2001).

8 "Berkeley Robotics & Human Engineering Laboratory," http://bleex.me.berkeley.edu/.

9 Mark Shwartz, "Wireless Power Could Revolutionize Highway Transportation, Stanford Researchers Say," *Stanford University News*, February 1, 2012, http://news.stanford.edu/news/2012/february/wireless-vehicle-charge-020112.html.

10 "BIG's Proposal for the Audi Urban Future Award," *ArchDaily*, September 10, 2010, http://www.archdaily.com/77103/bigs-proposal-for-the-audi-urban-future-award/.

11 Stelios Rodoulis, "The Impact of Autonomous Vehicles on Cities," *Journeys* (2014): 14–15.

12 Tan Cheon Kheong and Tham Kwang Sheun, "Autonomous Vehicles, Next Stop: Singapore," *Journeys* (2014): 6.

13 Bradley Berman, "Get Ready To Say Goodbye To The Traffic Light," *ReadWrite*, 2014, https://readwrite.com/2014/08/20/traffic-light-smart-cars-networked-roads/.

14 Thorsten Luettel, Michael Himmelsbach, and Hans-Joachim Wuensche, "Autonomous Ground Vehicles—Concepts and a Path to the Future," *Proceedings of the IEEE 100, no. Special Centennial Issue* (2012): 1832–34.

15 Jianqi Liu et al., "A Survey on Position-Based Routing for Vehicular Ad Hoc Networks," *Telecommunication Systems* 62, no. 1 (2016): 15–30.

16 Jordan Yerman, "V-Poles: Douglas Coupland Writes the Future of the Telephone Pole," *The Vancouver Observer*, July 26, 2013, https://www.vancouverobserver.com/life/technology/v-poles-douglas-coupland-writes-future-telephone-pole.

17 Kurt Dresner, "AIM: Autonomous Intersection Management—Project Home Page" (AI Laboratory, University of Texas, Department of Computer Science, 2018), http://www.cs.utexas.edu/~aim/.

18 Ibid.

19 Jason Koebler, "Autonomous Vehicles Will Bring the Rise of 'Spam Cars,'" *Motherboard*, June 18, 2014, https://motherboard.vice.com/en_us/article/pgak49/autonomous-vehicles-will-bring-the-rise-of-spam-cars.

20 Mario Gerla et al., "Internet of Vehicles: From Intelligent Grid to Autonomous Cars and Vehicular Clouds," in *Internet of Things (WF-IoT), 2014 IEEE World Forum On* (IEEE, 2014): 241.

21 "IDEO · The Future of Automobility," https://automobility.ideo.com/.

22 Hars, "Autonomous Cars: Breakthrough for Electric Vehicles," *Inventivio Innovation Briefs*, http://www.inventivio.com/innovationbriefs/2014-02/.

23 Donald C Shoup, "Cruising for Parking," *Transport Policy* 13, no. 6 (2006): 479–486.

24 Martin V. Melosi, "The Automobile Shapes The City" (The University of Michigan Dearborn & Benson Ford Research Centre, 2005), http://www.autolife.umd.umich.edu/Environment/E_Casestudy/E_casestudy.htm.

25 Rodoulis, "The Impact of Autonomous Vehicles on Cities," 16.

26 Fagnant and Kockelman, "The Travel and Environmental Implications of Shared Autonomous Vehicles," 8.

27 Sol You, "Autonomous Delivery Vehicle" *Behance*, https://www.behance.net/gallery/36680603/AUTONOMOUS-DELIVERY-VEHICLE-by-Sol-You.

28 Alex Davies, "Uber's Self-Driving Truck Makes Its First Delivery: 50,000 Budweisers," *Wired*, June 3, 2017, https://www.wired.com/2016/10/ubers-self-driving-truck-makes-first-delivery-50000-beers/.

29 Marcus Fairs, "Domino Launches World's First Driverless Pizza Delivery Vehicles," *Dezeen*, February 16, 2016, https://www.dezeen.com/2015/04/01/dominos-launches-worlds-first-driverless-pizza-delivery-vehicles/.

30 Martindale, Jon, "Autonomous Delivery Robots Could Shake Up Grocery Business in 2016," *KitGuru*, November 2, 2015, https://www.kitguru.net/channel/generaltech/jon-martindale/autonomous-delivery-robots-could-shake-up-grocery-business-in-2016/.

31 "Self-driving Cargo-I Can See It All Now," *Sqwabb*, March 10, 2016, https://sqwabb.wordpress.com/2016/03/10/self-driving-cargo-i-can-see-it-all-now/.

32 Dan Maloney, "Autonomous Delivery and the Last 100 Feet," *Hackaday*, March 13, 2017, https://hackaday.com/2017/03/13/autonomous-delivery-and-the-last-100-feet/.

Chapter 8
Public Transportation

Chapter 8
Public Transportation

The future of public transit is one of the most exciting topics surrounding AVs because of what is at stake: on the one hand there is the potential to re-imagine what public transit could be using this technology; on the other, the potential for the loss of public transit completely. Public transit is essential in order to provide mobility for all of the population, servicing those who may not otherwise have the ability or financial means to get around; it also has the benefits of reducing congestion and greenhouse gas emissions as well as promoting economic development. But public transit is too often associated with slow and inconvenient modes of transport[1] that do not take the rider to where they want to go but instead require the rider to move to where these services are deployed in the urban fabric (the 'last mile' problem). This is shown by the fact that 91.4% of trips in the US are taken by private car and only 3.7% by transit.[2] (Transit performs slightly better with commuters, where 5.1% of people take transit.[3,4])

However, there is great latent potential for transit ridership. Where transit is well set up and convenient, it is readily adopted. This can be seen in New York City, where 55% of people commute by transit[5] and in Copenhagen, where 28% use transit. In Zurich, 25% of the population are committed transit users and in Toronto and Montreal, 23.3% and 22.2% of commuters respectively make work journeys this way.[6] These cities cover a broad range of climates and urban patterns and all show high transit ridership when the service is of high value to its users.

Automated technology has the potential to address many of the negative aspects of public transit: last mile issues could be solved by on-demand shuttles, which pick up and drop off at the door, or by local SAV networks. Service at night could be maintained with on-demand systems providing better safety and service for those who need to travel at night either for work or recreation. Transit systems could adjust live to meet demand and deploy more vehicles as needed; advanced booking systems could even reserve seats so riders do not have to stand. Furthermore, the cost of public transit could be significantly reduced if driver salaries are no longer an overhead; while any loss of jobs is obviously a significant and problematic issue, it would nevertheless reduce the costs of transit and allow companies to invest more money into vehicles. Vehicles could be smaller because the system is more agile and responsive and this will allow more vehicles to be deployed to reduce wait times. These changes would revolutionize public transit and, through faster and more responsive services, create better value for the rider who will then be incentivized to shift modes. However, this optimistic scenario requires public transportation providers to retool their operations, adding new technologies and investing in autonomous technology. It is far from certain that this will happen quickly.

SAV networks *are* likely to proliferate quickly since they are likely to be backed by highly monetized international corporations, such as BMW, Mercedes, Uber and Waymo. The incentive for car-share services to include more than one passenger per trip will be high: on the supply side, this would reduce demand at peak times allowing more trips to be serviced with fewer cars; on the demand side, it would result in cheaper fares for customers with minimal inconvenience. At this point it becomes a question of whether these SAV networks will be considered as public transportation. If public transportation is defined by whether a public agency runs the service, then the term 'public transportation' would not be used for private companies and the 'shared mobility service' label would be more suitable. Shared mobility services could then be provided by a private or a public entity.

Transit Erosion

Private SAV services could completely replace public transit.[7] The impact of current car-sharing services has already been shown to reduce transit ridership by 6%.[8] If SAV services, or even private shared mobility services, are too much competition for public transit, then public transit will suffer as ridership will substantially decrease and private entities will limit their service to those areas which are most profitable.[9,10] This could leave less dense and less profitable areas out of the SAV service area, leaving public transit only non-profitable areas to service. The financial impact of this could be ruinous for already cash-strapped services, as they would face falling ridership and income; this situation could erode public transit further. The electric streetcar is an historic precursor to this discussion and serves as a warning of the potential problems here. As discussed in the next chapter, the mass production technology for the automobile developed in 1916 caused the automobile to become affordable to much of the population; investors no longer saw the streetcar as a good investment. This led to the traction companies being unable to raise the funds needed to build new lines and eventually they went out of business.[11] Government was left to

Driverless Mass Transit

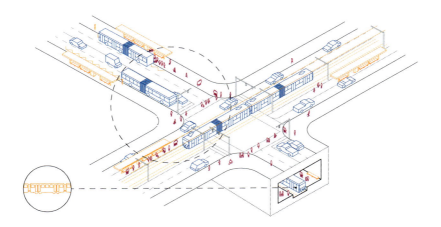

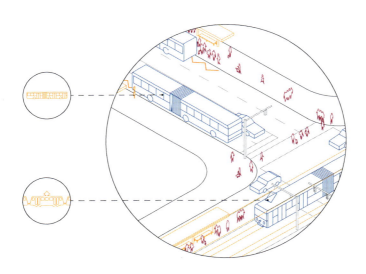

Urban mass transit cross-section: bus, tram and subway.

256   Chapter 8 Public Transportation

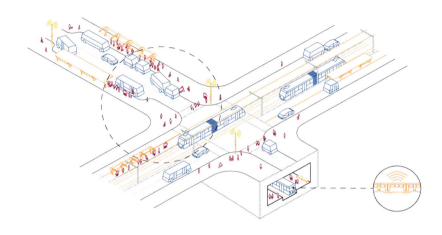

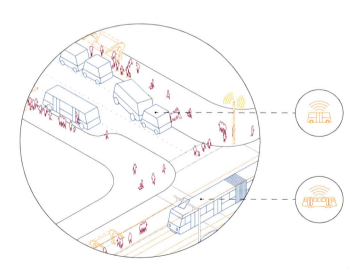

Autonomous mass transit cross-section: driverless shuttle, light rail and subway.

run the unprofitable services in areas where the streetcar was deemed to be essential to the communities. If public transit is eroded due to competition with private services, it is undoubtedly the poorest members of society that will be most impacted.[12]

Service Equity

Equity in public transit can be thought of in two ways: service equity—that is, how public monies get spent equitably across a geographic distribution to provide transit; and social equity, which views public transit as a means of improving equity across society. Both are important considerations. The service equity aspect always necessitates political discussion when investment in public transit is being made in a democracy. Outlying areas are more difficult to service with transit since the population is less dense, and it is usually much more expensive to create an equal level of service as compared to a dense inner city. Courts have weighed in on this and in general it is held that a government is required to provide the same level of monetary support geographically to their constituencies rather than the same level of transit service.[13] However, much of the public does not use transit; when they discuss equity, they are concerned with their region being treated equitably—that their tax dollars are being invested in their own area. The issue of equity in how money is spent

geographically often overlooks broader issues such as cleaner air and less congestion, and who benefits from these. Equity in public transit costs also frequently overlooks the significant subsidies that are provided to car users for their use of the streets.[14] What is still unclear is whether the use of automated mobility services will result in better and less expensive service for outlying areas. The possibility of better service lies in the potential for the driverless mobility to be used only when and where it is needed. Prospective cost savings in this case come, again, from the lack of a driver and the potential for the size of the AV to be customized according to demand across the day and region. It may be possible that the reduced number of vehicles required in outlying areas to produce the same transportation outcomes, in combination with the possibility of a central transportation dispatch centre to service outlying areas without additional costs, will even out service level disparities between areas.

Social Equity

There are many aspects to the social equity of transport; only a few are touched upon here as a way of introducing the conversation and of bringing attention to its importance. As noted by David C. Hodge, who studies the relationship between equity and transportation, "urban transportation is important to defining which social groups, which factions of capital, which geographic areas in cities are to gain and which are to lose."[15] As such, it is a vitally important discussion when talking about equity across our society.

It is generally accepted that a principal function of public transportation is to provide accessibility to all members of society, particularly to those who are transit dependent. The impact of AVs on transit dependence could be that people who have previously relied on public transport no longer do. This would include people such as the elderly, the physically disabled, the visually impaired and people who are too young to have a licence. These demographics are not necessarily transit dependent because of income, but because they are unable to operate a car themselves. From this perspective, equity will have already been improved by the AV technology. Social equity may also be improved if the cost of travel by SAV is lower than the cost of owning a vehicle: this would provide more people more access to higher value transportation at the same cost. However, public transit will still continue to be extremely important in order to allow access to transportation to those who cannot afford SAV service. It is these people who are most vulnerable if transit services are eroded or disappear.

With regard to equity and gender, it is well established that there are substantial differences between the travel patterns of men and those of women. In general, most studies have found that women work closer to home, travel less time to reach their jobs, and more often use public transit.[16] Data on carpooling is less clear; studies have found that in some areas women carpool more than men and in others this is reversed.[17] At present, detailed information on demographic choices between men and women is not sufficiently robust to understand travel behaviour and therefore what the impact of automation may be. The use of automated public transit may be less reassuring to women since there is no person 'in charge' in the vehicle. However, all transit AVs in current use do have cameras in the vehicle and it is anticipated that these would provide some level of security. The impact of this change to driverless transit, how the monitoring of the space works, what safety features are installed and so on, still needs to be resolved. Of course, it is not only women for whom personal security is a concern, and measures will be necessary to ensure general safety as well as psychological comfort during travel.

Garrett and Taylor have examined the issues of public transportation and social equity with regard to the interest from public transit organizations in attracting ridership amongst automobile drivers. They note that public transportation is generally utilized by transit commuters as well as 'transit dependents,' or those "who are too young, too old. Too poor, or physically unable to drive."[18] Their research indicates that funding is increasingly being spent to attract discretionary commuters to transit which involves increasing services for commuter rail and bus services. They see this as problematic because it is socially inequitable as well as inefficient:

> We conclude that the growing dissonance between the quality of service provided to inner-city residents who depend on local buses and the level of public resources being spent to attract new transit riders is both economically inefficient and socially inequitable. In light of this, we propose that transportation planners concerned with social justice (and economic efficiency) should re-examine current public transit policies and plans.[19]

This discussion also applies to automated transit and new investments in this area. The advent of autonomous technologies and their application to public transit, as well as the resources required for such investment, provides an opportunity to re-examine this issue and ask questions about equity and public transportation: how should fairness be defined in the context of public transit? Who is being served by the shift in transit investment to autonomous vehicles? Should public transit policy strive for greater geographic mobility, regardless of the available alternative modes of transportation, or would it

be preferable to improve accessibility for those with few private alternatives? Will these future investments increase or decrease social equity?

Congestion

Congestion is another critical discussion in regard to public transportation. Regardless of who operates it, shared mobility services are necessary if congestion reduction is a goal. One can get an idea of the impact of SAV networks with and without sharing rides (i.e. more than one person in the car) and public transit through a study carried out by the International Transport Forum[20] in 2015 on traffic in Lisbon, Portugal. Their findings show that if public transit disappears, and only SAV networks are left, the weekday traffic volume is estimated to increase to 190% of what it is today and 197% at peak hours.[21] If SAV networks accommodate more than one passenger at a time (autonomous shared mobility), the traffic is better but still expected to increase to 122% of today's levels. Under the transition scenario of 50% conventional drivers, the traffic would be 160% of the baseline condition. High capacity transit (subways in the case of Lisbon, but this could be rapid bus transit, etc.) with autonomous shared mobility would reduce this to between 106% (0% conventional drivers) and 129% (50% conventional drivers). High capacity transit is therefore essential to reducing congestion,

260   Chapter 8 Public Transportation

regardless of what other autonomous mobility services are available.[22]

Conclusion

Through discussions of accessibility to transit, social and service equity, and congestion, one can see the importance of public transit. While this is not new knowledge, the high impact, high risk position that AV technology brings to public transit brings the urgency of the discussion to the forefront. It seems clear that expanded public transit, especially of the high capacity variety, will be increasingly important as AV technology is introduced, both to provide equity but also to reduce congestion and pollution. What is required to facilitate this, however, are responsive and agile public transit agencies who can move to embrace the new technologies at a very quick rate. This is a high stakes social issue and, at this point, the outcome is still unclear.

Notes

1 Federal Highways Administration National Household Travel Survey, "Summary of Travel Trends: 2009 National Household Travel Survey (Document as Well as Data in XLS Format)," 2009, 48.

2 Federal Highways Administration National Household Travel Survey, Table 9.

3 Federal Highways Administration National Household Travel Survey, 46.

4 American Census Bureau, "American Communities Survey," Means of Transportation to Work by Selected Characteristics, 2016, https://factfinder.census.gov/faces/tableservices/jsf/pages/productview.xhtml?pid=ACS_16_1YR_S0802&prodType=table.

5 American Census Bureau.

6 Statistics Canada, "National Household Survey," 2011.

7 International Transport Forum, OECD, "Urban Mobility System Upgrade: How Shared Self Driving Cars Could Change City Traffic," 2015, 6.

8 Regina R. Clewlow and Mishra, Gouri Shankar, "Disruptive Transportation: The Adoption, Utilization, and Impacts of Ride-Hailing in the United States, Research Report—UCD-ITS-RR-17-07" (UC David Institute of Transportation Studies, 2017).

9 This can be seen by Car2Go's reduction of service area in Vancouver, Canada in 2016.

10 "Car2go Cuts Richmond, North Vancouver Coverage," *CBC News*, January 19, 2016, 2, http://www.cbc.ca/news/canada/british-columbia/car2go-cuts-richmond-north-vancouver-coverage-1.3343303.

11 Susan Hanson, *The Geography of Urban Transportation, Second Edition* (New York: The Guilford Press, 1995) 39.

12 International Transport Forum, OECD, "Shaping the Relationship between Public Transport and Innovative Mobility," 2017, 7.

13 David C. Hodge, "My Fair Share: Equity Issues in Urban Transportation," in T*he Geography of Urban Transportation Second Edition,* ed. Susan Hanson (New York: The Guilford Press, 1995).

14 Ibid, 364.

15 David C Hodge, "Geography and the Political Economy of Urban Transportation," *Urban Geography* 11, no. 1 (1990): 87–100.

16 Sandra Rosenbloom, "Differences by Sex in the Home-to-Work Travel Patterns of Married Parents in Two Major Metropolitan Areas," *Espace, Populations, Sociétés* 7, no. 1 (1989): 65–75.

17 Ibid, 71.

18 Mark Garrett and Brian Taylor, "Reconsidering Social Equity in Public Transit," *Berkeley Planning Journal* 13, no. 1 (1999): 6.

19 Ibid, 6.

20 International Transport Forum, OECD, "Urban Mobility System Upgrade."

21 Ibid, 20.

22 Ibid.

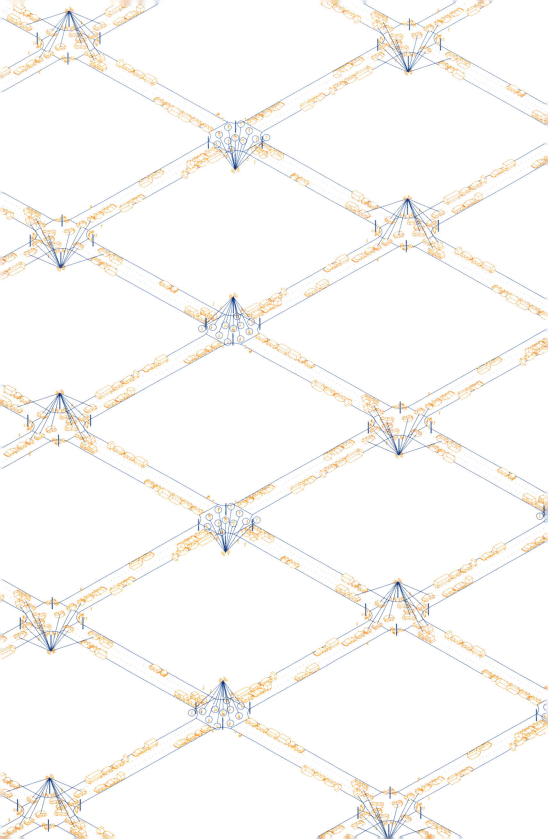

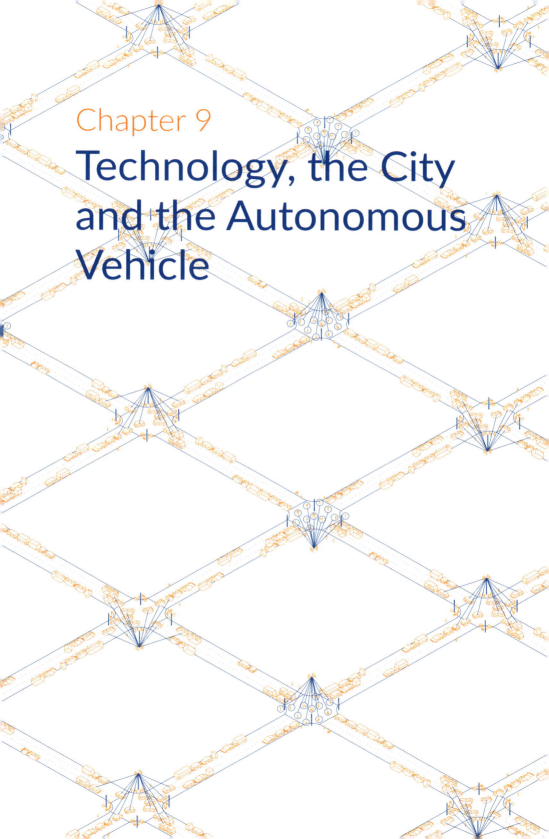

Chapter 9
Technology, the City and the Autonomous Vehicle

Chapter 9

Technology, the City and the Autonomous Vehicle

Introduction

The discussion in this book so far has mainly been about the intelligence of the car, with some discussion of the benefit of infrastructural intelligence; now we turn our focus to the simultaneous changes the city will be undergoing as a result of digital technology and how that will affect its relationship to the AV. Intelligence as described here is not intelligence in the sense that the car or city are sentient and can make decisions; it is intended to mean that each can make decisions based on inputs from a network and respond to those inputs based on preset programming. That is not to say that cities and cars could not develop sentience—this has been discussed by many others, most notably Antoine Picon in *Smart Cities*[1] and Mark Shepard in *Sentient City*,[2] as well as many in the SENSEable City Lab at MIT. Here, however, we will discuss ideas about how city intelligence could relate to the AV and what benefits or disadvantages this may bring to the citizens of these cities.

Benefit to AVs

The advantage of infrastructural intelligence—or intelligence provided by cities—in terms of AV functionality is that it can provide 'live' data about the streets, the network, surroundings generally and potentially other cars and actors in the vicinity. It can also provide local accurate mapping data for the area, decreasing the required memory and computing power for the vehicle. Detailed mapping of the urban fabric is a critical aspect of the AV environment. Whereas landscape mapping tends to be two-dimensional, the mapping that AVs require is three-dimensional: it is this mapping which connects the urban landscape to the digital framework. Maps for AVs are invaluable in facilitating the functioning of the AV and SAV networks, and cities where AVs are now being introduced are extensively mapped in aid of the AV navigation. But these maps are 'heavy,' meaning they need a lot of storage in the AV computing system. If accurate maps could be loaded live from city infrastructure, this would relieve the AV of having to store the data and update it if something changes. These maps could also include information on current unanticipated events in the city, for example where roads are blocked or protests or parades are happening. As such, infrastructural intelligence could increase reliability and accuracy of the functioning and routing of the AVs as well as decrease their need for memory storage and computing power.

Network Resilience

One potential disadvantage for the AV which is worth consideration is its dependency on an urban network. Systems can, and do, fail; if that system is a centralized control system for transportation upon which AVs are dependent, we can see that system failure would be highly problematic. That is not to say that engineers could not design a redundant or adaptive control system which could isolate areas that fail and then compensate; however, this type of engineering would be expensive as well as redundant, both qualities which perhaps run counter to traditional engineering methodologies that celebrate economy and efficiency. However, as the need for resilient software systems increases, approaches will need to be reconsidered. There is also the critical issue of network security and its vulnerability to intentional damage by terrorists, or other malevolent actors, who choose to target infrastructural systems—a

particularly significant concern today when seemingly every system is vulnerable to hacking.

Current design theories have dealt with this type of problem previously and may be applicable to the configuration of the network of AVs and its relationship with the network of the city. These theorists posit that the network design should be more like a natural system. For example, Stan Allen writes, "Complex systems [...] such as cities or natural ecologies, are robust and adaptive: they produce complex effects through the interaction of simple variables, incorporate feedback, and are capable of adjusting as conditions change."[3] He also cites Jane Jacobs, who states, "Cities happen to be problems in organized complexity, like the life sciences."[4] Thus, we note that designers are thinking about and theorizing the city as a robust natural network, even though it is human-made. The robustness attributed to the city is perhaps due to a more bottom-up system of building, with many actors and many redundancies. If we apply this theory to the design of an infrastructure network to support AVs in the city, what is posited is that a single controlled network could be more vulnerable than a dispersed network with many actors providing information. In terms of an AV network, we can compare this to V2I (vehicle-to-infrastructure) and V2V (vehicle-to-vehicle) informational systems where vehicles are providing information to infrastructure and other vehicles. If vehicles are to take information from infrastructure, it could be 'live' and also temporary—i.e. information would disappear after a designated timeframe when it is supplanted by other information. Should hacking of such a system happen, then potentially it could be highly localized: system design would need to support this set up. This is, however, not so much a 'control system,' which implies centralized control, as an information relay system with information being assembled from, and relayed to, many robotic actors. It begins to resemble a natural system, although somewhat limited in its scope as it has presently been envisaged. Engineers are beginning to discuss approaches such as the 'Resilient Systems of Systems' (SoS) approach[5] for AV infrastructure which has characteristics including: independent operation of each AV, emergent behaviour both of the groups of AVs and the networks themselves, geographic distribution, and evolutionary functions.[6] The discussion currently focuses mainly on technology, however, and not the political and social framework behind how such a technology may be implemented.

Network Disposition

It becomes apparent from the discussion here that ecologies are perhaps an apt metaphor for AVs and their relationship to their infrastructures and the larger urban environment. The action and reaction of natural forces seems to be a fitting comparison for a technology-related infrastructure, and particularly for an AV. To design an infrastructure is to design something which will serve as a catalyst—its purpose is to facilitate some kind of movement or action. In general terms, an infrastructure is that which supports human activity and its presence as such may be somewhat intangible.

This catalytic character of infrastructure is critical: the idea that the presence (or absence) of infrastructure can cause something to happen. This dynamic catalytic action of an infrastructural intervention can be seen in the example of subway stations, as density is created at these points by drawing people to the place and creating a population where previously there was none. This intrinsic character of an infrastructure is described by Keller Easterling as "active form" and "disposition." Easterling explains "active form" as the rules by which form abides—a zoning bylaw, for example. The bylaw dictates the form although we never 'see' a bylaw—we only see the result. She writes that "active forms describe the protocols by which some alteration performs within a group, multiplies across a field, conditions a population, or generates a network."[7] Easterling's theories are influenced by the work of cybernetician Gregory Bateson. Bateson sees the organization of activity in the integration of people and groups, neurons, natural systems and artificial programmed systems as having similarities of character. Easterling uses Bateson's work and theories to support her idea of the "disposition of infrastructure." She claims that if infrastructure creates organizations, and these organizations have a disposition, then they affect the urban (or other) realm in which they operate:

> An underground mafia organized as a hub and spoke organization fosters secrecy because of limited contact to administrative decisions. A television or radio organization of mass media similarly has a hub and spoke organization very different from contemporary networks of computation.[8]

As further examples we can look to the typologies of different computer networks themselves: there are hierarchical networks, ring networks, mesh networks and so on. Each of these facilitates, and thus suggests, certain uses and organization of information. We can also look to roads which demonstrate more and less hierarchical arrangements—the classic road network which includes local, collector, arterial and freeways is a hierarchical network and gathers and distributes traffic with a branching network similar to the hierarchical computer network. Quoting Easterling again, "the active forms or directions for activity have

a substrate of geometry or arrangement that shapes the disposition of the organization."[9] So if the design of infrastructure facilitates some things and prevents others, then the question to ask in embarking on the design of infrastructure for the AV becomes: what should we try to facilitate, and can we set the disposition of the infrastructure to favour those things which we value as a society?

Benefits to the Public

Within a plural society, whatever infrastructure we set up in the city must support a variety of viewpoints and uses. It must also benefit its occupants. Neutral networks are key to this; by this, I mean networks which are not owned by one corporation or private interest but shared by all. Typically, in a democracy, this would mean a government-controlled network. While this may seem obvious, there are examples of tech companies who are charged with being monopolies[10] and are at the same time taking over parts of cities: for example, the Sidewalk Labs initiative in Toronto where Google, the parent company, is also charged with three breaches of antitrust rules in the EU.[11] In other cases, large companies like Siemens and IBM are vying to take over city infrastructure in the name of helping the cities but are also making large profits by getting an advantage in either head starts on business initiatives or spin-offs through easier access to markets.[12] The benefit for cities in engaging a company and providing them with a monopoly on the city system(s) is that they achieve smart infrastructure in a 'turnkey' arrangement with a tech firm, with only limited capital or personnel investment to achieve their goals for city 'smartness.'[13] For a cash-strapped municipal government, the incentive for this type of relationship is strong. But monopolies have four well-documented disadvantages: they can price fix because there is no competition, they can supply inferior products, they lose the incentive to innovate, and they create inflation. As such, cities should avoid creating monopolies in any form and adopt the principle of keeping their networks neutral with relation to their digital infrastructure; if they do not, citizens will inevitably lose in the long run, even if the city shows a benefit in the short term. The city as a neutral network, with many actors working to innovate, will provide unforeseen benefits; this can be seen with other networks and in setups like Apple and Android where ecosystems of apps are sourced from a broad range of people with varied interests and viewpoints. It seems the idea that only companies can innovate has been popular recently but it is certainly not universally true: Amsterdam's Smart City (ASC) platform was initiated by the Amsterdam Innovation Motor (AIM), a collaboration between technology providers and the City of Amsterdam, while San Francisco's then mayor, Ed Lee,

commented in 2012 that the city is a 'convener' of technological potential.[14] The question, then, is how to set up such a network for a city; as we shall see, many cities are currently experimenting with many different models.

Martijn de Waal is a writer and researcher focusing on the relation between digital media and urban culture, with a specific interest in public space. He writes about the potential of the public sphere and the idea of the future city and its public sphere (including public and digital realms) going different ways. On one hand, de Waal argues, the city could work like the internet, where people see and connect only with like-minded people. He says that in a dystopian version, only people with the 'right' RFID sensors could enter places so that one could be sure to be surrounded only by like-minded people—a concept which Belgian philosopher Lieven de Cauter calls a 'capsular society.' On the other, more optimistic, hand, de Waal also discusses using the locative media to re-activate the public sphere; there have been a multitude of projects such as this put forward by artists and urbanists. Examples include the Murmure project, which was launched in Toronto's Kensington Market in 2003 and then taken to Montreal and Vancouver;[15] it asks the public to tag places with 'intimate commemoration'—stories and memories of what places mean

270   Chapter 9 Technology, the City, and the Autonomous Vehicle

to them. The Yellow Arrow project, based in Germany,[16] explicitly seeks to have 'alternate' understandings of place documented through yellow arrows in a 'guerilla map.' There are also projects which digitally connect the public with the history of the past through a smart phone or supplemented through digital projective art—examples include the Vancouver In Time app by Simon Fraser University's 7th Floor Media[17] and the Montreal Cité Mémoire project.[18]

De Waal also discusses the possibility of using technology to create 'issue publics,' or groups that draw together because they wish to protest something. Saskia Sassen, the political economist who coined the term 'global city,' supports this idea and states that digital networks allow the disadvantaged, outsiders and discriminated against minorities to gain presence in global cities by allowing them to be political actors.[19] These global networks enable interconnection to allow political activism, support local communities and initiatives, and create local alliances within communities. She says this is important when it seems that the notion of 'local' is losing ground to the global (she notes that digital networks are mostly thought of as global).[20] Sassen concludes by claiming, "Any large city is today traversed by these 'invisible' circuits."[21] The 'disposition' of the system can be set up to facilitate these things—or not. There is a broader public discussion of this 'disposition'

which needs to be had, and about the infrastructure of the city set up to facilitate this.

While this discussion may seem independent of the debate concerning the infrastructure for the AV, engineers are already working on infrastructure that will facilitate simultaneous human sharing and robotic sharing because the technology is the same.[22] This technology is also able to share entertainment content, which opens up its potential use to many more actors. Such types of technologies form urban platforms similar to iPhones, Wikipedia and other open-sourced or multiple input modes of digital sharing. This type of open but 'content reviewed' platform has been used as a successful business model by Apple, Android and others. In this model, the companies provide the hardware and people develop software, with the platform provider collecting enough revenue to allow for reviewing and operation. A platform developed on this model could provide cities with the potential to engage citizens by asking them to provide input (already common with some city apps internationally) or offer local history or information on local events. It is likely platforms will emerge with just this type of framework in mind and the physical place, the citizen and the digital realms will be more robustly related. GE (General Electric) has a platform for its smart street lights and is installing it in San Diego in collaboration with Intel and AT&T. The street lights have cameras,

Benefits to the Public   271

sensors for sound and sensors to monitor pollution. The system is able to locate gunshots, assess crowd data, and check vehicle speeds. It also includes an open software platform for which developers can create applications. However, this type of system is again built by a company for profit and developed as a municipal centralized control system to facilitate urban concerns such as city policing; it has not been designed with the intention of facilitating local interaction or communication either for humans or, at this point, for AVs.

Sassen also has important commentary on the implications of technology for the city. She observes that the problem commentators have in understanding these implications results from two analytic flaws: one "confines technological reading to the technical capability of the digital technology,"[23] which ignores the societal impact. Sassen argues that this reading leads to an analysis in which the place becomes a 'non-place,' by assuming anything in the digital realm has no social or cultural characteristics, neutralizing its social and distinct characteristics.[24] Secondly, she says the reliance on analytic characterizations from the past will lead to a tendency to conceive of things as either digital or physical/material. This binary precludes more complex readings of the "impact on material and place bound considerations."[25] Both arguments apply to the AV and its networks, a realm where place and

digital mapping are more intertwined than ever before, as the physical and digital are continuously informing each other as well as the location of the vehicle.

These viewpoints allow us to see our cities and their digital infrastructure in ways that were neither available nor necessary to view 20th century infrastructure; to speak of freeways we do not need to talk of how they relate to local and global political movements or multinational global monopolies. Yet this is the 'material' of the digital infrastructure of the city—a network connected to others and potentially controlled by actors external to the city and even the country—many of which have motives relating to making profit for their organization and/or positioning themselves to do so in the future.

Infrastructure and the Finances of the City

Some of the practical issues of the city will push it to adopt digital technologies. For example, with the advent of the AV and SAV networks, parking income for cities will drop because the cars no longer need to park. This means cities will likely need to make up the lost funds. One of the strategies for funding car infrastructure which is under discussion even now in many urban centres is road pricing; this is often under the guise of reducing congestion, which it also alleviates. Road pricing is in effect in many cities already and advanced network intelligence in a city facilitates it. The authors of *Splintering Urbanism*, Steven Graham and Simon Marvin, note that all major infrastructure networks—energy, telecommunications, water and waste, and much of transport infrastructure—are being opened to private sector participation. As a result, infrastructure is one of the most important sectors in finance and technology.[26] Sassen would say the infrastructure has been liquefied and is now distributed across the globe: the implication is that the profits from local infrastructure development go to the wealthy around the world. As such, it is necessary to carefully consider the equity implications of how the pricing of roads is applied, who owns the technology, who operates it and gathers data, what happens to that data and what happens to the monies accrued.

Even in fully developed countries, there is, and will continue to be, socioeconomic stratification due to access to different infrastructures. Let us consider toll roads: expanding rapidly in the 90s, a new series of urban highways developed around the world. Based on electronic road pricing (ERP), "highway space has shifted from being 'dead,' public and electromechanical; now it is 'smart,' digitally controlled, privatized and sold as a priced commodity in a market for mobility that is increasingly diversified

in both time and space."[27] The technologies mean that the roadway itself can be splintered into custom lanes, from HOVs to bus lanes, lanes for only cars fitted with transponders, etc. Road networks, then, become commodified computerized systems. But such practices, the authors argue, provide the basis for a framework that differentiates groups according to the power over space that they are seen to warrant within the new urban political economy. They write,

> [R]oad pricing, or other linear methods of controlling or excluding particular social groups from getting control over space, equally limits the power of some while propelling others to the explosive heights of controlling space, and thereby everything contained in it. Developed entirely by private firms to service only the most lucrative nodes within the urban fabric, these new premium urban highways are thus entirely commodified. Sometimes the price of the journey varies in real time with demand.[28,29]

Thus, the developer can ensure snarl-free traffic under any condition and the affluent can bypass the gridlock any time of day and enjoy the premium networked connection.[30]

Road pricing is clearly a regressive tax, but if taxes accrued from road pricing are distributed to offset the regressive effect then, in theory, all can benefit. In regard to taking this strategy to the space of the city, road pricing is a highly effective method of reducing congestion and also of raising income for a city—but it ensures that only the affluent car owners get premium service on the public spaces of the road. It is up to the public in a democratic society to decide whether this is a good way to distribute a public service: whether using a road in a car or an AV, for example, is a public right; or perhaps one can only use the road for free if you travel in public transit, by bicycle or walk. On the one hand, it uses the forces of economics to move people to potentially sustainable modes (depending on whether fuelling is sustainable), but on the other, it takes a historically free space and monetizes it, either taxing it for government revenue and/or capitalizing it for the benefit of a company's shareholders.

The issue of the AV's digital umbilical cord to the city is still an open question, and therefore one that requires robust public input and debate. There is likely to be some kind of interaction between AVs and the city infrastructure and the question is how this infrastructure and communication protocol can be best set up to support the purposes of the city and its occupants. If cities are places for people to meet and exchange ideas, goods and money, then the infrastructure should support this interchange. Transportation routes and modes are the arteries and veins of a city; without healthy and highly functional transportation, the city will not flourish. So, using the network to ensure healthy transportation modes in multiple ways and to support throughput is key. But while considering transportation, how else can we support the purposes of the city? If the mode of connecting the AV to the city is through fixed infrastructure like the Compass Pole shown in Chapter 7, can we enable them to be used for other forms of communication or to facilitate other social action? In our illustration of the Compass Pole we have shown this infrastructure with the ability to provide graphics (holographic in this case); these could facilitate highly localized histories, banners, or information on local events. The pole could also charge smartphones or cars, potentially providing access to electricity for street people. The potential is only beginning to be seen.

Notes

1 Antoine Picon, *Smart Cities: A Spatialized Intelligence* (Chichester: Wiley, 2015).

2 Mark Shepard, *Sentient City: Ubiquitous Computing, Architecture, and the Future of Urban Space* (Cambridge: MIT Press, 2011).

3 Stan Allen, "Urbanisms in the Plural: The Information Thread," in *Fast Forward Urbanism: Rethinking Architecture's Engagement with the City* (New York: Princeton Architectural Press, 2011).

4 Jane Jacobs, *The Death and Life of Great American Cities* (New York: Vintage Books, 1961), 433.

5 Azad M. Madni et al., "Model-Based Approach for Engineering Resilient System-of-Systems: Application to Autonomous Vehicle Networks," in *Disciplinary Convergence in Systems Engineering Research* (Springer, 2018), 365–80.

6 Ibid.

7 Keller Easterling, "Disposition," in *Extrastatecraft: The Power of Infrastructure Space* (Verso Books, 2014).

8 Keller Easterling, "The Action Is the Form," in *Sentient City: Ubiquitous Computing, Architecture, and the Future of Urban Space* (Cambridge, Massachusetts: MIT Press, 2011), 158.

9 Ibid.

10 Franklin Foer, "Why Governments Should Protect Us from Barely-Taxed Tech Monopolies," *The Guardian*, October 19, 2017, http://www.theguardian.com/technology/2017/oct/19/surveillance-capitalism-government-big-tech-privacy.

11 Mark Scott, "Google Fined Record $2.7 Billion in E.U. Antitrust Ruling," *The New York Times*, June 27, 2017, https://www.nytimes.com/2017/06/27/technology/eu-google-fine.html.

12 Tuan-Yee Ching and Joseph Ferreira, "Smart Cities: Concepts, Perceptions and Lessons for Planners," in *Planning Support Systems and Smart Cities* (Springer, 2017).

13 Ibid.

14 Ibid, 152–54.

15 Mike Crang and Stephen Graham, "Sentient Cities: Ambient Intelligence and the Politics of Urban Space," *Information, Communication & Society* 10, no. 6 (December 1, 2007): 808.

16 Ibid.

17 Simon Fraser University 7th Floor Media, "Vancouver In Time on the App Store," App Store, https://itunes.apple.com/us/app/vancouver-in-time/id480547811?mt=8.

18 "Cité Mémoire," *Montréal En Histoire*s (blog), http://www.montrealenhistoires.com/en/cite-memoire/.

19 Saskia Sassen, "Unsettling Topographic Representation," in *Sentient City: Ubiquitous Computing, Architecture, and the Future of Urban Space* (Cambridge, Massachusetts: MIT Press, 2011).

20 Ibid, 189.

21 Ibid.

22 Jianqi Liu et al., "A Survey on Position-Based Routing for Vehicular Ad Hoc Networks," *Telecommunication Systems* 62, no. 1 (2016): 15–30.

23 Sassen, "Unsettling Topographic Representation," 186.

24 Saskia Sassen, *Territory, Authority, Rights: From Medieval to Global Assemblages* (New York: Princeton University Press, 2008). See Chapter 7.

25 Sassen, "Unsettling Topographic Representation," 186.

26 Stephen Graham and Simon Marvin, *Splintering Urbanism: Networked Infrastructures, Technological Mobilities and the Urban Condition* (New York: Routledge, 2001), 91, 95.

27 Ibid, 250.

28 Graham and Marvin, 251, quoting E. Swyngedouw. "Communications, Mobility and the Struggle for Power over Space" in *Transport and Communications in the New Europe* (Belhaven: London, 1993): 323.

29 Graham and Marvin, 251.

30 Ibid.

Chapter 10
Utopian Visions

Chapter 10
Utopian Visions

When we talk of utopia we evoke a long history of figures who have proposed alternative futures: from religious figures (Sir Thomas Moore, 15th century), social theorists (Owen, 19th century), architectural visionaries (Modernists, 20th century) to cinematic story tellers (science fiction, mid-20th century), all of whom put forward alternative social orders and alongside them, the future cities to support these societies. Currently there is a re-emergence of utopian visions put forward by leaders of the large technology firms: Google, Amazon, Microsoft and Tesla amongst others. Elon Musk (Tesla), for example, could be viewed as selling shares not in a car company, but rather in a techno-utopian future—a future that, as evidenced by the unexpectedly high share price, people are buying into at a great rate. Bill Gates has bought land in Arizona and is proposing to build a new smart city there.[1] Google's sister company, Alphabet Inc., through an entity called Sidewalk Labs, has put forward a vision for the planned Quayside neighbourhood of Toronto. Their plans outline the idyllic (and yet inexpensive) comprehensive development of an entire neighbourhood including driverless public transit; robotic trash removal; integrated digital infrastructure; censored streets and responsive public space; prefabricated, sustainable and inexpensive development; local shops and plenty of amenities.[2] It is unlikely that these firms consider themselves as utopians, nor do they propose their solutions as utopian visions. However, they are being referred to here as utopian in the sense that they offer a comprehensive alternative organization of the built environment and contemporaneously the social and political context needed to produce it.

This gleeful general acceptance of the new techno-utopias put forward by these extremely well-monetized, very large international technology firms and their owners should demand some serious soul-searching in light of how past utopian ideas have had significant negative consequences on cities. While this chapter does not do soul searching, it does begin the very interesting discussion of what a utopia is and what past visions of utopias may tell us, and provides a lens through which to view this re-emerging utopian discussion.

What is a Utopia?

In order to put more recent utopian proposals into an historical context, it is necessary to understand what the concept of a utopia means, how it has historically been defined, and what the criteria are for something to be called a utopia. Earlier utopias by Thomas More (1478–1535), Charles Fourier (1772–1837), William Morris (1834–1896) and others, outline social systems and new ways of organizing society to address the problems that were endemic at those time periods. The term "utopia" itself is taken from the creation of the term by Thomas More in 1516, when he wrote about a society on an island called Utopia (the word originates from the Greek meaning "no place").[3] The society More wrote about is often referred to as an ideal one, but it is not clear that More intended for it to be viewed as such; rather, he wrote *Utopia* as a critique of the societal order at the time and as a proposal for a better future. A re-imagining of the social order is a fundamental attribute of utopias, as well as the idea that the proposed social order is a critique of the current social order at the time of writing. In general, utopian visions are proposing new social orders intended to relieve the human suffering that is viewed as a fundamental problem of the time and improve quality of life overall. Utopias have re-emerged in writing in various time periods and are usually in response to a societal crisis.

In addition to their general goal of responding to a social crisis, there are several other commonalities or criteria necessary for a proposal to be considered utopian, one of which is the concept of 'Identity and Difference' put forward by the philosopher Hegel (1770–1831).[4] This criterion necessitates that the proposed society is radically different from the current society. For example, in More's *Utopia*, several propositions are made: a republic as opposed to the feudal system of the time; common property as a solution for exploitation, greed and conflict; everyone (including women) works a little as opposed to some working a lot and others (women, nobles) not working; and that the adoption of technology will lead to societal prosperity at a time when technology was distrusted and thought of as temporary.[5] This was thus a radically different societal proposition in comparison to the society of the time. The sociologist Karl Mannheim (1893–1947) also comments on the principle of 'Identity and Difference,' stating that in order to be utopian, an ideology has to be "incongruous with the state of reality within which it occurs."[6] Mannheim further clarifies that not every state of mind that is incongruous with reality is a utopia—for an idea to be utopian it must, if it were to happen, "tend to shatter, either partially or wholly, the order of things prevailing at the time."[7]

When we look at each of the proposals put forward by tech companies today, we can see they meet these criteria since the point of these proposals is to put forward something radical and disruptive in order to challenge the prevailing status quo. In the case of Google's Sidewalk Labs and Gates's Smart City, they are to reimagine the city through the use of advanced technologies and the benefits they can bring. In Musk's future, the entire fossil-fuel-based energy ecosystem is changed to sustainable sources, a change which would disrupt not only the car industry but also the oil and gas supply chain as well as the way we use electricity domestically and the relationship of the house to the energy system. Musk also proposes colonizing Mars, a utopian future firmly established in the utopian genre of science fiction.

Mannheim also discusses the relationship between ideology and utopia: in *Ideology and Utopia*, he writes that ideologies can be thought of as "situationally transcendent ideas which never succeed de facto in the realization of their projected contents."[8] Mannheim continues, "Though they [ideologies] often become the good-intentioned motive for the subjective conduct of the individual, when they are actually embodied in practice their meanings are most frequently distorted."[9] He also states, however, that it is immensely difficult to tell the difference between an ideology and a utopia since the

judgement about whether something is utopian depends on whether the person making the judgement considers the utopian vision to be possible to achieve.[10] Accordingly, the term 'utopian' as used today essentially implies that the idea is in principle unrealizable.[11] As such, however, perhaps it is not so important to judge at this point whether the future being put forward is utopian (realizable or not), since time itself will tell. Furthermore, utopias as discussed today are those which are always in the past—meaning that they have not been attained—and ideologies are generally those that have been implemented and failed. It is, however, necessary to further clarify that in order to be utopian, an idea must be intended to be realized. It is this intention of realization that gives the utopian its power and further differentiates it from an ideology or vision.

Another argument put forward by the architectural historian Manfredo Tafuri (1935–1994)[12] is that what shifts the 'utopian' view to the 'ideological' is that of work, in the sense of labour. All utopian plans from the 19th and 20th century were trying to deal with the issue of labour and who was to do it. Finally, the avant-garde of the early 20th centuries, unable to avoid the topic and likely influenced by Marxism, decided labour was a necessity; having accepted this, they then moved it to being acceptable because it was done for the greater or collective good. 'Work' with regard to this discussion of utopias is used specifically to address the means of production so the question for utopias is: who is in charge of the means of production? When we look at the large multinational organizations putting forward ideas it is worthwhile looking at who is in charge of the means of production. In the case of Elon Musk, his means of production is the robot. He has liberated the production of the car and eliminated the need for assembly line workers completely—the production of the future has taken over. Google and Microsoft have not been explicit about their means of production but their cities are set up to facilitate the industries of the 'knowledge worker' of today. This knowledge worker is engaged in work, but not the physical 'labour' of an assembly line worker; rather, in an intellectual undertaking. In previous utopian discourse, such intellectual work is positioned in opposition to the 'labour' that needed to be carried out after the Industrial Revolution and into the 20th century—when we last saw comprehensive utopias proposed.

The issue of work and its association with utopias bears further examination for this discussion. Is it necessary that utopias be visions whereby means of production is controlled by the worker? It is a strong association, as many utopian visions included such socialist principles; however, as we will see from Frank Lloyd Wright's Broadacres project, this is not a precondition of what we consider a utopia. The association between utopias and socialism is also strong due to the 'socialist utopias' that were proposed prior to the 20th century by theorists such as Charles Fourier, Robert Owen, Henri de Saint Simon, and Étienne Cabet. Socialist utopias insisted on the removal or mitigation of 'work.' These utopias sit in contrast to Marxism and the scientific utopians who criticized what they called 'socialist utopias.' The scientific utopians explain how the utopic state is to be achieved and how it would function. They did not believe in socialist utopias (despite the fact that we now call them socialists). In *The Communist Manifesto*, Marx and Engels argue that the socialist utopians "reject all political, and especially all revolutionary, action; they wish to attain their ends by peaceful means, and endeavor, by small experiments, necessarily doomed to failure, and by the force of example, to pave the way for the new social Gospel."[13] They thought that this type of approach was unscientific and unrealistic. Their belief in the necessity of the revolution is in support of Mannheim's insistence that a utopia must be deemed to be socially unachievable from the viewpoint of the society from which it is proposed. Only a revolution, or some kind of radical social upheaval, will attain the proposed utopian vision.

Other theorists, such as Tafuri, supported the idea that revolution was necessary to utopias and believed that to propose a utopia without a revolution was to doom it to failure. In Tafuri's opinion, the utopian proposals of the Modernists (discussed below) suffered because they could never be realized in the fabric of a capitalist society; instead, they became distorted into an image of an ideal (the 'ideology of the plan'). However, Tafuri's viewpoint is not universal—he was writing to explain the failure of the Modernist utopian plans. The socialist utopias of the early 19th century did not believe revolution or class struggle was necessary to achieve utopia. It is useful to note that the socialist utopian theorists did not think of themselves as 'utopian' and that the term was applied to them by Marx and Engels in order to discredit their ideas as naïve. The term 'utopian,' similar to 'ideological,' has thus generally been used to refer to past plans that have been unsuccessful.

Through these criteria we can judge the proposed techno-utopias of today: Google and Gates's visions are of a completely independent city (or part thereof) including radical ideas of infrastructure and city development. They are envisioning a city that supports and provides agency to the worker in their everyday lives, decreasing costs of living through addressing innovative models of housing and transportation. They have not addressed labour directly but, as their proposed transportation and waste systems are automated,

there is an implicit reduction of labour. Musk is not taking on the city as a whole so much as the transport and energy systems—however, there may very well be a larger vision behind his radical and, in some cases, cohesive proposals. Although he does not mention the worker, he has eradicated manual labour entirely in his production methods. All of these schemes are possibly attainable but it is unlikely they will be under the governmental and social organization that currently exists. The one thing that may allow Google, Gates and Musk to achieve these radical futures is a massive amount of capital. The capital involved in all three ventures is almost unimaginable to the average person. The schemes are put forward by men who have succeeded in technological ventures and through them have amassed vast fortunes that exceed many government budgets. One other criteria that Google, Gates and Musk meet: all intend to carry these visions out and build the world which they have invented.

The Utopian Visions of the Modernist Era and the Similarities to Today

The similarities between the Modernist utopias and today's emerging utopias are striking. In the Modernist period (late 19th and early 20th centuries), many people were captivated by the advances being made and imagined a brighter future.

Modernist thinkers believed that technology was going to radically change the world and they were very optimistic about these changes and the benefits they would bring to society.[14] The Modernist period was responding to the rapid technological development of the 19th and early 20th centuries and large changes in society including the express train, radio and telephone, the elevator (thus the skyscraper) and, of course, the automobile. These inventions created massive disruptions in how society functioned—even more so than our current disruptive technologies. The telecommunications and the automobile are of course the biggest similarities between the Modernist era and our own in terms of technological advances; today we also envision tourist space travel, Hyperloop train travel and medical advances as other areas of great technical advancement and similarity with the innovations of the Modernist era. Again, a techno-utopian viewpoint is proliferating in the general sense of optimism about the possibility of technology to advance society.

Utopian visions offer a way of coming to terms with technological advances and their impact on society. Whether or not the visionaries were themselves enamoured with the technologies, they clearly understood their inevitability and therefore used the potential of the technology to envision a better future in their utopias. Le Corbusier, for example, very much appreciated the craftsman skills he had learned as a youth and the traditional artisan community; however, although conflicted, he recognized that an artist had to create with the technologies of his time and so designed a city and an art with these new technologies. His cities and architectures break with the past and propose a future which takes the artisan principles and attempts to apply them to the new technologies. This was not always successful; in fact, each of the utopian societies put forward by the visionaries have arguably done significant damage to our society through dysfunctional planning and transportation schemes.

There are three visionaries worth examining because their utopian visions were so influential on the current forms of our cities. It is worthwhile looking at how these utopias came about and what people at the time did—and did not—see as problematic about them.

Utopian City Projects of the Modernist Movement

Garden City by Ebenezer Howard (1850–1902)

In Chapter 4 we looked at the Garden City, its influence on the suburb and its proliferation across England and North America. Howard produced this urban form as part of a utopian vision of a community with a comprehensive plan for social reordering. He believed his utopian town offered a better solution to the chaos and squalor of the city of his time and that through the form of the new community, people could be relieved of suffering and achieve their potential—the potential he saw wasted in the cities. He imagined that humans living in harmony with nature would create a better society. These thoughts were outlined in his manifesto, *To-Morrow: A Peaceful Path to Real Reform* (1898, republished with modifications as *Cities of To-Morrow* in 1902). This was a comprehensive treatise and took on the issue of land ownership and its role in the oppression of the poor. Howard's utopian community was to be funded by capitalists who would get a fixed profit over a period of years from rental income and then hand the property over to the community who would maintain it from the collective rents. However, in order to realize his ideas he had to raise capital; after great effort, and through the help of a prominent Liberal lawyer, Ralph Neville, he was successful in securing funding from several business magnates including George Cadbury and W. H. Lever.[15] The philanthropic capitalists who funded his plans, however, would not agree to his utopian funding ideas and Howard faced a dilemma—to build under the financial model dictated by the investors or go back to scratch and try to raise funds again. Howard believed that the form of the community itself would

improve lives and once people saw that this worked, he would have the opportunity to build others that could then be more in keeping with his utopian ideals.[16] The utopian funding model did not proliferate but aspects of his urban form were indeed very influential[17] and adopted by many communities in North America—resulting in massive urban sprawl and the greenhouse gas emissions that come with it. Howard's idea was only in part realized: for example, he proposed walking and train transportation in his communities, which did not materialize. Indeed, in Howard's vision each city was to have all the necessary community facilities so that one did not have to travel elsewhere for goods or services. If put into place, these aspects would have mitigated most of the negative effects that resulted from the adoption of the Garden City model. The outcome here demonstrates that if one is not attentive to the implementation of an ideal, and the political and social context of that implementation, unforeseen or unknown consequences may—and usually will—result.

Broadacre City by Frank Lloyd Wright (1867–1959)

Similar to Howard, Wright observed the polluted, dirty and overcrowded conditions of the city of his day and believed that the city was unhealthy and crushed the human spirit. With the advent of the automobile and the telephone, he saw the future in a highly individualistic, decentralized urban form which brought people closer to nature and allowed each their own space. His decentralization was more radical than Howard's because of the technology of the car: Howard was relying on the technology of the train to access his development and walking was imagined as the mode of transport while in the community. In contrast, Wright's Broadacre City was based on the burgeoning technology of the car and the ability of the telephone to keep people connected over distances. Wright believed in democracy and individualism and, through these ideals, abundance for all. He maintained that the new technologies had mastered time and space and that great cities were therefore obsolete: people no longer needed to live in crowded conditions in close proximity, but instead could have their own space and reconnect with nature. Like Howard, he believed that inequality in land ownership was the source of poverty and suffering and if this problem were solved then society's ills would be cured: if everyone owned land and became independent farmers and proprietors, this would create equality and wealth for all which, in turn, would lead to a harmonious society. Wright's plans also proposed that everyone worked as a farmer, mechanic and intellectual in equal measures and the equality between people's work and the variety of tasks performed would reinforce social harmony. He was also a great believer in the family as the social unit and the home as the headquarters of this unit. Wright rejected the notion of government as he thought it was unnecessary, and so no government rules over his citizens. He also proposed a monetary system where money devalued over time, thus reducing inequality as well as interest rates and encouraging people to spend it instead of hoarding it.[18]

Wright's vision for Broadacre City also extended to theories on education. He believed centralized education was a threat to individualized thinking and proposed that schools have no more than 40 students and operate independently. His vision of higher education took the form of small institutes whose fellows did pure research and design institutes: it was this idea that he manifested into his own design school at Taliesin.

Wright proposed Broadacre City as a response and an alternative to the degraded conditions of many less fortunate people's lives in the city. His proposal, like Howard's *City of To-Morrow*, contributed to suburban thinking and urban sprawl, broadly influencing thoughts about the ideal American city. Besides its contribution to sprawling city formation and dependence on automobile travel, it is also patriarchal, anti-intellectual, and bereft of institutional support for dissent.

The Contemporary and Radiant Cities by Le Corbusier (1887–1965)

Howard and Wright were not without critics at the time, including Le Corbusier and CIAM (Congrès Internationaux d'Architecture Moderne). In his *Ville Radieuse* (1935), Le Corbusier says,

> Let us not accept the illusory solution of the garden-city, that palliative conceived in panic by authorities who, alarmed suddenly by the noise of the approaching storm, think that they can turn the linked energies of a great city into a scattered dust of uprooted, immobilized and broken men. The fallacious benefits of an illusory countryside. The same stupid compromise that has already created the suburban commuter, drawn and quartered the city, and made innumerable people wretched at one and the same time.[19]

Le Corbusier put forward several utopian visions for cities—The Contemporary City and The Radiant City—which, like Wright and Howard's visions, also seek to liberate people. Unlike Wright and Howard, however, Le Corbusier sought to achieve his aims not through individualism and decentralization, but through the pursuit of individualism through other mechanisms—either a centralized authority which could create the conditions for harmony, equality and prosperity for all, or through corporations and/or syndicates. Le Corbusier, like other intellectuals of his time, had seen the failure of democracy to deal with the Great Depression and was concerned that a democracy could not produce a coherent and well-thought-out future. He was interested in a charismatic leader who could unite people behind a positive message and overcome the fractious interest-politics of the parliaments of the time, as Le Corbusier believed that only such a leader would be equipped to build the city of the future. His views on government changed over time but generally Le Corbusier left politics out of his utopian cities and focused on the logistics of the society and its physical form. He believed that after this form of the city was built that it would run itself harmoniously and not require government.

Le Corbusier, similar to Wright, glorified the technology of the time—the car—and built it in as a central tenet of his utopian city. His transportation system includes elaborately designed networks of superhighways, access roads, subways, bicycle paths and pedestrian walkways. At the centre of his Contemporary City is the central terminal and the interchange where the two superhighways meet. He believed that speed and the efficient communication and exchange of ideas and information was imperative for the creation of a successful society in the future, and he set out to design a city which would facilitate such a society. His central terminal and interchange were surrounded by sixty-storey high-rises which contained 'the brains' of the city. These high-rises were conceived as vertical streets which freed the landscape to allow space and light on the ground, thus dealing with the dark, overpopulated, unsanitary conditions that he saw in the streets in Paris of the time. He, like Wright and Howard, also believed that the city of the time was outdated and served society's needs poorly. Le Corbusier's solution was a radical replacement of the city with a new form, engaging all the technologies available in the new era. He clearly positioned his city proposal as a utopian vision:

> These plates [...] constitute the positive elements of a theory for the planning of machine-civilization cities. Being purely theoretical products, they make it possible to express the fundamental principle of this matter in an ideal form, removed from the hurly-burly of everyday life. Can such a theory emerge from its utopian framework and confront the world as it is in reality?[20]

Le Corbusier's interest was in the 'creation of harmony' and to do this he wanted to harness and manage the aspects of life that were new and felt out of control. He writes, "We must provide all these forces that have so recently and so rapidly been unleashed upon us with a rhythm, an order that will permit us to harness them efficiently. And by efficiently, I mean so that everyone receives a merited share in their benefits."[21]

These forces include technology and the benefits that he believed would accrue from them.

Le Corbusier also carefully thought through how his utopian society would work on many levels. Unlike Wright, who proposed to merge work and leisure, Le Corbusier thought that labour should be balanced with leisure and he suggested eight hours of each per day. He proposed facilities for sports and physical recreation as well as crafts and other hobbies in order to facilitate leisure. His Radiant City had housing for everyone, called 'Unités'; this provided housing based on the size of the family as well as collectively funded amenities, on the premise that collectively everyone could live more luxuriously than on their own. The Unités had gyms with pools, tennis courts and sandy beaches, as well as restaurants, cafés, shops, and workshops for traditional handicrafts. Each also had a daycare, nursery and primary school, and collective laundry facilities. Le Corbusier based his society around the family but believed that men and women would be equal partners and share the job of earning the family income.[22] The programming in the building was intended to support the family and provide the services they needed for when they were away at work.

Le Corbusier developed his ideas for the Radiant City in the 1930s, but they were extended and worked on throughout the 30s and 40s. As they evolved they were informed by different political and social ideas. He managed to build his ideas and the Unités for Marseilles and Chandigarh were completed in 1952 and 1960 respectively. However, like Howard, the final built form was isolated from the social system to which it was in service. Unité Marseilles was so expensive that it discouraged others from following the model and Chandigarh, unlike the advanced Western industrial societies for which Le Corbusier had conceived his designs, was built in an unindustrialized area in India.

Le Corbusier's legacy, along with CIAM and others of his time, has been blamed for the ills that came with the 'slum clearing' of the mid-20th century. This resulted in isolated buildings floating in large, program-less fields which degenerated into poorly maintained and socially problematic areas of the city. Similarly, the building of highways into cities, which destroyed city fabric and isolated neighbourhoods, can be seen as a direct lineage from this type of utopian vision. The problems arise in part from the insertion of only fragments of the utopian plans as well as the temporal and scale oversights, combined with a lack of concern for the integration and relationship between the old and the new. The classic utopias, from More onward, have an island mentality (or what today we might term a 'gated

community mentality'). In addition, many of the problems resulted from the political disengagement with respect to the project's intentions and community concerns, and a failure to predict the problems associated with the technology due to the enthusiasm about the technologies themselves. It is these failures that foreshadow the fulfillment of today's utopian visions.

Modernism and Capitalism

What finally discredited the Modernist utopias, however, was not so much the failings of the urban planning which came from their visions, since that was not yet fully realized, but rather their relationship with capitalism. In *Architecture and Utopia: Design and Capitalist Development* (1973), Tafuri charts this problematic history from the decline of the social utopia to the rise of the "utopia of form."[23] Tafuri breaks this decline into three stages:

1. formation of urban ideology
2. artistic avant-garde develop ideological projects
3. architectural ideology becomes the 'ideology of the plan'

It is the third step, which requires capital, where the problems really begin to arise. It is only through the engagement with the capitalist system that the projects were brought into reality—but it was that same

288   Chapter 10 Utopian Visions

engagement with the capitalist system that rendered the utopian social model and related financing irrelevant. We can see this evolution in all of the Modernist projects discussed above. The consequence of this, as Tafuri points out, is that everything else become secondary to the plan, which was the element that lived on as the ideological model. Since the building of the city can never be separated from the money required for development, except in an authoritarian government structure, the Modernist utopian model would always be at ideological odds with its mode of financing.

Further, the image of Modernism, which eschewed any historic decoration and became synonymous with technical progress, was increasingly adopted enthusiastically by companies as a way of portraying a modern and technologically advanced image to the world. This ambient association further discredited the utopian visions of the time period as the Modernist movement became irretrievably linked with capitalism.

Post-Modern or Science Fiction Utopias

One could speculate that it was the failure of the Modernist utopias that doomed the utopia and caused it to vanish from public thought for almost 40 years, but in fact during the post-Modern period we still see

architectural utopias and visionary projects being put forward. Visionary projects, unlike utopias, are not reconceiving the entire social order but rather offering social commentary in order to critique current social phenomena or to propose alternatives for how the future could be. Sometimes these point the way to a positive future and sometimes warn of a negative one, but many carry some critique of capitalism. These utopian visions are sometimes referred to as the science fiction utopias[24] as they evolved alongside the development of the increasingly popular genre of science fiction. Science fiction is a genre that often deals with a utopia in some form, and utopias have been proposed as being a subset of the larger genre of science fiction.[25,26] The significant role science fiction has played in directing society's approach towards scientific research and progress cannot be understated. However, these many texts do not provide blueprints of built form and were themselves intended to stimulate commentary on our societal situation and evolution, especially with regard to technology. They have that in common with the following projects.

The following proposals may be classified as visionary projects rather than utopias in that they do not in all cases reconceive the entire social order. However, they do require something of a break with reality in order to achieve their visions. In many cases, their visions are not meant to be achieved but rather to produce a social commentary. As such, they would be considered as informed by ideologies since they are not meant to be implemented; however, they are still worth mentioning as they put forward ideological visions, in the form of a built environment, which criticize aspects of our society and propose solutions.

Metabolists

The Metabolists were highly influential and provide a continuous link between Modernism and the post-Modern visionaries. Metabolism was a post-war Japanese architectural movement that was interested in natural processes and the city. They integrated ideas about biological growth and regeneration with architectural megastructures. They first presented internationally at CIAM's 1959 meeting and so are connected with the lineage of the Modernists.

The Metabolists proposed a "utopia of resilience."[27] They were responding to the devastation of Japan in World War II and envisaged a regenerating architecture employing biological metaphors and techno-scientific images.[28] They also promoted individuality and harnessed this belief with their large resilient technical infrastructures and institutions, designed to organize and support the individual as well as be able to change and adapt over time. Like other visionaries

of their time, they are known more for their ideas than their built work. Most of the work built was during the 1970 World Exposition in Osaka. One of the leaders of the movement, Kenzo Tange, was responsible for the master planning of the site.

Superstudio

Superstudio, founded by five architects in Florence in 1966, had a series of 'visionary projects,' none of which were meant to be built. Superstudio is still a highly influential, highly poetic group and their design critiques the spread of globalism. The drawings show a never-ending white grid which comments on the spread of globalism and the stripping of local cultures in the wake of the force of global capitalism.

Archigram

Archigram was a collective of architects who were fascinated with technology and drew images which proposed extreme future cities. Most of the images show the city as some sort of complex machine in which people enjoy themselves in various forms. The city is generally portrayed as an infrastructural frame outfitted with imagined future technology of various descriptions which serves the human inhabitants.

Projects included the Plug-In City by Peter Cook (1964), a mega-structure which was essentially a massive framework into which dwellings could be 'plugged in.' The dwellings were prefabricated units and all elements could be relocated by cranes. The Walking City (Ron Herron, 1964) was a proposition of walking cities that would congregate where their power was needed and then disperse. They were conceived as giant intelligent robot-like buildings which could travel on legs. The form was a combination of insect and machine. Each roaming pod was independent, but could plug in to recharge itself and exchange goods and citizens. The world these walking cities lived in was a world destroyed by nuclear war.

Yona Friedman

In Ville Spatiale (1956) and Utopies Réalizables (1975), Yona Friedman set out the principles of an architecture capable of understanding the constant changes that characterize 'social mobility' and based on 'infrastructure' that provides housing. Friedman's utopic ideas were based on user participation and allowed people to adjust their circumstances. It was also concerned with providing large amounts of housing. Friedman is also credited with proposing a pluralist utopia that allowed individuals to associate with other individuals with whom they agreed to create their own cities.[29] They were free to move between these cities with different social ideals. All the cities governed themselves and there was no centralized government, only an association between cities.[30]

Buckminster Fuller

Buckminster Fuller, on the other hand, put forward utopian ideas about society's use of materials and how we form our environment. He was considered the "architectural conscience for social technology"[31] because he was critical of society being too wasteful. He focuses on visual and structural models of a complex set of elements and connections which define a new sort of living.

Summary

As Michael Hays points out, Superstudio, Archigram and Yona Friedman's visionary projects are:

> [F]oremost ideological criticisms of the cultural codes and conventions of an emerging consumer society—anti-utopias whose proper functions are antagonism and disruption, using the new as a radical and systemic break with the present. Technology and social program are preoccupation but architectural form [...] is still a primary concern [...] And though these architects' work certainly contains serious propositions, it trades more freely in irony, paradox and aesthetic negativity. Superstudio's Continuous Monument, in particular, is a pure practice of negation, a revolt of the object—the laying to waste of tradition through relentless repetition and counterpoint.[32]

Post-Modern or Science Fiction Utopias   291

These propositions have now left behind the intention of being carried into practice but instead are acting as cultural critique.

Colin Rowe calls the projects of Superstudio, Archigram and Friedman the "Science Fiction utopias."[33] He critiques these:

> [T]he results of science fiction, whether systemic or neo-Futurist, usually suffer from the same conditions which plague the Ville Radieuse—disregard for context, distrust of the social continuum, the use of symbolic utopian models for literal purposes, the assumption that the existing city will be made to go away: and, if the Ville Radieuse is now supposed to be evil, productive of trauma and disorientation, it is not easy to see how science fiction, which would seem to compound the ills, is in any position to alleviate the problem.[34]

These ideological visions (not utopias by our definition) were not intended to solve problems but point them out. They are meant to break with the present to offer a better (or at least different) future and, by offering it, put the present into context. By providing us a context which is different from the one in which we exist, it helps us see our own context with more clarity. In some ways, they are not fully described utopian futures, but they do engage the tools of utopias and present themselves as visionary or idealistic for the most part.

Capitalists Take Over Utopia

The utopias presented today by Musk, Google and Gates, are operational ones; like the Modernists, they intend to put them into practice. Their rhetoric and purpose is to save the planet from environmental degradation and to improve people's lives. They intend to do this through applying technology: accelerating green technologies, improving connectivity and making life cheaper, safer, more productive and more enjoyable. As such we have now come full circle: it is the capitalists who not only utilize the symbols of utopian visions but are now proposing the utopias themselves. The intention currently is that they will also build these utopias—Gates, through his smart city, and Google through Sidewalk Labs Toronto Quayside project, have already invested millions of dollars in these designs.[35]

Politics and Utopias

The relationship between politics and utopias becomes even more relevant in light of the above discussion about capitalism and utopic generation today. The association between utopias and politics is unresolved but it was the connection between socialist politics and utopias that doomed them to unpopularity after the 1970s , which saw the rise of the Chicago school of economics promotion of free markets and the neo-liberal politics of Margaret Thatcher and Ronald Reagan.[36] There seemed no natural enemies to late capitalism and the fall of the Soviet Union and Eastern Germany sealed the fate of the communist visions, once so popular in Europe. In the meantime, social safety nets had been abandoned, unionization dismantled and pensions privatized as the free market has dominated.[37] Science fiction was the last we had seen of utopias until the recent techno-utopian ideals, now emerging from the most unpredictable of places: the capitalists themselves.

But the connection between politics and utopias is ambiguous and it is by no means certain that utopias are all politically connected to socialist ideals. Wright's utopia was not a socialist construction; neither was Le Corbusier's, although he had community-type approaches to social activities. The conscious construction of a utopia is forwarded by an individual or group as an attempt to challenge the current system with a vision of a better future, but these futures do not necessarily have to be socialist or have socialist values. That is not to say that the association of the utopia with socialism historically is not without validity—More's original *Utopia* did away with money and property and this eschewing of money and property rights is a consistent characteristic of many utopias as they try to deal with the issues of inequality and poverty.

The problem with the current capitalist system is that there is no utopia to challenge it: the utopian imperative seems to have been lost since the 1970s and the rise of neo-liberal politics. One could see this as a lack of invention in society; more likely it is the lack of the necessity of invention. The utopian and the inventor have much in common—both invoke creations to respond to specific fundamental problems. Both are convinced that they have resolved the problem through their invention and both persistently put forward their ideas as those which will solve society's problems.[38] Thus we can see here how Musk's pollution-free energy and transportation and Google's future city of seamless transportation and affordable housing fit into utopian ideals. Neither of these organizations proposes to address political issues. Both are products of a late capitalist society that is highly supportive of a culture of invention and arguably has developed a cult following of the personalities of the utopian inventors themselves. As yet, however, it is not completely clear if there are social reordering ideals behind these new utopias, but in the Google future city there is an overarching sense of a benevolent technology 'entity' in control of the technological system who will ensure its smooth functioning. Google goes so far in their proposal as to say that the government agencies should waive regulations in the name of innovation.[39] Musk seems to be operating within the current capitalist system; however, it could be posited that he is exploiting it in a type of Robin Hood way—to steal from the wealthy and give to society—in the name of his utopian vision. His Tesla company is significantly overvalued and its likelihood of turning a significant profit for its shareholders anytime in the near future seems remote.[40] Furthermore, the integration of his Solar City company into Tesla was not so much a corporate strategic move to make the company more profitable as a way of keeping the Solar City company funded so that his vision of a sustainable world could be forwarded. All of Musk's future visions are funded by a capitalist mechanism but none seem to have any intention of creating profit for this system; rather they are exploiting the capitalist system to obtain unlimited funding to further advance the many utopian visions of its inventor.

Our Context

This technological catalyzation, particularly of the Modernists, into utopic visions is critical to our discussion because, once again, we have a rapid technological revolution happening that may be the impetus for imagining new utopic or ideological futures. The catalyst is again the automobile, but in its current iteration as the autonomous automobile, harnessed with the communications speed of the internet instead of the telephone. Again, we see the enthusiasm with which our civilization approaches the new technology, wanting to apply it to solve the problems of society, with a lack of concern for the unintended consequences of the implementation of such a technology.

When we so willingly uptake any new technology, it is important to realize the significance of the positions we are taking. These technologies could prove to be utopic—but all the utopic visions we have seen to date have been dystopic in outcome. As such, we should carefully examine our proposals to look for the unanticipated but possibly dystopic outcomes. Similar to Le Corbusier's plan for the Radiant City, which received significant opposition when it was presented, there is currently backlash to at least one of the current proposals (Toronto Quayside) in terms of the implications of the use of private data[41,42] and its replacement of the City in terms of governance.[43] As Jathan Sadowski, an academic in the field of the ethics of technology, says,

> It is easy for city leaders to step aside and allow technocrats and corporations to take control, as if they are alchemists who can turn social problems and economic stagnation into progress and growth.
> But cities are not machines that can be optimized, nor are they labs for running experiments. Cities are not platforms with

users, nor are they businesses with shareholders. Cities are real places with real people who have a right not to live with whatever "smart solutions" an engineer or executive decides to unleash.

These partnerships cannot be a way for city governments to abdicate responsibility and accountability to citizens by handing over (parts of) the city to corporations. Nobody elected Alphabet or Uber or any other company with its sights set on privatizing city governance.[44]

As such, it is with some form of general trepidation that we should approach the techno-utopian visions for the AV and the city of the AV which are being put forward today— even those within this book. Not least of our concerns should be the agendas of the extremely well-funded, global and socially powerful authorities who are proposing the utopias and yet their primary purpose is to make money within the capitalist system.

However, having now looked back and studied the past and the mistakes made in the past, perhaps we can approach the future with a more balanced, optimistic and thoughtful attitude. We can take forward the spirit of the Modernists—who recognized that new technologies were inevitable and did whatever was in their means to promote these technologies for the benefit of all in society—while recognizing with

humility that we are almost certainly making serious problems for future generations. It is with this spirit that I hope you leave this book—engaged, and with the intention of using the technology as wisely as possible for a better world.

Notes

1. Bianca Buono, "Bill Gates Buys Big Chunk of Land in Arizona to Build Smart City,'" *KGW*, November 10, 2017, http://www.kgw.com/mobile/article/amp/news/bill-gates-buys-big-chunk-of-land-in-arizona-to-build-smart-city/491135744.

2. Sidewalk Labs, "RFP 2017-13 Innovation and Funding Partner for the Quayside Development Opportunity" (Sidewalk Lab, October 17, 2017).

3. Thomas More, *Utopia,* Transcribed from the 1901 Version by David Price (Online: Project Gutenberg, 2005), https://www.gutenberg.org/files/2130/2130-h/2130-h.htm.

4. Georg Wilhelm Friedrich Hegel, *Encyclopedia Logic, Book Two,* "Essence" (1817) (Oxford University Press, 1975).

5. Thomas Moore, *Utopia,* transl. Paul Turner, (Harmondsworth: Penguin, 1965), 38–39.

6. Karl Mannheim , *Ideology and Utopia* (New York: Routledge, 2013, published originally in 1936), 173.

7. Ibid, 173.

8. Ibid, 175.

9. Ibid.

10. Ibid, 176.

11. Ibid, 177.

12. Manfredo Tafuri, *Architecture and Utopia: Design and Capitalist Development*, trans. by Barbara Luigia La Penta from the 1973 Edition (Cambridge, Massachusetts: MIT Press, 1976).

13. Karl Marx and Friedrich Engels, *The Communist Manifesto* (Penguin, 2002).

14. Reyner Banham, *Theory and Design in the First Machine Age* (Cambridge, Massachusetts: MIT Press, 1960), see introduction.

15. Robert Fishman, *Urban Utopias in the Twentieth Century: Ebenezer Howard, Frank Lloyd Wright, and Le Corbusier* (Cambridge, Massachusetts: MIT Press, 1982), 59.

16. Ibid, 62.

17. Forest Hills Gardens by Frederick Law Olmsted Jr (1909), Radburn, New Jersey (1923), Suburban Resettlement Program towns: Greenbelt, Maryland, Greenhills, Ohio, Greenbrook, New Jersey and Greendale, Wisconsin (1930s).

18. First proposed by Swiss economist Silvio Gesell.

19. Le Corbusier, *The Radiant City*, Translation 1967 (New York: Orion Press, 1933).

20. Ibid, 156.

21. Ibid.

22. Fishman, *Urban Utopias in the Twentieth Century*, 232.

23. Tafuri, *Architecture and Utopia*, 48.

24. Colin Rowe and Fred Koetter, *Collage City* (Cambridge: MIT Press, 1983), 38.

25. Fredric Jameson, *Archaeologies of the Future: The Desire Called Utopia and Other Science Fictions* (New York: Verso, 2005), xiv.

26. The invocation of science fiction and its utopias of course deserves many pages of discussion but falls outside the scope of this work. The reference is made here and can be taken up in future books and papers.

27. Meike Schalk, "The Architecture of Metabolism. Inventing a Culture of Resilience," in *Arts*, vol. 3 (Multidisciplinary Digital Publishing Institute, 2014), 279–297.

28. Ibid.

29. Jameson, *Archaeologies of the Future,* 218–221.

30. Yona Friedman, "Utopies Réalisables, Yona Friedman," *Lyber Eclat*, 1975, http://www.lyber-eclat.net/lyber/friedman/utopies.html.

31. Michael Hays and Dana Miller, *Buckminster Fuller: Starting with the Universe* (New York: Taylor & Francis, 2009), 11.

32. Ibid, 17.

33. Rowe and Koetter, *Collage City*, 38.

34. Ibid.

35 Sidewalk Labs, "RFP 2017-13 Innovation and Funding Partner for the Quayside Development Opportunity."

36 Jameson, *Archaeologies of the Future*, xii.

37 Ibid.

38 Ibid, 11.

39 Sidewalk Labs, "RFP 2017-13 Innovation and Funding Partner for the Quayside Development Opportunity" (Sidewalk Lab, October 17, 2017), 20.

40 Tom Randall, "Tesla and Wall Street Have Never Been Further Apart," *The Globe and Mail*, February 21, 2017, https://www.theglobeandmail.com/globe-investor/investment-ideas/tesla-and-wall-street-have-never-been-further-apart/article34096939/.

41 Bianca Wylie, "Think Hard Before Handing Tech Firms The Rights To Our Cities' Data," *HuffPost Canada*, November 8, 2017, http://www.huffingtonpost.ca/bianca-wylie/think-hard-before-handing-tech-firms-the-rights-to-our-cities-data_a_23270793/.

42 Torontoist, "Civic Tech: On Google, Sidewalk Labs, and Smart Cities," *Torontoist*, October 24, 2017, https://torontoist.com/2017/10/civic-tech-google-sidewalk-labs-smart-cities/.

43 Jathan Sadowski, "Google Wants to Run Cities without Being Elected. Don't Let It," *The Guardian*, October 24, 2017, http://www.theguardian.com/commentisfree/2017/oct/24/google-alphabet-sidewalk-labs-toronto.

44 Ibid.

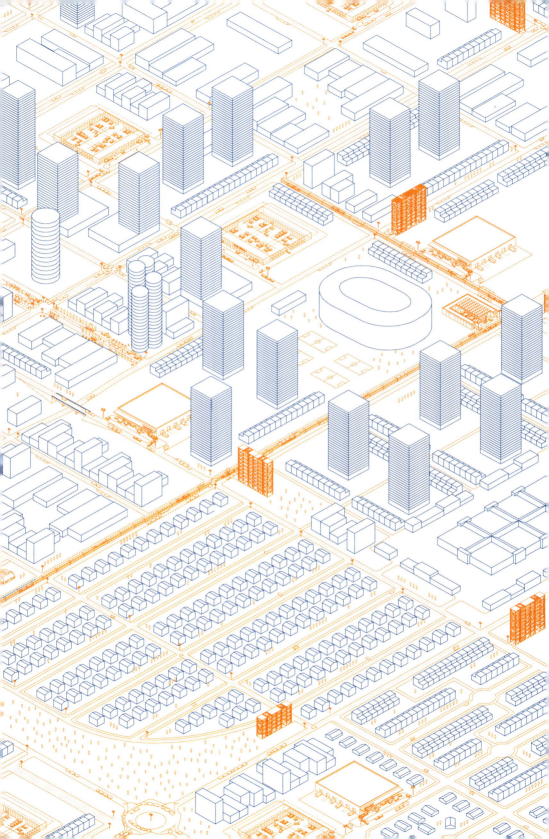

Index

Page numbers in *italics* show illustrations, **bold** indicates a table

Adams, John S. 116
Alberti, Leon Battista 96–97, 161–162
Alessi, Galeazzo 97
Allen, Stan 171, 172, 267
alternatives futures method (Townsend) 40
American Automobile Association 92
Amsterdam 270
Apple's AV designs 6
Archigram 290–291
architecture: agency and discursive visions 29–30; digital technology's influence 30–32; drawing practices and the automobile 28–29; Post Modern visionary projects 290–292; speculative alternatives 32–34, 40; street design, innovations and theories 161–163
Automated Vehicle Coalition 20–21
automobile revolution: car growth, street safety and use 91–93, 186; streetcar demise 94, 255, 258
autonomous vehicle (AV): charging facilities *231*, 232, *237*, 238; charging technology 203, *205*; classifications and applications 5, 7–10, *9*; general design features 5–7, *7*; infrastructure and intelligence systems 13–15; ownership models 10–13; safety and deployment of technology 18–21; social and urban impact 3; standards, technology and urban infrastructure 15–18, 23n30; tech industry's societal vision 2–3; vehicle-to-grid power systems 136, *136–137*, *237*, 238
AV city design, cultural theories: ecological urbanism 174–178; landscape urbanism 167–174; projective ecological models 178–179
AV infrastructure and safety programs: bike lanes and traffic integration 74, *76*; pedestrian-vehicle interface challenges 173–174, 187; pop-up crosswalk 223, *225*; Smart Tarmac 74, 203, *205*; traffic intersection management 77, 213, *215*, *217–218*, 219
AV pods 7–8
AV transportation scenarios, research approach: decision-making matrix 49, *52*, 54; drawings, design objectives 33–34; factors' network of influence 45, *46–47*; key factors and driving force analysis **42–43**, 44–45; overview 41, 44; scenarios, theoretical testing *53*, 54; scenario variances, structuring process 45, 48–49, *50–51*
AV transportation scenarios, user narratives: commercial trader (Pro AV) 80, *82*, *84*; commercial trader (Pro Public Transit) 81, *83*, *85*; elderly (Pro AV) 68, *70*, *72*; elderly

(Pro Public Transit) 69, *71, 73*;
overview 55; student (Pro AV) 74,
76, 78; student (Pro Public Transit)
75, *77, 79*; suburban family (Pro
AV) 56, *58, 60*; suburban family (Pro
Public Transit) 57, *59, 61*; urbanite
(Pro AV) 62, *64, 66*; urbanite (Pro
Public Transit) 63, *65, 67*

Banham, Reyner 171, 179
Bass, John 33
Bateson, Gregory 268–269
Batlle, Enric 171
Bélanger, Pierre 166
Bing, Alexander M. 101
Boston Dynamics 9
Britain: Garden Cities 100–101,
283–284; London's congestion
charge 127; Picturesque movement
100; road width standards 97
Broadacre City (Wright) 28, 284–285
Brown, Hilary 174–175

Canada: Google's Sidewalk Labs
269, 278, 280, 294; mass transit
commuting 254; public space and
digital interactions 270–271
car-share and ride sharing 11–12
Cauter, Lieven de 270
children, independent mobility:
personal AV 56, *60*; public transit
57, *61*
CIAM (Congrès Internationaux
d'Architecture Moderne) 98, 102,
286, 290
'Cité Industrielle' project (Garnier)
99–100
commuting: AV share program 56,
58; mass transit, high use cities
254; personal AVs 81, 154, *155*;
streetcar/trolley era 93–94; urban

growth patterns and AVs 116, 118,
120, *121*, 122, *123*
compass pole, multifunctional 14,
213, *214–215*
Contemporary City (Le Corbusier) 28,
102, 286–287
Contested Futures (Brown et al.) 29
Cook, Peter 290–291
Corner, James 167, 171
Cramer, Florian 32
Cuff, Dana 162
Cupers, Kenny 30
cycling, urban areas: bike lanes and
traffic integration 74, *76*; lane
allocation by speed *201*, 202

Deep Ecology 176
delivery services: building drop-off
issues 9; commercial delivery zone
242, *244–245*; delivery robots
242; dispatch hub 226–227, *229*;
grocery drive thru 226–227, *228–
229*; home delivery box *246–247*,
248; lane allocation by speed *201*,
202; robotic delivery 242, 243,
247, 248; SAV courier services 23;
shipping technology 242
delivery services (scenarios): door
to door shipping 80, 81, *84, 85*;
trackable compact AVs 80, *82, 84*;
transport share service 81, *83*
Doucet, Isabelle 30
drawing practices: architectural
agency and future discourses 29–
30; speculative alternatives 32–34;
technology as pervading influence
30–32; urban architecture and the
automobile 28–29

Easterling, Keller 15–16, 17–18, 31,
268–269

300   Driverless Urban Futures

ecological models, projective tools 178–179

ecological urbanism: ecosopophy and 'existential ecologies' 177–178; human interests and nature 175–176; infrastructure ecologies 174–175; theory evolution 174; urban form approaches 176–177

ecosopophy and 'existential ecologies' 177–178

elderly and disabled: customized AVs 68, *70, 72*; public transit, personal accessibility 69, *71*

Engels, Friedrich 281, 282

engineering and street design 163

Fagnant, Daniel 132

Forstall, Scott 6

freeways and beltways 103–104

freight delivery 10

Friedman, Yona 291

Fuller, Buckminster 291

functional hierarchy (street design) 97–98

Gaia hypothesis 176

Garden Cities, ideology and impact 100–102, 283–284

Garnier, Tony 99–100, 102

Garrett, Mark 259–260

Gates, Bill 278, 280, 281, 282

GE (General Electric) 271–272

Gehl, Jan 95, 160, 195

gender and travel behavior 259

Giddens, Anthony 29

goods transportation: AV's and delivery issues 9; private rental 74, *78, 79*; vehicle classification 9; *see also* delivery services

Google: car testing 19; delivery robots 242; monopolies

infringement 269; Sidewalk Labs, Toronto 269, 278, 280, 294; techno-utopian cities 278, 280, 281, 282, 293

Graham, Steven 273

Guattari, Félix 177–178

Hays, Michael 291

Hegel, Georg 279

Herron, Ron 291

highway interchange efficiency *206–207*, 208

Hilberseimer, Ludwig 98, 102

Hodge, David C. 3

Howard, Ebenezer 100–101, 283–284

IBM 269

individually dedicated AVs 13

infrastructure and intelligence systems: AV optimized road network 140, *140–141*; movement ecologies 144, *144–145*; network resilience, failure limitation 267–268; pop-up crosswalk 223, *224–225*; Smart Tarmac 74, 203, *204–205*; structures and communication 13–15; traffic intersection management *216–218*, 219; traffic mapping and management 170; urban fabric and network mapping 266–267; virtual zoning, flexible traffic rules 142, *142–143, 220–221*, 222

infrastructure systems, AV cities: complex interconnected ecosystems 172–173, 176; ecosopophy concepts 177–178; finance strategies 272–274; landscape urbanism approach 168–169; network disposition and 'active form' 268–269, 272, 274; neutral network and corporate

Index   301

limitations 269–270, 271–272; pedestrian-vehicle interface challenges 173–174, 187; public sphere and digital interactions 270–272; systems of systems approach 268; traffic mapping and management 170; urban fabric and network mapping 266–267

intelligent transportation systems (ITS) 13–14

International Transport Forum, 2015 260

Ives, Jony 6

Jacob, Sam 32
Jacobs, Jane 267
Jobs, Steve 6

Kalra, Nidhi 19–20
Kockelman, Kara 132
Kreiger, Alex 164–165
Kwinter, Sanford 175–177, 179

landscape architects 166–167
landscape urbanism: AV cities, design potential 168; biological complexity 172–173; infrastructure system integration 168–169; space-time frameworks 171–172; system non-boundaries 170–171; theory evolution and innovations 167–168

Larson, Kent 187
'last mile' issue 110, 156n1, 172–173
Le Corbusier: architectural vision 283, 293; *Contemporary and Radiant Cities* 28, 102–103, 286–288; negative impacts 288; planning critiques 95, 102; urban planning 98, 161
Lee, Ed 270
Lister, Nina-Marie 178–179

Live/Work/Play Nomadism 154, *155*
Lovelock, James 176

Mannheim, Karl 279, 280
Marvin, Simon 273
Marx, Karl 281, 282
mass mobility: vehicle classification 8–9, *9*; vehicle design 8–9
McHarg, Ian 166
McLuhan, Marshall 39, 41
Metabolists 290
Microsoft: Gates's Smart City 278, 280, 281, 282
mobile AV offices: company vehicle 62, *64*, *66*; shared support buildings 233, *234–235*
modalities: city movement patterns and modality 147, *148–149*; door-to-door mixed mode, shared AV 152, *152–153*; private AVs and Live/Work/Play Nomadism 154, *154–155*; public transit, AV integrated 150, *150–151*; transport development paths *146*, 147
Modernism: Capitalist finance and discreditation 288–289; Howard's Garden City 100–101, 283–284; Le Corbusier's utopian cities 102, 286–288; negative impacts 288; urban planning 97–98, 102–103; utopian visions, present day parallels 282–283; Wright's Broadacre City 284–285
More, Thomas 279, 293
Morris, William 101
Motordom lobby 20, 92–93, 186
Muller, Peter O. 116
Mumford, Lewis 100–101
Musk, Elon 278, 280, 281, 282, 293–294
Nash, John 100

New Urbanism 165
Norton, Peter D. 20, 93

Olmstead, Frederick Law 100, 166
on-demand services: shared mobility
options 11–12; subscription model
12–13, 56, *58*
ownership models 10–13

Paddock, Susan M. 19–20
Palladio, Andreas 97
Parker, Barry 101
parking, spatial and temporal:
automobile issues and AV
alternatives 126, *128*; day/night
optimization 132, *132–133*;
ownership and function typologies
129; parkades and SAV storage
130–131; parking-free density
islands 134, *134–135*; revenue loss
and road pricing models 126–127;
space conversions 194, 226;
street parking and AV idling 130;
vehicle-to-grid power systems 136,
136–137, 237, 238
personal mobility AVs: children,
independent journeys 56, *60*;
commuting 81; company vehicle
with office space 62, *64, 66*; Live/
Work/Play Nomadism 154, *154–
155*; parking issues 127, 130, 134;
vehicle classification 7–8, *9*
Picturesque movement 100
planning discipline 164
public sphere and digital interactions
270–272
public transit: AV and congestion
reduction 260–261; AV integrated
modality 150, *150–151*; AV
systems, positive changes 254–255;
present to AV system *256–257*;

service equity, cost and routes 258;
service erosion due to private SAVs
255, 258; social equity, user options
and safety 258–260
public transit (scenarios): AV
reservation for specific use 75, *79*;
extensive day and night services
75; flexible and fixed route options
63, 64, *67*, 75, *78*, 81; navigation
apps 63, 64, 69, *71*; public transit
57, *59*; suburban family use 57,
59; wheelchair accessibility 69, *73*;
working on the go 63, *65*

Radiant City (Le Corbusier) 102, 286,
287–288
Reed, Chris 178–179
research methodology (scenarios):
alternatives futures method critique
40; future-visioning methodologies
38, 39–40; projective user
scenarios 38; scenario learning 41,
44–45; Shell method 40–41, 44,
45, 49
road networks: AV optimized
modification/installation 140,
140–141; AV's self-organizing
potential 138; current hierarchy and
controls 138, *139*; responsive traffic
flow 144, *144–145*; virtual zoning,
flexible traffic rules 142, *142–143*
road pricing 126–127, 272–273
road safety: AV pedestrian-vehicle
intersections 213, *215, 217–218*,
219, 223, *225*; bike lanes and
AV traffic integration 74, 76;
pedestrian rights, 1920s America
91–92; pedestrian-vehicle interface
challenges 173–174, 187; self-
driving technology 18–21; Smart
Tarmac 74, 203, *205*

Robinson, Michael 10
Rodrigue, Jean-Paul 147
Roig, Joan 171
Rowe, Colin 292

Sadowski, Jathan 294–295
Sassen, Saskia 271, 272, 273
'Science Fiction' utopias 289–292
Self-Driving Coalition for Safer Streets 20
Sert, José Luis 165
shared autonomous vehicle (SAV) and mobility services: car sharing incentives 255; car sharing, tiered subscription model 12–13, 56, 58; customized for elderly/disabled users 68, 70, 72; day/night optimized parking 132, 132–133; family ownership and uses 56, 61; network optimization 124, 194; on-demand, commuting 56, 59; on-demand, family use 57, 61; on-demand, uptake factors 11–12; ownership models and mobility networks 10–11, 152, 152–153; reservations for specific uses 74; stop-off zone benefits 193, 194; vehicle classification 8, 9
Sherman, Roger 162
Sidewalk Labs, Toronto 269, 278, 280, 294
Siemens 269
Sitte, Camillo 95–96, 102
skeumorphism 6
Smart Tarmac 74, 203, 204–205
social equity and transit options 258–260
Southworth, Michael 18
standards: 'disposition' of AV cars 16–17, 23n30; ISO's role 16; urban infrastructure and AV's 15, 17–18

Starship delivery robot 242
Stein, Clarence 101–102
Strang, Gary L. 167, 169
streetcar/trolley 93–94, 255, 258
street design: disciplinary authority contests 160–161; functional hierarchy 97–98; modern road construction 97; professional disciplines and AV 163, 164, 165–167; road classification and widths 97–99; Roman to Modern 95–97
street design professions: architecture 161–163; engineering, dominant role 163; landscape architects 166–167; planning 164; transportation planning 163–164; urban design 164–166
street scale impacts: AV and pedestrian prioritization 186–187; cars' historical impact 91–93, 186; regulated public space 3
street scale impacts, building typology and program: charged carport 236–237, 238; charging station and fast food 230–231, 232; dispatch hub/grocery drive thru 226–227, 228–229; garage & frontage conversion 239, 240–241; mobile office dock 233, 234–235
street scale impacts, road infrastructure: block-end stop-off 192–193, 194; boulevard reclamation 195, 196–199; flat street 188–189, 190–191; highway autodrome 206–207, 208; lane relay 200–201, 202; Smart Tarmac 203, 204–205; twin carriageway, phased adaption 209, 210–212
street scale impacts, shipping: commercial delivery zone and delivery station 242, 244–245;

delivery technology projects 242; home delivery box *246–247*, 248

street scale impacts, traffic and interaction infrastructure: compass pole, multifunctional beacon 213, *214–215*; pop-up crosswalk 223, *224–225*; traffic intersection management *216–218*, 219; virtual traffic control *220–221*, 222

Superstudio 290

Tafuri, Manfredo 280, 281–282, 288–289

Tange, Kenzo 290

Taylor, Brian 259–260

Tenner, Edward 39

Tesla *see* Musk, Elon

three-way through road (AV) 195, *197*

Townsend, Anthony 40

Transportation Infrastructure and Public Space Lab (TIPSlab) 12–13, 38

transportation infrastructure and urban form: AV impacts, street level 98–99; cars' historical impact on streets 91–93; freeways, suburbs and infill 103–104; Garden City adaptions 101–102; Le Corbusier's networks 102–103; social welfare motivations 100, 101–102, 103; streetcars, land and social impacts 93–94; street scale interrelationships 94–97; urban fabric, evolution of 99, 104–105; zoning developments 99–100

transportation planning 163–164

United States: Garden City adaptions 101–102; modern road networks 98; Picturesque movement 100;

road width standards 97; San Francisco's tech potential 270; smart street lights, San Diego 271–272

Unwin, Raymond 101

urban design 164–166

urban form: AV impacts, street level 98–99; buildings and street-linked networks 94–95; cars' historical impact 91–93; Freeway Era 103–104; Garden Cities, ideology and impact 100–102; Modernist perspectives 98, 102–103; Picturesque movement 100; road's functional hierarchy 97–98; streetcars and suburban growth 93–94; street design, Roman to Modern construction 95–97; zoning trend 99–100

urban growth patterns: AVs and expanded commuting 116, 118; exurban AV enclaves 122, *122–123*; shared-AV densification 124, *124–125*; spatial structure developments *119*; sprawl, car to AV led developments 120, *121*; sprawl objections 116; transportation and urban form, US city 116, *117*

urbanite, personal AV mobility 62, *64, 66*

urban scale impacts: modalities *146*, 147, *148–155*, 150, 152, 154; parking 126–127, *128–129*, 130–131, *132–137*, 134, 136; road networks 138, *139–145*, 140, 142, 144; urban growth patterns 116, *117*, 118, *119–125*, 120, 122, 124

urban scale impacts, research overview: conceptual framework **112**, 112–114, **113**, **115**;

Index   305

drawings, design objectives 110,
114; transport transformation,
comparative approach 110–112
urban sprawl 116
utopian visions: *Broadacre
City* (Wright) 28, 284–285;
Contemporary and Radiant Cities (Le
Corbusier) 286–288; *Garden City*
(Howard) 101, 283–284; ideology
and realization 280; Modernism's
discreditation 288–289; Modernist
and present day parallels 282–283,
294–295; political relationships
292–294; Post Modern visionary
projects 289–292; socialism links
281–282; technology firms and
projects 278, 280, 281, 282, 293–
294; utopias, fundamental criteria
279; work and means of production
280–281, 282

vehicle ad hoc networks (VANETs)
13–14
vehicle classification: autonomous
vehicle (AV) 5, *9*; conventional *8*
Vehicle Miles Travelled (VMT) 11
vehicle-to-infrastructure (V2I)
communication 13–14
vehicle-to-vehicle (V2V)
communication 13, 14
Vitruvius 95–96, 161–162

Waal, Martijn de 270–271
Waldheim, Charles 165, 170, 171
Wall, Alex 171
Waymo *see* Google
'Woonerf ('living yard') 189
Wren, Christopher, Sir 161
Wright, Frank Lloyd 28, 161, 281,
284–285, 293
Wright, Henry 101–102